THE
LONG ROAD
HOME

On Blackness
and Belonging

DEBRA THOMPSON

Published by Scribner Canada

New York   London   Toronto   Sydney   New Delhi

SCRIBNER
CANADA

Scribner Canada
An Imprint of Simon & Schuster, Inc.
166 King Street East, Suite 300
Toronto, Ontario M5A 1J3

This Scribner Canada edition September 2022

SCRIBNER CANADA and colophon are
trademarks of Simon & Schuster, Inc.

For information about special discounts for bulk purchases,
please contact Simon & Schuster Special Sales at 1-800-268-3216
or CustomerService@simonandschuster.ca.

Interior design by Lewelin Polanco

Manufactured in the United States of America

3   5   7   9   10   8   6   4   2

Library and Archives Canada Cataloguing in Publication

Title: The long road home : on Blackness and belonging / Debra Thompson.
Names: Thompson, Debra (Debra E.), author.
Identifiers: Canadiana (print) 20220166978 | Canadiana (ebook) 20220167109
| ISBN 9781982182465 (softcover) | ISBN 9781982182472 (ebook)
Subjects: LCSH: Thompson, Debra (Debra E.) | LCSH: Black people—
North America—History. | LCSH: Black people—Race identity—North
America. | LCSH: Black people—North America—Politics and government.
| LCSH: Women, Black—Canada—Biography. | LCSH: Women college
teachers, Black Canada—Biography. | LCSH: North America—
Race relations. | LCGFT: Autobiographies.
Classification: LCC E185.625 .T46 2022 | DDC 305.896/073—dc23

ISBN 978-1-9821-8246-5
ISBN 978-1-9821-8247-2 (ebook)

This book is dedicated to:

First, my ancestors in the space between worlds.

Second, organizers, activists, and
resistance fighters, with gratitude.

Third, my students, who teach me in turn.

Fourth, my loves, still/always/forevermore.

Fifth, all those who believe we can remake the world.

Contents

[Y]ou don't write about racism, you write about life. It is life you must write about. It is life you must insist on.

—Dionne Brand,
A Map to the Door of No Return

THE
LONG ROAD
HOME

We Came Back Too Soon

In the early days of 2020, months before George Floyd's murder in Minneapolis sparked the kinetic uprisings across North America, my father said, "You know, Debra, your daughter was the first Thompson born in America since Cornelius Thompson escaped slavery. It's been over a hundred and fifty years, and some days I think we came back too soon."

My father was born in 1944 and spent the first years of his childhood in Shrewsbury, Ontario. It's a tiny town about fifty miles east of Detroit on the shores of Lake Erie. It, and other neighboring towns such as Buxton and Dresden, were among the last stops on the Underground Railroad. In 1850, the United States Congress passed the Fugitive Slave Act as part of a larger series of political compromises made between the southern enslaving states and the free northern states. It required law enforcement officials to arrest people suspected of being runaway slaves based on little or no evidence and penalized any official who dared not comply. Any person found aiding a runaway slave by providing food or shelter was liable to six months imprisonment and a $1,000 fine.

Monetary awards were offered to anyone who captured a fugitive slave. Those suspected of being runaway slaves were not eligible for a trial and could neither testify on their own behalf nor defend themselves against the accusations. The result was the legalization of a national program of mass kidnapping and enslavement of free Blacks across the United States. But the Fugitive Slave Act did not extend to Canada, and to Canada thousands fled, including my grandfather's grandfather, Cornelius Thompson.

Many of the people who escaped to Canada went back to the United States after the Civil War to find the loved ones left behind, stolen from them, or lost along the way. But generations of those descended from Black American refugees from slavery still live in southwestern Ontario, including my father's family. Because the communities were rural and segregated, my kin have the most wonderful way of speaking, their southern intonations inflected with unambiguously Canadian accents. My father says "thee-ater" and pronounces the "w-h" in *white*. He talks in the same rhythmic riddles that characterize barbershop talk in African American communities and cultures. He says things like, "You know, Debra, those politicians got nothing more than a nodding acquaintance with the truth." But he is also staunchly, proudly, fiercely Canadian, and his accent appears plainly in words like *about* and *sorry*.

Dad doesn't know where Cornelius or the others in the overgrown Shrewsbury graveyard escaped from. He thought he heard someone talking about West Virginia or Alabama once, "but Debra," he said, "you're looking for ghosts. You're looking for evidence left behind by people who were trying to hide, and whose lives depended on how well and for how long they could do it."

So many of our stories are ghost stories. How could they not be? African-descended people in the Americas are connected by the horrors of the Middle Passage—the point during the triangular route of the transatlantic slave trade when Africans were violently kidnapped from their traditional territories, commodified as objects, forcibly transported to the "New World," and sold as property. So, too, the deep of the Atlantic, the goddess Yemaya's domain, holds a place in our collective memory. There is blood in the water; it is the fathoms of the dead.

When I decided to move to the United States more than a decade ago, I thought the ghosts of my ancestors would welcome me home. I felt like I was returning to the land of my ancestors' birth, the country they built, where they prayed, and sweated, and toiled, and were tortured, and resisted, and fought, and wept as their children were stolen and sold, and were traumatized as they were raped for profit and murdered for sport, the country where they died, the places they still haunt. They escaped and I returned to lay claim to the opportunities and the humanity they were refused. I thought I was going home.

I was wrong. But not in the way you might think.

In the opening pages of *The Souls of Black Folk*, published in 1903, the prolific African American sociologist W. E. B. Du Bois identified the so-called "Negro problem" as the unasked question of white America. "They approach me in a half-hesitant sort of way," he writes, "eye me curiously or compassionately, and then, instead of saying directly, How does it feel to be a problem? they say, I know an excellent colored man in my town; or, I fought at Mechanicsville; or, Do not these Southern outrages make your blood boil? At these I smile, or am interested, or reduce the boiling to a simmer, as the occasion may require. To the real question, How does it feel to be a problem? I answer seldom a word."[1]

I grew up in Oshawa, Ontario, and spent most of my life in Canada not exactly as a problem per se, but rather as the Only

One—the only Black person in any space, anywhere, anytime, every time. There were so few Black people in my life growing up that if I was not literally the Only One, then I was figuratively the Only One—being one of the few in these majority white spaces. It was only after I moved to the United States in 2010 that I often found myself thinking about Du Bois's infamous question. Between 2010 and 2020 I lived in four very different places, each with a complicated history of racism. My initiation to American life was in Cambridge, Massachusetts, on the outskirts of Boston, the birthplace of American freedom. Next I lived for four long, challenging years in Athens, Ohio, a very small, very white college town in the poorest county in the state, nestled in the foothills of the Appalachian Mountains. In 2015 I moved to Chicago, Illinois, the great Black Metropolis, and bore witness to the colliding legacies of Emmett Till, Fred Hampton, and Michelle Obama. My last years in the United States were spent in Oregon, founded as a white ethno-state, where the clash between the rugged frontier and the untamed coast mimicked the disparate ideological forces at play in state politics.

How does it feel to be a problem? Riding the Red Line to Harvard Station, I watched young Black men get on the subway, laughing and joking as teenagers do. I watched as the white people in the vicinity surreptitiously moved away and avoided eye contact with them.

I thought of this question when I began my first teaching position at Ohio University. I was running along the Hocking River path when a pickup truck zoomed by and a man's voice screamed, "HEY NIGGER!" It wasn't the first or the last time something like this happened. But the worst was yet to come, and it would come from my white liberal colleagues, so desperate to be seen as progressive and tolerant to my face, but resentful and vindictive behind my back.

"Deb Thompson? She's just so full of herself. Like a bull in a china shop. Not very collegial," they told the other faculty throughout the university.

How does it feel to be a problem? Du Bois coined the phrase "double consciousness" to describe the "twoness" of being African American and American at the same time; a conflict not of loyalty or allegiance, but one characterized by hard truth that the core ideas of American national identity—life, liberty, the pursuit of happiness—were only made possible to white Americans because of the torturous and deadly subjugation of Black people. Double consciousness is also a description of the psychic weight of constantly viewing one's own Black identity, experiences, behaviors, and potential through the eyes of the white people who probably hate and fear you. It is an utterly exhausting tactic of Black survival, defined by the necessity of being neither here nor there and yet nowhere and everywhere at the same time.

Americans often think of their country as exceptional—one of the world's oldest democracies, the birthplace of revolutionary freedom, the only remaining superpower, the last line of defense against a world constantly threatened by dictators and demagogues. But from the vantage point of African Americans who reside in what Du Bois called the Black lifeworld, the United States isn't exceptionally free or equal. American racism is all the more tragic, cunning, and ruinous precisely because it exists alongside but in direct contradiction with the idealism of the American Creed, the pervasiveness of the American Dream, and the homogenizing power of American national identity.

And to those that observe American history in the making from abroad, the United States is exceptional only in terms of how utterly, unforgivably, uncompromisingly racist it is.

———

The idea of American *racial* exceptionalism is particularly powerful in Canada. American racism is understood as real and morally repulsive, and in comparative terms Canadian racism either does not exist, or if it does, it is less harmful, less depraved, less entrenched, and less traumatic than the racism in the United States. Comparison is routinely, frequently, faithfully used in the service of Canadian deniability. It is a national pastime, an obsession that works to simultaneously hide and entrench the persistent racial inequalities that define nearly every socioeconomic indicator in Canadian society. The cognitive dissonance required to be righteously indignant about anti-Black racism in America, but defensive when the perpetrators are the "us" and not the "them," is itself a peculiarly Canadian form of racism.

A central idea in this book is that there is an innate value in the exploration of Blackness, belonging, and the broader politics of race in Canada and the United States, not in contrast, but rather in relation to each other. Ideas and inspirations, people and profits, goods and grievances have crossed the border for centuries. Black freedom dreams, as well, have never been limited by the geographical boundaries of the nation. And while others have compared racism in the United States to more obvious circumstances of legalized racial apartheid like in South Africa or Nazi Germany, the insistence in Canada that racism happens somewhere else or happened long ago requires a kind of national ignorance that is worthy of careful examination. Extreme cases have much to tell us, but so, too, do unsuspecting ones, and Canadian peculiarities make for interesting politics.

Black communities in Canada are both very old, predating Confederation by more than a century, and very new, growing exponentially in the mid to late 1990s. The population is quite small, at just 3.5 percent of the national population, but significant in cities such as Toronto, Montreal, Halifax, and Ottawa. We are the diaspora of the diaspora, so to speak: both old and new Black communities are products of the global collusions and imperial collisions of colonialism and the transatlantic slave trade, but we have neither the level of political or cultural recognition of African Americans nor the sheer magnitude of the millions who comprise the African-descended populations of the Caribbean and South America.

We also have a unique kind of racial consciousness, the result of multiple formulations of Blackness in Canada that are criss-crossed with nationality, ethnicity, generational status, language, class, religion, and more, but which are also shaped by conver-gences, amalgamations, frictions, translations, and intersections with shifting contours of Canadian culture, politics, and society. Organizing and creating a sense of solidarity among Black people in Canada is difficult but is also full of the potential that comes with the recognition of multiple, overlapping, authentically con-tradictory Black experiences.[2]

Blackness in Canada also exists within the crucible of Cana-dian exceptionalism. That is, Canada the exceptional, Canada the clearly not-racist, Canada the good, Canada the white savior, Canada the successful multicultural experiment. The dismissive-ness is part of the appeal, because if we are the global exception to the multitude of polities that rule by, through, and according to race, then we have no need to examine our exceptionally Cana-dian racial rules. It's a red herring, of course, because Canadian racism is shaped not just by a global history that gives it a familiar force and feeling, but also by those peculiarities that make it Ca-nadian born and bred, just like me.

It's an open question, then, about how Canadian racism is shaped by Canadian democracy, Canadian political structures, Canadian liberalism, Canadian whiteness, Canadian politeness, Canadian public policy, Canadian political parties, Canadian political culture, Canadian popular culture, Canadian urban centers, Canadian regionalism, Canadian ruralism, Canadian media, Canadian peacekeeping, Canadian war-making, Canadian bilingualism, Canadian settler colonialism, and the Canadian national inferiority complex. There's a lot we don't yet know about the nuances of Canadian anti-Blackness. It's hard to research what is so consistently jettisoned to the realm of the unthinkable.

This is part of the reason why a sense of real *belonging* was, at least for me, always elusive in Canada. The kind of belonging I always wanted in the country of my birth, I instead sought in the country that enslaved my ancestors.

In early 2020 I was teaching a class called "Black Lives Matter and American Democracy" at the University of Oregon. The classroom was packed; when the sixty spaces of the course filled within the first five hours of the registration period, I pulled some strings and added an additional thirty seats. At a predominantly white university with only five hundred Black students, and somewhere around a dozen Black faculty, it was heartening that so many young people of all backgrounds wanted to learn about Black Lives Matter. It's not exactly *pleasant* to spend ten weeks reading about racism and police brutality. They came to my classroom nevertheless, every Tuesday and Thursday morning, without fail. There were no participation grades and I didn't take attendance, and they all showed up anyway.

But in those early days of 2020, I had begun to wonder if I should be teaching about Black Lives Matter in the past tense. More than five years after Ferguson, Missouri, police officer Darren Wilson shot and killed Michael Brown in August 2014, what was different, *really*? In spite of a murder that made the tiny city of Ferguson, with a population of just over 21,000, known throughout the world, a scathing U.S. Department of Justice investigation into the Ferguson Police Department, and a consent decree that required significant changes in Ferguson's approach to policing, little had changed.

Black Lives Matter activists throughout the United States were still doing the on-the-ground work, but the public's attention had waned. It wasn't because the police had suddenly stopped killing Black people. In September 2018, for example, twenty-six-year-old Botham Jean was shot in his own apartment by an off-duty police officer. She claimed she mistook his apartment for her own, a floor below. But shootings like these, as racist and preventable as they were, were still just one more injustice in an avalanche of bad news. The Trump administration made a daily habit of political assaults on the impoverished, the undocumented, the disenfranchised, and the vulnerable. The president was impeached in December 2019 and *it didn't matter*. It was hard on the soul to be outraged all the time. The anger was so overwhelming, so all-consuming, we couldn't help but become desensitized to the ongoing tragedies. I knew it, my father knew it, my students knew it. Despair breeds indifference.

Then, during the final week of the semester, COVID-19 hit home.

In an instant, the campus became a ghost town. Oregon governor Kate Brown declared that all K–12 schools would be closed from March 16 to March 31, 2020; they never reopened. Working parents scrambled to figure out how to work full-time and care for their children. Businesses shut down. The economy fell off a cliff. The governor issued a shelter-in-place order. Congress scrambled to put emergency funding in place for the 30 million new unemployment claims filed between March and April. If you listened hard enough, you could hear the hum of the phrase "flatten the curve" everywhere you went. Horror stories started to emerge from New York City, the early epicenter of the pandemic. March was the longest month in human history. April wasn't much better.

And then. On May 25, 2020, George Floyd was murdered by the Minneapolis police. The last moments of his life, spent being slowly tortured to death as a police officer kneeled on his neck for eight minutes and forty-five seconds, were recorded by bystanders. The video went viral.[3]

Did you know that George Floyd started to cry when he saw the police approaching him? Did you know that one of the police officers, Thomas Lane, pulled his gun within fifteen seconds of encountering Floyd, who was sitting, minding his business, in a parked car? Did you know that George Floyd begged officers not to kill him? That he repeatedly called them "sir" and "Mr. Officer" and told them he could not breathe at least twenty-five times? Did you hear the spectral echoes of Eric Garner's last words in George Floyd's last moments?

Floyd's murder followed on the heels of two other high-profile, shocking, unjustifiable killings. Ahmaud Arbery was jogging in Glynn County, Georgia, when three white vigilantes chased him in their truck before shooting him with a shotgun. Breonna Taylor was sleeping in her home when three plainclothes officers from the Louisville Metro Police Department broke down the door. Taylor's boyfriend, Kenneth Walker, assumed they were intruders and shot at the officers once; in response, they fired thirty-two rounds into the home, hitting Taylor five or six times.

Then in New York's Central Park, Amy Cooper—a white woman *from Canada*, it turned out—called the police when bird-watcher Christian Cooper asked her to restrain her dog; her fake, manipulative hysterics went viral and added a sense of liberal, middle-class indignation to the emerging unrest. Pundits connected the dots between Christian Cooper and George

Floyd—how easily one could have become the other. It added to a growing understanding about how exhausting, how unfair, how disproportionate, how arbitrary these dangers are for Black people—how a chance encounter with a white woman who is unafraid to weaponize her privilege to get her way could so easily end a life.

Minneapolis exploded. The embers spread to major American cities and then around the world. On June 6, 2020, the peak of the protests, half a million people turned out in more than five hundred cities across the United States. The protests were bigger, more diverse, occurred in more places, and lasted for longer than any form of collective action we've ever seen.[4]

The demands made by protestors were not new, but they were gaining more traction than they ever had before. Many echoed the call to defund the police. Concessions were won in key battlegrounds, including Minneapolis, where the city council pledged to dismantle the police department. Confederate monuments were toppled. Seattle removed the police presence from its schools. *Cops*, the worst show on television, was temporarily cancelled. Police reform bills were introduced in the House of Representatives and more than twenty state legislatures. The struggle was resurrected; change seemed, for the most fleeting of moments, possible.

And, I left.

After spending a quarter of my life in the United States, at exactly the same moment as the COVID-19 pandemic exposed our collective vulnerability and mass uprisings against racial injustice rocked cities around the world, I fled, as did my ancestors before me, to Canada.

The timing was curious, but coincidental. A plan of return, two years in the making, was already in motion. With my American partner, our two children under five, and the Artful Dodger, our anxious rescue mutt, in tow, I began a cross-continent, international move from Eugene, Oregon, to Montreal, Quebec. I didn't feel a sense of relief when I stepped off the plane and into the usually packed Pierre Trudeau International Airport, now eerily silent because of the restrictions the Canadian government had placed on all nonessential travel from abroad.

I was instead, and once again, unsettled.

⸻

This is a book about the peculiar nuances of racism in Canada and the United States and the power of freedom dreams that link and inspire Black people across national borders. I offer insights from the perspective of someone who has deep ties and loyalties to, critiques of, and hope for both countries. I am not so unlike those who came before me. For my ancestors, Canada was the Promised Land. It was a refuge from American slavery; a chance to access the rights of citizenship, make lives for themselves and their children, and start anew as recognized members of a political community. For me, the United States was the birthplace of the struggle against racism, the geographic core of Black cultural identity, and the originator of a blood debt owed to my kinfolk for generations of bondage.

But some truths only reveal themselves while we're in transit from one place to the next, and, one hundred and fifty years apart, my ancestors and I found ourselves as inside-outsiders in both countries. Though we could, in some ways, make parallel claims about how much we belonged in and to our adopted homes, our membership in these nations was always troubled and incomplete. Always a problem.

America could never quite be all that I wanted it to be. The land and the people are still haunted by what leading African American Studies scholar Saidiya Hartman calls the "afterlives of slavery." More than four hundred years after the beginnings of chattel slavery in British North America, more than one hundred and fifty years after the Thirteenth, Fourteenth, and Fifteenth Amendments to the American Constitution ended racial bondage and granted Black people the rights of citizenship, Black lives continue to be put in peril by a centuries-old racial calculus.[5] The formerly enslaved were promised forty acres and a mule at the end of the American Civil War. Instead they and their descendants were given morphing forms of state-sanctioned racial domination: convict leasing, exploitative sharecropping arrangements, Jim Crow, lynch mobs, the prohibition of access to various mechanisms of creating intergenerational wealth, such as higher education, bank loans, and home ownership, redlining, the assassination or forced exile of an entire generation of Black leadership, de facto discrimination, institutionalized racism, the system of mass incarceration, and no choice but to share a country with people who refuse to acknowledge the irreparable damage of these structures, or do much of anything to mitigate their effects.

And so, the struggle for citizenship—not just citizenship on paper, but rather the intractable, irreversible political, social, and economic inclusion into the polity—has been the defining characteristic of African American social and political life for centuries. Black Lives Matter is, at least in some ways, the most recent iteration of this struggle.

Still, I refused to be enamored with Canada, the home I left behind. I was too critical of nationalism, too annoyed by the façade of multiculturalism, and too cognizant of the possibility of a dystopian future in which a national sigil might determine which cage I was put in, and so I could never imagine going down the road of having a maple leaf anywhere on my body, like so many Canadian expats. Instead I got a tattoo of a compass rose, pointing north. Not for Canada, but in memory of the path travelled by my ancestors. *Left foot, peg foot, travelling on, follow the drinking gourd.*

The act of moving across borders—forced and freedom-seeking, escape and exile—is central to the African diaspora. The scattering of African-descended peoples in the Americas originates in the traumatic, violent, and forced departure of the transatlantic slave trade. To be enslaved was to have your movements regulated, surveilled, and criminalized. Black history is full of forced relocations, mass population removals, displacements, segregated spaces, zoned existences, and escapes.

Black migration has also been done in defiance. In his award-winning book *Freedom as Marronage,* political theorist Neil Roberts reminds us that between enslavement and freedom, there is flight; physical movement often must precede the shift from one social status (unfree) to another (free).[6] The very idea of the fugitive slave is powerful. An enslaved person flees their captivity and breaks an unjust, inhumane law in order to do so. The act is, technically, one of theft, but the property stolen is *oneself*. A fugitive slave steals herself, and in the act of fleeing slavery frees herself. Fight and flight are one and the same. Even leaving America has sometimes been a strategy of Black liberation—Liberia and Sierra Leone were founded as colonies for freed Black people when many countries still traded in human lives. James Baldwin, Paul Robeson, W. E. B. Du Bois, Richard Wright, and Josephine Baker all left and found peace and humanity elsewhere, even when it was temporary. Exile has, at times, been emancipatory.

The meaning of home, one of the central questions I'm trying to think through, is full of tensions, complications, and contradictions. There are no easy answers. Home is, of course, much more than a physical location. It's not just about where you land or where you live. It's also about membership in a community, a sense of belonging, the people that you claim as your own and those who claim you. The desire for home is natural, recognizable, understandable; it is the most basic of human needs.

Home is a particular place at a moment in time even as our conceptions of it transcend both time and space; it encompasses desire and nostalgia, brings together memories and longings, our future children and our ancestors long gone, democratic processes of conflict and consensus, the local and the global, inclusion and exclusion, the material and the ghostly, the corporeal and the intangible. Our understandings of home frequently clash with the rigid boundaries and bindings of the citizenship regimes enshrined in law, as immigrants, refugees, exiles, diasporic groups, and those who are stateless or nationless change the meaning of membership in a political community through their access to it, or lack thereof.[7] The very idea of a "return" may be little more than wishful thinking; a wistful dream that we can go back to a place where we once were, but no longer are, and yet desire to be. Paradoxically, mobility and constraint exist in tandem; it's entirely possible to be homeward bound and yet bound by a peculiar sense of home.

And, to tangle things even further, it is crucial to recognize that we cannot even begin to speak of homelands, homecomings, or homegoings without acknowledging that these territories we now call Canada and the United States never did belong to us. I can only claim an uncomplicated return to this land if I am willing to ignore our ongoing complicity in the violence of settler colonialism. Slavery is often cast as America's original sin, but North America was founded on Indigenous dispossession and genocide.[8]

These tensions between home and abroad, fixity and mobility, the familiar and the foreign, travel and habitat, rootedness and displacement hold a special meaning in Black political thought.

They manifest most obviously in our attempts to articulate Black life in the timeless, space-defying afterlives of slavery, what Black Studies scholar Christina Sharpe formulates as the wake—of a ship, from a slumber, during the rituals in honor of the dead. But the tensions also live in the generations of people and the generation of ideas that move back and forth across lands and oceans. The tensions bleed hybrid cultural formations that take inspiration from Black genius around the world. They animate British cultural theorist Paul Gilroy's idea of the Black Atlantic as a space continually crisscrossed by Black people most tragically as commodities, but also as explorers, pirates, activists, and archivists engaged in redefining their understanding of and relationship to the modern world. Even within the bounds of the nation-state, the freedom to stay and the freedom to move are, as migrant rights activist Harsha Walia argues, foundational to any conceptualization of social justice.[9]

But, as the saying goes, what if I can't *really* go home again? What then? What now?

Home is a calling for many, but my understanding of home is rife with ambiguity. I want to articulate some of the story of what it was like to have been in the United States, the land of my ancestors, a country that is and isn't mine; to be doubly unwanted as an immigrant and a Black person, but there by choice and protected by incredible class privilege; and then, at a moment when Black uprisings once again called the meaning of American democracy into question, to leave to return to Canada. I want to provide a lens onto the unrepentant structural racism of American society while not negating the subversive, insidious racism of Canada; to share my bewilderment and awe at African Americans' love and hope and pride in their country, their dedication to making it better, even as it has, more often than not, refused to love them back.

I seek to articulate how, even though I returned to the country of my birth, a nation that prides itself on multiculturalism, a place that sells the mythology of the Promised Land and the imagery of racial diversity, I still feel as though my acceptance into the Canadian mosaic is conditional. But, much like Dorothy's quest to find the Wizard of Oz or Alice's trip down the rabbit hole to Wonderland, you first have to leave home to know where—and what—it really is.

More than anything, this is a story about what it means to be in a place, to have ancestral ties to a place, to be haunted by the ghosts tethered to the land, water, soil, and swamp, but to be not *of* that place. These are the questions I have asked myself for more than a decade, as I try to think through whether I can and should lay claim to America, whether I can or should lay claim to Black freedom dreams that might have been born there, but which have also travelled around the globe, whether Canada is capable of welcoming me home, and what these claims might mean in the broader context of belonging in and to the African diaspora.

I can't guarantee you'll find any concrete, confident, or declarative answers in these pages. I have been told that I can be frustratingly elusive as a writer. As a person. It causes more trouble—more heartbreak, really—than I'd like to admit. More problematically, the insistence on finding more, better, deeper questions, including questions that do not have clear answers, animates a peculiar kind of dilemma, when precisely the power you seek to challenge insists on claiming your ideas in the service of its own aggrandizement and consolidation. That's the price of the ticket, though, because once you put your writing, whether elusive or absolute, out into the world, it's no longer yours. People will understand it as they see fit, it will speak to them in different ways, they will do with it whatever they please. I can spin these words, but if you're reading them, they don't belong only to me anymore. They're yours now, too. It's a beautiful gift to be a teacher and a writer, to have this privilege to bear witness to how complete strangers may take up and translate, absorb and adapt this spark. I can only hope that these words resonate and will serve you well.

CHAPTER 1

The Great White North

(Shrewsbury, Ontario)

W here are you really from?"

This time I'm in the lobby of Mount Sinai Hospital in Toronto, wasting the hours between bloodwork appointments for the mysterious autoimmune disorder that is still, to this day, trying to kill me. It's 2007. I am in my mid-twenties and my hair is in braids, which, together with the tri-striped Adidas superstars I wear everywhere, make me look younger than I am. The questioner is an elderly white man, whom I have been chatting with for the past ten minutes. He had opened with a story about his recently deceased wife. I figure he's lonely and I can fake extroversion when necessary. He asks if I am a student, and I tell him I'm working toward my doctorate in political science. He asks what kind of political science, and I reply that I am researching the politics of race in Canada and the United States. He glances at the book I'm reading and his eyes kind of light up as he leans back in his chair.

"I've got a question for you, then," he says. Oh no, I think, but he continues without noticing. "Why is it that I never see any Blacks in the library?"

I cringe, and then sigh. "Oh, we go to the library, just like everyone else." I gesture to my book, wishing that I could get back to it.

He looks at me, skeptically. "Tell me," he asks, but of course it is more of a demand. "Where are you from?" He is unsatisfied with my initial response of "here," and I know what's coming.

"No. Where are you *really* from?"

For those whose presence in Canada has never been questioned, it may be hard to hear the presumption in the query's premise. The insinuation. Where are you really from, because I can see that you're not one of us. Where are you really from, because you don't seem to fit in here. Where are you really from, because how long you've been here will tell me something about your place in this country. Where are you really from, because my whiteness means that I am entitled to your time, your benevolence, your patience, your attention, and your respect. Where are you really from, because my curiosity is more important than your comfort or safety. Where are you *really* from, because you can't possibly be from *here*.

To this day, the question has a paralyzing effect, a mnemonic albatross of childhood anxiety. In my youth, my knee-jerk reaction was to claim belonging through longevity. I'm from *Canada*, I insisted. I'm fifth-generation Canadian on my father's side and fourth-generation on my mother's side. Some of us, I would say, alternating between shrill indignation and what I hoped sounded like a wry cynicism, have been here for a very long time.

I remember feeling at the time like it was absolutely crucial that the questioner knew about my deep roots in Canada. It was important, for some unknown reason. As if the amount of time my family had been in the country would be able to tell others something about me—who I was, who I would be, could be, if they just knew that we had been here for generations. As if time itself was a marker of true Canadian-ness.

Every summer during my childhood there was a weekend when my parents would pile me and my three siblings into our rusty, wood-paneled yellow station wagon and trek from the eastern outskirts of Toronto to my father's hometown of Shrewsbury, Ontario. It felt like the trip was as far as the gates of hell and probably just as hot. I have vague childhood memories of the scorched, dusty earth that surrounded a red schoolhouse, and the graveyard down the road that always stole the sound of our footsteps in the long, untended grass between the stones. My grandparents moved my father and his siblings to Toronto sometime in the late 1950s, but to my dad Shrewsbury would always be home. The house he grew up in was long gone. Condemned and demolished, probably. But the schoolhouse still stood, and that was where we gathered for a weekend each July, without fail.

In my mind's eye the school looks like a barn from the outside, but that could just be because of the clearer memories of high ceilings of the single room in the building, and the stagnant, musty smell of a space seldom used. The screen door creaked when opened and banged itself closed. The folding tables around the perimeter of the room would be piled high with potato salad, iced tea, coleslaw, slow-roasted pork for sandwiches, and fruits that tasted like summertime. Someone would always buy a few buckets of Kentucky Fried Chicken—I remember that very clearly in the way that fuzzy childhood memories are sharpened when they involve food. There was always a display of pictures from long ago that featured people I didn't know. My father would place an iron grip on my shoulder and stand me in front of an elder, saying, "Now, you remember so-and-so, don't you?" I never did.

The students of S.S. Harwich No. 13, 1929. First row, seated:
Marion Patterson, Gertrude Lewis, Elsie Willerton, Addie
Thompson, Janet Lewis (my grandmother), Ethel Burns, Au-
drey Goffney. Second row, kneeling: Sam Hartford, Douglas
Lewis, Oswald Lewis, Douglas Patterson, Bill Hartford, Lloyd
Patterson. Third row, standing: Mary Goffney, Grace Patterson,
Velma Lewis, Beulah Harding (teacher), Andrew Thompson
(my grandfather), Constance Patterson, Nellie Harris, Ruth
Goffney. Fourth row, standing (school trustees): Louis Murphy,
William Thompson, Clem Patterson.

My sisters were always much better at that kind of thing; Jessica is
good with details and Leisa is good with people. I am neither, but
the elders couldn't tell we three girls apart, anyway, so I figured
we were even.

The gathering wasn't just for family; those who attended included kinfolk of a different order. It was a reunion for the students of the schoolhouse, S.S. Harwich No. 13. Built in 1861, it
was one of the first racially integrated schools in North America.

Every year, long after the school's creaky, banging door was
shuttered, the denizens of the schoolhouse would come back and
reminisce together. It was more than a school reunion—it was
an annual veneration of the power of education in a place built
by those who were denied it. It's no coincidence that education

has been on the front lines of the battles for Black equality for hundreds of years; we are the only people in North American history who were legally prohibited from learning to read or write. Education is dangerous. It creates the ability to question why the world is, how it came to be, and whether it should be this way. Freedom is born from the most daring of ideas.

My siblings and I, the children of teachers, had no choice but to take seriously the incendiary potential of knowledge. I knew what the words *segregation, integration,* and *slavery* meant before I could do a proper cartwheel—though, of course, I didn't understand what they *meant.* I knew that the graveyard down the road from the schoolhouse was for Black people like us, that you never stood on someone's grave, and that it was silent and still because that's how the spirits liked it. I knew that the white people who insisted on a separate cemetery must have had to live with a hatred so intense that they couldn't fathom the idea that the Black dead be laid to rest in the same space.

There is, of course, a long history of Black migration to Canada. The Black presence in Canada began as early as the first decades of the 1600s, when Mathieu Da Costa, a free Black African, is believed to have travelled to Canada with Samuel de Champlain and served as an interpreter between French and Indigenous peoples. A few years later, in 1628, a nine-year-old boy stolen from Madagascar, who was later baptized Olivier Le Jeune, was the first Black person to be bought and sold in what is now called Canada.[1] We know little else about him. His namelessness and invisibility, even centuries later, are integral to the logic and cruelty of slavery, a system predicated on captivity and brutal violence, these forces mobilized with the ultimate goal of denying the personhood and humanity of the enslaved.

Many Canadians still don't know or acknowledge that slavery existed here, for more than two hundred years. Our national ignorance about slavery in this country is only possible because of the inexorable specter of American slavery. Even as those who wrote the U.S. Constitution in 1787 avoided using the word *slavery,* it was nevertheless baked into every legal, political, and economic institution at the founding. Article I, Section 2 of the Constitution stipulated that enslaved people were to be counted as three-fifths of a person in the calculation of congressional apportionment. It was a compromise that made the American union possible; a deal struck among white men about the subhuman status of nearly 700,000 enslaved Black people—somewhere around 18 percent of the total population of the original thirteen states. The American Revolution was fought over lofty ideas of freedom and equality but founded a country with an ideological core corrupted by exploitation and forced captivity of the Black population.

The political economy of slavery literally built the United States. Cotton, grown on plantations and extracted by the forced labor of enslaved Black people, was the nation's most valuable export for decades. Enslaved people physically built cities and streets, capitol buildings and transcontinental railroads, and the profits made from the unpaid labor of the enslaved—always, without exception, performed under the threat of violence and death—helped finance prestigious universities.[2] Slavery as an institution "helped turn a poor, fledgling nation into a financial colossus," creating vast fortunes for white people in both the North and the South and making the young nation a global competitor on the world economic stage.[3]

The United States was certainly not the only society that profited from the lives and labor of enslaved Africans. In fact, more than 95 percent of the captives of the international slave trade disembarked in the Caribbean and South America. Brazil, not the United States, was the last country in the Americas to abolish slavery. But American slavery casts a long shadow across time and space. Slavery is frequently called America's "original sin," a contradictory blight on the otherwise powerful democratic ideals of the nation. This interpretation of American history is profoundly dismissive. Slavery wasn't just a sin or a blight; in 1860, on the eve of the American Civil War, there were 3.9 million enslaved Black people in the American South. There were more Black people enslaved in the southern states in 1860 than the entire population of Canada in 1871. It took a war that lasted four years, nearly tore the United States apart, and killed an estimated 750,000 people to abolish slavery. In terms of its impact on the nation's collective memory and mythology, the Civil War is second only to the American Revolution; in fact, Pulitzer Prize–winning historian Eric Foner's recent book on the Civil War and Reconstruction calls the period "the second founding."[4]

Slavery in British North America—what we now call Canada—was much smaller in comparison, but still objectively horrific. There truly is no such thing as humane slavery. Life in bondage is cruel by its nature. It steals children from their parents, punishes the enslaved for forming bonds of friendship or intimacy, extracts and exploits the labor of the unfree, and operates under the constant, relentless threat of violence and death. In her 2006 book, *The Hanging of Angélique,* historian Afua Cooper reveals, in painstaking detail, the "untold story of Canadian slavery" through the life and death of Marie-Joseph Angélique, a Portuguese-born enslaved woman who was accused of starting a fire that decimated Old Montreal. Marie-Joseph Angélique spent her last days on earth being tortured into confessing that she set that fire.

Many enslaved people, including "Panis," the enslaved people of Indigenous descent, attempted to run away from their captivity, or died young. Enslaved people had neither rights nor freedom to choose where or how to exist. For example, in March 1793,

Chloe Cooley, an enslaved woman, was violently removed from her home in Queenston, Upper Canada (now Ontario), beaten, bound, and tossed into a boat by Adam Vrooman, who claimed ownership over her. Though she "screamed violently and made resistance," Vrooman successfully rowed the boat across the Niagara River and sold Cooley to an American buyer in New York.

In 1793 the lieutenant governor of Upper Canada, Colonel John Graves Simcoe, learned of what happened to Chloe Cooley from a Black Loyalist named Peter Martin. Martin, knowing he would not be believed on his own, brought William Grisley, an additional white witness, to report the incident to the Executive Council of Upper Canada. A supporter of the growing antislavery movement in Great Britain, Simcoe initially pushed for the total abolition of slavery in Upper Canada. Slaveholding members of the parliament opposed these efforts, and Simcoe compromised with a law that prevented the introduction of new slaves into the province, meaning that enslaved people could not be imported into the province, and provided for the emancipation of the children of the enslaved once those children reached the age of twenty-five. But current slaves would remain in bondage and the act did not prevent the sale of enslaved people across the Canada-U.S. border.

Canada's national mythology has long positioned our country as the Promised Land for enslaved Americans. In 1991 there was a "Heritage Minute" commercial on the Underground Railroad. It opened with a young Black woman expressing fear that her father had been caught by slave catchers; she and her brother are inconsolable even as two white women try to calm them. As the Black woman, "Eliza," sees a church pew used to smuggle her father, sealed in a hidden compartment, being brought to their location, a narrator says, "Between 1840 and 1860, more than 30,000 American slaves came secretly to Canada and freedom. They called it the Underground Railroad." The father and his children are re-united, and he joyfully exclaims, "We're free!" Eliza responds, "Yes, Pa! We's in Canada!" I sat wide-eyed in front of the television and absorbed the messaging like a sponge. America is where we escaped from. Canada is where we escaped to. Good white Canadians made it happen. We should be grateful. Canada is the national embodiment of the benevolent white savior.

The rhetoric and messaging of that Heritage Minute commercial, the first time I had ever seen Black Canadians be part of the thing we called Canadian heritage and so resonant that I still remember it word for word thirty-one years later, failed to mention that several northern states, including Pennsylvania, Massachusetts, New Hampshire, Rhode Island, Connecticut, and the territories claimed by the Northwest Ordinance of 1787 (Michigan, Indiana, Ohio, Illinois, Wisconsin, and part of Minnesota) abolished slavery long before Upper and Lower Canada. The great paradox of the original Underground Railroad is that enslaved people from the United States could become free by landing in Canada, while those enslaved in Upper or Lower Canada were forced to seek freedom from bondage by escaping to find refuge in the free northern states.[5]

Beyond those enslaved by British and French colonialists, the first significant wave of Black migration to Canada occurred in the aftermath of the American Revolution. In 1775 the royal governor of Virginia, Lord Dunmore, offered freedom to any enslaved person willing to fight for the British in the war against the American rebels, and in 1779 the British commander in chief, Sir Henry Clinton, promised that any person who escaped their American enslavers would have freedom and security behind British lines. At the war's end approximately three thousand Black people were transported from New York to Nova Scotia, along with white British Loyalists who brought enslaved people with them when they fled to Canada.

As fictionalized in Lawrence Hill's best-selling novel and CBC miniseries *The Book of Negroes,* the Black Loyalists faced incredible hardships in Nova Scotia. In nearly every circumstance, the Black settlers were segregated and their land allotments, if they were received at all, were smaller, rockier, and less fertile than those provided to their white counterparts. Many did not reach the province until late autumn and had neither the clothing nor housing to get them through the winter. White Loyalists, angry at economic competition from the Black laborers, attacked and destroyed Black communities. There were persistent rumors that free Blacks were being sold back into slavery and transported to the Caribbean. Those who could not eke out subsistence by farming their small allotments of land became exploited as sharecroppers or tenant farmers for their white Loyalist neighbors.

Disappointed by the failed promises of freedom in Nova Scotia, many Black Loyalists felt their grievances would not be heard or addressed no matter how long they persevered in British North America. In 1792 nearly half of the Black Loyalist population, around 1,200 people, took the British government's offer of transport back to Africa, where they founded the community of Freetown in Sierra Leone.[6] Nearly 60 percent would be dead or dying within six months of their arrival. A few years later rebels ousted from Jamaica were sent to the Maritimes as punishment for their political insurgency, but in 1799 British administrators plotted their deportation. By August 1800, more than 90 percent of the Jamaican Maroons were forcibly removed to Sierra Leone.[7]

Formerly enslaved Black Americans of the mid to late nineteenth century comprise the second wave of Black migration to Canada.[8] Slavery was abolished in Canada as it was throughout the British Empire in 1833, and so crossing the border meant freedom. In 1849 Josiah Henson, who had escaped to what is now the province of Ontario and founded a settlement for Black fugitive slaves near Dresden in Kent County, published his autobiography, *The Life of Josiah Henson, Formerly a Slave, Now an Inhabitant of Canada, as Narrated by Himself.* The book inspired the titular character in Harriet Beecher Stowe's highly impactful antislavery novel, *Uncle Tom's Cabin* (1852).

By the 1850s, Black leaders of the abolition movement established newspapers in Canada West (Ontario), such as the *Provincial Freeman* and *Voice of the Fugitive*, and used these outlets to urge for Black settlement in Canada. Mary Ann Shadd's 1852 pamphlet, *A Plea for Emigration; or Notes of Canada West in Its Moral, Social, and Political Aspect,* made the case that Black Americans should seek refuge and settlement in Canada, where their political and legal rights were protected. The records are sketchy, but estimates suggest that up to 40,000 refugees from American slavery may have fled to Ontario and Quebec, though only 10,000 to 20,000 chose to remain at the close of the Civil War.[9]

The first traces of my family in Canada are from this period, in the years leading up to the Civil War, and so this is where—and when, I suppose—my Canadian roots begin.

My family's history is a story full of holes, conjecture, folklore, and misdirection. Neither of my grandfather's paternal grandparents, Cornelius Thompson nor his wife, Rebecca, appear on the 1861 census, but according to a land registry he was sold half an acre on the southwest side of Albert Street on December 1, 1863. The record of Cornelius in the Canadian census is riddled with inconsistencies; he was apparently thirty years old in 1871, forty-seven in 1881, sixty-six in 1901, and ninety-five in 1921. An article in the *Montreal Gazette* on September 18, 1922, announced his death two days earlier, at "the great age of 100 years." If his actual birth date was within the range of his lies, Cornelius was somewhere between twenty and forty when he escaped the American South. While it's reasonable to assume that someone who was born into slavery may not know their exact birth year, the twenty-year spread in these official records to me suggests a purposeful deception.

"Buxton was full of upstanding citizens," my father confirmed. "But Shrewsbury? That's where you went if you were hiding. And you best believe they'd do whatever they needed to do to stay hidden."

In Cornelius's obituary, he is remembered for appointing himself a reverend and how "he was always proud to narrate that in the days before he escaped from slavery he had been put up for sale and brought $800 on the auction block."

I couldn't find any evidence of him or Rebecca in the database that houses thousands of "runaway ads" posted in local newspapers by the enslavers who were enraged that their property had

taken flight. My father's cousins think that Cornelius and Rebecca escaped from the Spy Hill Plantation in King George County, Virginia, which was once owned by George Washington's family. But proof is hard to come by. Even my last name could be a fabrication; it's a possibility that is more appealing than the likely

My grandfather's grandfather, Cornelius Thompson, date unknown.

alternative, that it was the name of the family that enslaved us. And of Rebecca, we know practically nothing, other than that she was born in the United States, perhaps in 1844, according to the errant statistics of the era.

The ancestors who lived and died in Shrewsbury can be arranged on a family tree that ends up looking far more like a spider's web. There were Thompsons, Lewises, Murphys, and Griffiths, all interspersed and intermarried.[10]

"Everyone in the county is related to my cousin Duane, and some of us are related to Duane in four different ways," laughs my father.

Some folks inexplicably disappear from the official record from one decade to the next. Family legend has it that at least one of my relatives was so light-skinned that he cut off all contact and disappeared into the wilds of Michigan to live the rest of his life as a white man. Another rumor is that someone a few generations back—Elizabeth Lewis, my grandmother's grandmother, perhaps—was Indigenous, though census-takers refused to count her as such because she married a Black man. More folklore that I can't prove. Being indiscernible and avoiding the gaze of the state has long been a strategy necessary for Black survival.

It's a funny thing, given how central slavery is to the African American experience, to have no information about my family before they won their freedom. According to my father, Cornelius and Rebecca both searched for their families when they reached Canada. A wife, a husband, a lover, siblings, parents, children who may have been sold before their escapes, or perhaps they were separated somewhere in the wilderness between the Mason-Dixon Line and the northern shore of Lake Erie. We only know because in the late 1960s, Toronto Argonauts kicker Dave Mann and his co-owners opened the Underground Railroad, a soul food restaurant in Toronto; according to an article in the *Montreal Gazette,* one of the items that adorned the walls of the establishment was a nineteenth-century public notice from Reverend Cornelius Thompson, asking for information on the whereabouts of his and his wife's families. History shows up in strange places, sometimes.[11]

During my PhD I spent a few months in various archives and libraries in Washington, D.C.—what academics call "fieldwork." My dissertation was on the creation of racial classifications on national censuses and I was looking for archival records that might reveal why the United States Census Bureau decided to count by race in the shifting, contradictory ways that it did. On the weekends I visited the monuments and museums, feeling . . . not patriotic, exactly, but some combination of the layered emotional vibrations of curiosity, pride, deep sadness, anger, disbelief, and awe.

On my way to one of the Smithsonian museums, amid the blooming cherry blossoms and the chattering tourists, I saw a homeless Black family. There are homeless people in Toronto, and practically every other Canadian city, but I had never seen homeless children before. There was a mother, who looked maybe a few years older than I was then, and two beautiful Black children, both with huge brown eyes.

I wish I could tell you more about them, about the conversation I know I had with the mother, but I was young and naïve and completely stunned by the idea of homeless children living on the streets of the capital of the richest country in the world. But there they were, sitting on the ground, begging for money amid the grandeur of monuments and statues and museums, unnoticed by those who regularly entered the halls of power—the White House, the United States Capitol, the Supreme Court—mere blocks away from where I sat with them. I wish I could remember what I said to the children, whose huge brown eyes remain emblazed in my mind. It bothers me now that they are still and silent in my memory of them, but they haunt me, nevertheless. I gave them all the cash I had—it wasn't much, and I felt terrible about it. I still feel terrible that I couldn't do more. So, when I looked at the original Declaration of Independence at a museum later that day, eavesdropping on white middle-class parents telling their white middle-class children that American freedom was written *right there,* on that paper, I felt rage at the sheer hypocrisy of it all. And a great despair for all that could have been but wasn't.

In a different dimly lit room, I happened upon a register of marriages, an ancient volume with neat, slanted writing that filled rows of yellowed paper, encased in a glass tomb. A small plaque to the side of the display case detailed the work of the Freedmen's Bureau, a short-lived government agency that provided temporary assistance in finding food, shelter, health care, and jobs for recently freed African Americans and impoverished whites. It also registered and legitimated thousands of marriages among the formerly enslaved.

Slaveholders routinely broke up Black families, sold children away from their parents, raped enslaved women, and denied any responsibility toward their offspring, whose existence was simply added to the ledgers of the enslavers' assets. And, of course, enslaved people could not legally marry—the ability to enter into a contract is a right that could only be exercised by people, not property. More than a mere contract, the right to marry recognizes the basic human desire to maintain intimate, dedicated, long-lasting connections with one another.

I stepped closer to read the entries. There, on the left page, the Bureau recorded the marriage of Samuel and Mary Thompson. My heart skipped a beat and I looked around frantically. I half-expected someone to be staring at me, waiting for this kind of reaction. As usual, I was alone—fieldwork is a solitary, lonely part of writing a dissertation. There was no one to tell. Could these be my people?

African American genealogy is purposefully untraceable. Several proposals to record more details about the enslaved population on the 1850 census, such as names, children, family ties, and place of birth, were soundly defeated by southern members of Congress. It made the enslaved seem too human, they argued. It's more likely to find evidence of familial relations in private bills of sale than in the official record of the state. But I had never been able to find anything to augment family lore and the knowledge of our lineage always came to a grinding halt the minute Rebecca and Cornelius crossed the border. I stared at the ink on paper, trying to will the seasoned pages into revealing more. They didn't. As I slowly left the museum, I decided that even if these Thompsons weren't my kin, they were still my people, and I was glad, in that moment, that they were able to legalize their relationship. Loving another, especially in an existence full of trauma, terror, and loss, is an act of resistance; a solidification of humanity in the face of its denial.[12]

These two groups of Black migrants to Canada, the ancestors who risked everything to follow the North Star and those whom renowned sociologist Daniel Hill named the "freedom seekers," were the last substantial Black immigration to Canada for a hundred years. Both arrived in Canada and claimed political asylum from tyrannical rule and a brutal, violent regime premised on the destruction of their minds, bodies, communities, relationships, and souls. In their escape to Canada, they sought the right to live and die freely. But much like the fractional freedom that characterizes how African Americans were left out of American democracy throughout the nineteenth and twentieth centuries, Black Canadians were not full participants in Canadian social and political life. Many lived in and regularly crossed the ambiguous territory of the border, a line that never cuts as clearly in reality as it does on a map. In their movements back and forth across borderlands, they reshaped the territories, cultures, demographics, and democracies that they transgressed.

Many of those who escaped to Canada eventually found it necessary to escape from Canada as well. Black emigration from Canada was not exactly "forced migration," but was something more akin to "strongly encouraged migration." Or, "subtly coerced migration." Or migration under the false, state-endorsed pretense that Black belonging is impossible in Canada, because Black people cannot possibly be from here. Some of the refugees from American slavery crossed the border once again in search of the loved ones left behind or lost along the way. Others, like many Black Loyalists, chose to leave Canada, once described by French explorer Jacques Cartier as "the land God gave to Cain," to seek a better life than the lies the British Crown had offered. To speak of Black migration in terms of "waves," then, is surprisingly accurate; an initial advance onto new soil, followed by an inevitable ebb back from whence we came. Canada may have provided temporary, reluctant refuge, but elsewhere, often the United States, was *home*.

Those who stayed, an estimated 21,000 people at the end of the nineteenth century,[13] faced the experience of being unwelcome and unwanted, both familiar to other Black populations in the diaspora and, simultaneously, unique to the Canadian national project.

What was it like in the Great White North, I often wondered, for those eighteenth- and nineteenth-century refugees from American slavery who chose to stay in Canada? I once posed this question to my father's mother. She was born Janet Lewis in 1920, the third of four children (like me), had a short-lived marriage to someone we don't know of or talk about (for the record, also like me), and then remarried to my grandfather Andrew Thompson in 1942. What was it like to be Black in Canada during the decades of unabashed racism and segregation? What was it like to be a Black woman during the era when the Famous Five successfully petitioned Britain's Judicial Committee of the Privy Council to include women within the meaning of "persons" in Canadian law, but publicly advocated for eugenics and pushed for legislation that resulted in the forced sterilization of thousands of Indigenous women? What was it like for those Black men who worked as train porters, whom white passengers dismissively called "George" regardless of what their actual names were?[14]

Gram was a tiny thing with a wry sense of humor, perfectly done hair, and a tinkling laugh. She also didn't suffer fools gladly and she told me to mind my business and let the ghosts rest in peace. Gram died in 2009, about a year after the election of Barack Obama to the American presidency. Sitting with her in a nursing home in Scarborough one Sunday afternoon, I told her that a Black man had won the election and would be the incoming president of the United States. She never did believe me. It could have been the dementia. But it might also have been the decades of struggle and the intimate, lifelong experience with the durability of racism.

The Black population of Canada was quite small for most of the twentieth century; this was by design as successive Canadian governments made substantial efforts to maintain a white settler society through restrictive immigration policies. The Immigration Act of 1910 provided the federal Cabinet with more discretionary powers to prohibit the entry of any immigrant deemed "unsuitable to the climate or requirements of Canada." In 1911,

Prime Minister Wilfred Laurier invoked this power in an order-in-council that "prohibited . . . any immigrants belonging to the Negro race." Though the regulation was never written into the Immigration Act, it was an official, executive addendum to several other, indirect, and highly effective methods, such as the selective enforcement of obscure regulations, deception, bribery, and campaigns of dissuasion, used by border agents and other Canadian immigration officials to prevent Black immigration to Canada. Standard medical and "character" examinations at the border crossings in the prairie provinces were easily manipulated to ensure that Black immigrants were denied entry, while the government claimed, publicly and repeatedly, that race was not being used as a criterion in immigrant admissions.

These immigration controls meant that the Black population of Canada remained low and steady throughout most of the twentieth century. A small influx of approximately three thousand Black women from the Caribbean were able to come to Canada under the exploitative conditions of the West Indian Domestic Scheme between 1955 and 1967. But the largest and most recent wave of Black immigration to Canada occurred after 1967, when the federal government amended its explicitly racist immigration policy and implemented a points system, which gives priority to migrants who already speak English or French, can contribute to designated areas of the economy, and are highly educated.

In 1971 the Black population was tiny, at just 34,400 people. My father used to joke that in those days, if you saw another Black person in Toronto, there was a good chance you were related to them. But between 1981 and 1991 the population grew significantly, from 239,500 to 504,300, and by the time of the 2001 census Black folks comprised the third-largest "visible minority" group in the country.

Between 1996 and 2016 the number of African-descended

people in Canada doubled; however, at just under 1.2 million people (3.5 percent of the total population) there aren't that many of us compared to the Black population of the United States, which census estimates put at 46.9 million, or over 14.2 percent of the population.[15] According to the 2016 Census of Canada, Black immigrants hail from over 170 different places of birth, including Jamaica (19.7 percent), Haiti (14.8 percent), Nigeria (6.6 percent), Ethiopia (5 percent), Somalia (4.1 percent), the Democratic Republic of the Congo (3.9 percent), Ghana (3.6 percent), Trinidad and Tobago (3.4 percent), Cameroon (2.9 percent), and the United States (2.3 percent). The vast majority—94.3 percent—of the Black population of Canada lives in urban centers: nearly 40 percent live in Toronto, representing 7.5 percent of Toronto's population, and more than 6 percent of the respective populations of Montreal and Ottawa-Gatineau are Black.[16] Statistics Canada projections suggest that the Black population could reach 5 percent of the Canadian population by 2036, mostly because of immigration.

But *some of us,* I would insist angrily, have been here for a very long time.

⸻

I wonder now why I felt that it was so important to convey that I wasn't a newcomer. What was it about me, my life, my humanity, my potential, that the questioner would know if I could convince them that I had roots in Canada? Why would the number of generations we can trace in Canada matter? What does the claim to being here for a long time mean?

Claims about longevity, generational status, and time are frequently mobilized in ideas about who belongs and who doesn't, the definition of rights and responsibilities, the barriers to and conduits of integration, and political debates about redress, reconciliation, and reparations. I know that many people think that asking others where they are really from is just born from genuine, innocent curiosity. Or maybe it's an attempt to get to know someone better, to seek and find common ground. I get it. But that doesn't change the fact that the question is most often posed to racial minorities, and that asking this question fits a long-standing pattern in which claims about time are used to give white populations the ability to assert dominant ownership of territories, and primary, original belonging in the nation. White people—especially those who now view their origins as American or Canadian rather than the far-flung territories of their ancestors—appeal to ideas about time as a determinant of national belonging *constantly*.

My younger self's insistence about my family's deep roots in Canada wasn't so different from these declarations, that the country belongs the most to the white people who have been here the longest. At the time I felt it was so important, so critical for others to understand that the history of this country had involved my people. But really, it was about making a clear distinction between those of us who had been here for a long time—and thus belonged—and those who were new, who came from elsewhere, who shouldn't be able to make those same claims until they had some generational standing, like me. It's not unlike those who complain they are being "treated like foreigners" in their own country. The idea rests on the same underlying racial logic that foreigners *should* be treated differently. That even as we claim that we believe in the equal moral worth of every human being, we also believe some people are just worth *more* in and to our nation based on the unearned privileges afforded by the march of time. And yet, it still conveniently ignores and denies that Indigenous people have been here since time immemorial. These claims are steeped in the contradictory calculus of settler colonialism, and they are morally indefensible.

Of course, time works in other ways to shape Canada's national imagination. Nations have collective memories, but these are always contested, always up for debate, always shifting in accordance with who has a seat at the table. The flip side of the celebration of a nation's collective memories is the way that nations are also created and maintained through collective forgettings, denials, and erasures. Michel-Rolph Trouillot, in his important book *Silencing the Past*, argues that all historical narratives are produced by individuals and groups that have unequal access and power to the means and the ability to create, replicate, and reify those narratives. Some narratives are made possible through the silencing of others; remembering and forgetting are both perpetually bound with relations of power. Ideas of erasure, silencing, or denial are more purposeful and calculated, still. I don't want to give the impression that these processes are always intentional; that's clearly not the case. But national memories reflect whose voices are valued, what events can be most readily and efficiently absorbed into national narratives, and which ones fit with how we see and understand ourselves.

For years, Black Canadian scholars have explored the "absented-presence" of Blackness in Canada. The "absented" part describes the ways that Black people in Canada are assumed to not exist, or if they exist, to be recent arrivals to what has always been a majority-white country. Black Studies scholar Katherine McKittrick writes that Blackness in Canada is always unexpected, always surprising. "Blackness is surprising because it should not be here, was not here before, was always here, is only momentarily here, was always over there (beyond Canada, for example). This means, then, that black people in Canada are also presumed surprises because they are 'not here' and 'here' simultaneously. . . ."[17]

So, read this way, the question "Where are you really from?" is an attempt to address the shock and astonishment of seeing

Blackness in a place where it is not supposed to be. The question assumes the necessity of defining Blackness as from elsewhere, because, as McKittrick continues, Black existence is an actuality that takes on several forms that do not—surprisingly to some— always align with or conform to the idea of Canada.

But Blackness in Canada is not just absent (and it's worth asking, absent to whom and what?) but *absented*. I'm not suggesting that the act of disappearing an entire population is a conspiratorial, elite-driven rewriting of history with the intention of erasing all traces of Black people and experiences from the founding and evolution of Canadian life and culture. Instead, to be absented, rather than just absent, implicates the involvement of political processes that have unfolded over time and a series of actions that bring conditions into being, as opposed to a description of what has always been.

The "presence" part of "absented-presence" implicates the ways that narratives of Canadian identity depend on the existence of Black Canada, even as they erase it. The idea of Canada as the Promised Land, the destination for fugitive slaves who followed the North Star, a safe haven from the tyranny of American racism, a contemporary multicultural paradise that demonstrates, far more than America, Brazil, or even South Africa ever could, the potential of a multiracial democracy that celebrates its diversity— these are fundamental, foundational parables of the Canadian imagination. They all depend on the historical presence of an allegorical Black Canada. Just . . . not *too* many Black people, of course. And certainly not *angry* Black people, or *radical* Black people, or *loud* Black people, or *ungrateful* Black people, or Black people who remember the razing of Africville in Halifax and Hogan's Alley in Vancouver, or Black people who point out the many ways that Canada tolerates Blackness only begrudgingly.

There is also something quite unique about Blackness in

Canada, something fundamentally relational. Unlike African-descended peoples in the United States or Brazil, Black Canadians are not a national minority, even as we've been in the country since its founding. Black Canada is also on the edge of the African diaspora, in spite of our proximity to the assumed cultural hegemony of African American ideas of Blackness. In our efforts to think through the absence, presence, and absented-presence of Blackness in the Canadian imagination and the imprecise and disruptive narratives that never quite align with the multicultural ethos, an equally interesting question is the place of *Canada* in the Black diasporic imagination.

Canadian Blackness has confronted the joints and fissures of the African diaspora in ways that are unique, nuanced, and prescient: How might we understand slavery and colonialism as the dual yet interconnected racial formations that shaped the modern world? Are Black people settlers, and what is our responsibility in dismantling settler colonialism and allying with Indigenous peoples? What does it mean to have a truly diasporic consciousness that refuses to be subsumed by the primary claims of loyalty to, hope for, or belief in the liberatory potential of the nation-state?

Where are we *really* from?

CHAPTER 2

The Only One

(Oshawa, Ontario)

Y ou know, Debra," my father sometimes says, "hindsight is twenty-twenty because any fool can turn around and look behind them."

There's something both settled and unsettling about the ability to look back on one's life in ten- or twenty-year increments. It's a perspective that highlights with tragic and triumphant clarity who we once were in relation to who we are now. It's only in hindsight that the layered, compounding nature of everyday moments becomes meaningful. It turns out that the mundane is often much more consequential than the spectacular.

I have a clear memory of a Friday night like any other, hanging out with my grad school friends at some scuzzy bar on Yonge Street in Toronto, around the time when Barack Obama, then a junior senator from Illinois, had launched his campaign for the American presidency. I was talking to a friend about one of the central struggles in my research, namely, how to compare the dynamics of racism in Canada and the United States.

"But you've at least got to admit that multiculturalism resolves some of the issues that they have in the States," she countered. It was an ordinary, typical, forgettable moment, and hers was an ordinary, typical, standard response that I had heard before. But she was a friend—and is still one of my very best friends, actually—and she loved me, and I thought she might be willing to see the world turned upside down, so I decided to try a different tack.

"Jenn," I said. "Have you noticed that I'm the only not-white person in this bar?"

I remember her exact expression. Her eyes widened a little and she froze, lowered her beer bottle, and slowly turned in a circle, her eyes scanning each corner of the room. She faced me once more, a look of shock on her face.

"No, I didn't notice that at all," she said.

I took a sip of cheap, flat beer. "If our positions were reversed, and you were the only white person in a room of Black people, do you think you'd notice then?"

"Yeah. Yeah. Yes, I definitely would," she replied.

I shrugged and we let it be. Years later, I did, in fact, take her to a bar where she was the only white person in the room. She reminded me of this conversation—by then it was just one moment among the thousands that comprise our friendship, but she never forgot it. The first time she saw through the invisibility of whiteness. Neither did I.

During the first three decades of my life in Canada, I was often the Only One. The only Black student in any class, grade, and school. The only Black kid on the soccer team. The only Black employee in the branch of Indian and Northern Affairs Canada, where I worked for several years before leaving the civil service for a life in academia. The only Black graduate student in the political science department. The only Black person in any space, anywhere, anytime, everywhere, every time. And if I was not the Only One, I was certainly one of the very few in a sea of white.

Being the Only One didn't make me feel particularly unique or successful or special. It made me think that there was something inherently wrong with Black people and that I had to fight against it every single day to defy what the fates had in store for us. These weren't conscious thoughts, of course. They were the undercurrents of being, seldom spoken aloud.

"I don't know why they've got to have their pants hanging off their ass," my father used to mutter while watching the Toronto police arrest young Black men on the evening news.

And the local Toronto news, with its dramatizations depicting young Black men as the perpetrators of all kinds of social ills, alongside American television serials like *Law & Order*, was where most of my information about Black people came from. Caribana, as Toronto's summer street festival celebrating Caribbean culture was called then, was regularly portrayed in the media as a space of interchangeable Black revelry, violence, and danger. The Canadian media provided endless messaging of Black people as deviant, as criminals, as gang members, as pathological, as threatening to white safety and sanctity. The intersection of Jane and Finch was racial code for an American-like ghetto that existed out of time and out of place in the postracial diversity of Toronto.

Those were the stereotypes I felt I was up against. Every time someone exclaimed how well-spoken I was, how very articulate, how refreshingly smart, what an achievement it must be for my parents to see me in university at all, it was always said with a coy smile that hinted at the surprise of finding me in spaces where I clearly didn't belong. Praise always came with a side of gaslighting.

But I didn't see it then for what it was. Instead, it just made me more desperate to prove myself worthy. It's only in hindsight that I see this drive to excel as born of the same internalized racism at the heart of respectability politics. The measure of Black worth is determined by how readily, how easily, how often, how durably we can assimilate into white society. Assimilation is never a neutral process. It's not possible to be absorbed into a world that was built by theft and genocide, torture and mass murder without letting the many and varied excuses for these horrors infiltrate your logics and rationalizations for why things are the way they are. Whiteness always sees itself as benevolent, allowing all into its fold, if only we're willing to try. As if behavior alone could grant access to the heavily patrolled and guarded borders of whiteness.

"We have liberal democratic values here," whiteness tells us sagely. "Your presence will be tolerated as long as you adhere to our values and obey our laws. What? Well, yes, our laws were written exclusively by white people, but they are fair and applied equally. It's just that Black people commit more crimes. And yes, we are a democracy and you are free to assemble and protest! But don't you dare inconvenience capitalism while you're doing it. And the police can legally and legitimately beat and arrest you for speaking out. And we will condemn, belittle, and harass you for exercising these democratic rights, because you are really just *ungrateful* that we have so kindly permitted you to live here, among us, on this land that we stole from Indigenous people and in this wealth and prosperity that your ancestors were forced to build for free."

When whiteness speaks, it's always within a decibel of threat. Part of the trickery of white supremacy is in masking the threat of violence in a cloak of fragility and insecurity. Whiteness is so unstable, so easily stained that just one drop of Black blood used to be enough to ruin it. Assimilating into a predominantly white society therefore necessitates a disdain for those elements of Blackness that were created in defiance of white supremacy's demands for obedience and conformity. Respect is earned, we are told. Respectability can be wrangled, unwillingly and incompletely, from the clutches of whiteness by performing white-approved behaviors.

But, of course, mimicry always carries a temporal lag and facsimiles can never truly attain the power and persona of whiteness. For Black people, wresting these breadcrumbs of respect comes at the low, low price but high, high cost of hating Blackness.

And I was *so very* respectable.

But it was more than that, and worse—I bought into the respectability politics embedded in the idea that Black people must work twice as hard to get half as much.

"You cannot just be good," one of the few women of color in a faculty position at the University of Toronto told me in the early days of my doctoral program. "You're a woman and a woman of color, and that means you need to be much, much better than everyone else."

As I smoked a cigarette and drank a cup of coffee on the benches outside Sidney Smith Hall at the University of Toronto, ten minutes before the orientation to my PhD program was to begin, I decided that even if I wasn't the smartest person in the room, I could work the hardest. I had to. It seemed like I was once again one of just a small handful of Black students in the entire program, which had more than a hundred PhD students actively registered at any given time. Work twice as hard, hope for the best, be ready to fight the worst. That was just the way it was going to have to be. I knew that it wasn't fair, but I also knew there was no getting around it. The benefit of the doubt is for white people, not for we Only Ones.

I honestly don't know why my parents moved to the suburbs in the late 1970s from East York, the part of Toronto where my father had spent his teenage years and where my oldest sister was born. I also don't know if it's accurate to call Oshawa, Ontario, a suburb. It's outside of what is now a sprawling Greater Toronto Area, about fifty kilometers east of Toronto proper but close enough to be connected to the downtown core by a commuter train, the station of which was built on the fields where we used to pick strawberries each summer.

In the 1980s and 1990s, Oshawa was a small city, known for and proud of the General Motors plant that drove the local economy, providing well-paying, unionized jobs for folks who often had, at most, a high school education. When Ed Broadbent was our member of Parliament and leader of the federal New Democratic Party (NDP), the city was a working-class stronghold for the party. But Oshawa was also characterized by the kind of ideologically conservative streak that is often found in small towns that are neither urban nor suburban, but also not exactly rural. White supremacist organizations like the Heritage Front had a shadowy presence, making local headlines just infrequently enough to validate my parents' insistence of caution and vigilance around people we didn't know.

Canada proclaimed itself a multicultural nation in those last few decades of the twentieth century, but a full fifteen years after Prime Minister Pierre Elliott Trudeau stood in the House of Commons to set out the official multiculturalism policy, there were hardly any people of color in Oshawa. Or Canada, for that matter. According to the 1986 census, the Black population of the country was still tiny—less than 1 percent of the population. Even in Toronto, Black people comprised around 3 percent of the total population. And in Oshawa, just 840 people of more than 123,000 identified as Black in 1986. Five years later, in 1991, Oshawa's population grew by thousands but its self-identified Black population dropped to 825. There was no Black community to speak of, just individuals, maybe families. Strangers who nodded to one another on the street, but nothing more.

Leisa (age five), me (age two), and Jessica (age seven) in 1982. Jonathan wasn't born yet.

The rhetoric of Canadian multiculturalism was everywhere in the 1980s and 1990s, which was incredibly confusing for me and my siblings as we navigated countless situations where we were the only Black people in sight. Like so many Black children who grow up in predominantly white spaces, I was probably four or five when I learned from the other kids in my neighborhood that I was Black and that Black was ugly, stupid, and unwanted. Slur-worthy, slur-able Blackness. It's so odd to now listen to white parents worry that their white children are too young and too innocent to learn about race or racism, when it was white children and the prejudice and ignorance they learned from their white parents that terrorized my childhood.

Children can be cruel, but at least they were blunt about it. The prejudice of my teachers was harder to pin down. Maybe my teachers didn't think I was smart because I wasn't actually all that smart. Maybe the school librarian wouldn't let me take books from a higher reading level because she really believed that "rules are rules"; but that doesn't explain why the rules that were rules only seemed to apply to me and not my white classmates. Maybe I

really wasn't good at math. Maybe I really wasn't "university material." Maybe they were right. Or maybe they were racist. That's
the thing about the colorblind racism of the last decades of the
twentieth century, what sociologist Eduardo Bonilla-Silva calls
"racism without racists"—it always operates under the cloud of
plausible deniability.[1]

My parents were not interested in using my siblings and me
to challenge what I'm sure they suspected was the blatant racial
biases baked into teachers' perceptions of us, and the education
system as a whole. My father was a teacher at a different school
in the district and so could usually deal with any explicit racism
through the back channels available to those in the know. The
way that teachers treated me noticeably changed when one of my
father's good friends became the vice principal at my elementary
school. He was also my sixth-grade teacher and for the first time
in my life I had a white teacher who just assumed I was smart.
What a world of difference it made.

Equally important, I think, was that my parents were unnecessarily strict, overly invested in the idea of appearing "respectable," and were in many ways dismissive of the idea that we
could—or *should*—do anything to challenge the structural dis-
advantages we faced. I don't think my mother—white, Jewish,
frequently plagued by feelings of being the odd one out, overwhelmed with the task of raising four children on a modest teacher's salary, abandoned by some in her extended family that could
not forgive her for marrying a non-Jewish Black man, and full
of white fragility—ever really understood what we went through.
I am not convinced she could have understood, even if she had
wanted to.

My father, on the other hand, knew that Black people had to
work twice as hard to get half as much, and so he unapologetically adhered to the "that means you should be working twice as

hard" model of child rearing. He was also adamant that we defend each other. Most weeks at least one of us would come home crying about something some aspiring racist said or did. We were regularly targeted, teased, and beaten by white kids in the neighborhood.

"That's why I had four children," Dad would respond. The next day we would track the kids down and beat them up. There were four of us and so we usually, though temporarily, outnumbered them. They were always so conveniently regretful when they were about to be pummeled by our violent family tradition. But, all told, there were dozens of them, with, it seemed to me, family traditions of trying to humiliate and intimidate Black children.

Canadian multiculturalism was an integral part of our national identity in those years, but I could tell you stories for days about how little multiculturalism did to protect me from either individualized or structural racism. Or the many, subtle messages that I was never quite enough. How I was skipped over for promotions at my part-time jobs because I had "a problem with authority"; the security guards who followed me around department stores; the flippant, easily flung cruelty of my high school classmates; the city buses that passed me by if I was the only one standing at the stop; the fact that I couldn't find foundation that matched my skin tone until 2005.

And I could write an entire book on the trauma of white people talking about, mocking, and trying to wash, cut, or style my hair. When I was very young, a friend of my mother's cut my hair and used to say in complete earnestness that cutting my hair helped sharpen her scissors. White people—young, old, friends, total strangers, it didn't matter—used to just walk up to me and touch my hair without asking, patting me like I was some kind of domesticated animal, frequently laughing as they did. As a teenager, I once walked into a salon at the mall to get my hair trimmed and was refused service because the women who worked there were "too scared" to try to cut my hair. While I was in university, I tried to get a relaxer done at a random salon in Ottawa and the stylist left the chemicals on for too long, burning the skin around my hairline. When I once wore hair extensions to a bar, a white friend in my undergrad program asked if my hair was real. I told her it wasn't, and she said, "I didn't think so, it looks too nice to be your hair."

When I moved to Toronto to do my PhD, I found a college student originally from Jamaica to braid my hair. I drove to her house in Scarborough, where we would watch six hours of BET as she wove extensions into my hair, dry and damaged from a decade of chemical straightening. I was twenty-five years old, and it was the first time in my life that I got my hair done and didn't feel anxiety or shame.

These experiences were born of a particular time and place, and so I can't say for certain how generalizable they are—though, I think it's a pretty safe bet that most Black people in Canada my age and older (and probably younger, too) have been called the n-word at some point in their lives. These memories are also deeply personal and individualized, in the sense that so many of the slights, insults, and slurs were whispered in passing and therefore experienced in isolation, as I stood with a frozen smile on my face, frequently too shocked, but more often too hurt to reply. As the Only One, I just didn't have the vocabulary to articulate the relationship between my private, disjointed, individualized experiences of racism and the wider institutional and structural factors at play.

I couldn't name my experiences as racism in part because of Canadian multiculturalism, which encases the crucible of racial gaslighting. "Deb," my white friends, enemies, frenemies, teachers, coaches, managers, *everyone* used to say, "I don't even notice that you're Black," or "I just don't see race," or "Race doesn't matter at all," or "Aren't we all just human?"

This always made me feel . . . something. I didn't know what, exactly. Dismissed, deflated, defeated. A little insane. Like there was something wrong with me, like I must have deserved the differential treatment I knew I was getting. Like the racism I knew I experienced must not have really happened, or must not have happened the way I remember it, or was probably just some small misunderstanding, or I think you're being too sensitive, Debra, are you sure you're not just misinterpreting things? Like the order of things—no Black teachers, all-white environments, being the Only One in almost every situation—was preordained, natural, and normal, and that the only thing out of place was me. Somehow everything, and yet nothing, and yet everything was about race.

Canadian multiculturalism wasn't designed to make Canada a more inclusive place for racial minorities, and it certainly wasn't meant to benefit Indigenous peoples. This isn't to say that multiculturalism made Canada an openly hostile society, of course. Multiculturalism makes for a great marketing campaign. It sells even better than it deflects. But multiculturalism is not a magic bullet, and it does nothing to change the fact that non-white people in Canada are still considered interlopers to this great white settler social experiment, late additions to be absorbed by Canadian national identity, even as the rhetoric of multiculturalism depends on our existence.[2]

In hindsight, I can see how much I was a product of this environment. And in those days, before the internet enabled marginalized people to grow communities anywhere, our main source of information about the violence of colonialism and white supremacy was the colonial, white supremacist state. I didn't learn a single, solitary fact about Black Canadian history in school and the only Black teacher I ever laid eyes on was my father. More troubling is that in Oshawa, the name itself taken from an Ojibwe word that means something to the effect of "s/he goes across by boat,"[3] anything I learned about Indigenous peoples falls too solidly in the category of pro-genocidal propaganda to repeat here. As a teenager I played competitive soccer for the Whitby Iroquois Soccer Club the next town over, completely oblivious to the callousness of using a nation of people as mascots. These silences and erasures are critical to a national discourse that celebrates multiculturalism while deliberately avoiding any discussion of race, racism, or settler colonialism.

Our national identity is also heavily invested in a strategy of relational denial. The United States looms large in the Canadian imagination. America's foundational ideas, beliefs, identities, narratives, obsessions, and psychoses have enormously influenced the formation of our national identity. Look, it's just hard to share a border, language, culture, ideological tradition, media, and popular culture with the world's only superpower. I eventually came to think of it as akin to the Freudian theory of the "narcissism of minor differences," which suggests communities that have adjacent territories and close relationships are likely to be hostile and contemptuous because they are hypersensitive to the tiny differences between them. In Canada's case, the contempt seems to go only one way. Americans don't seem to think about us at all.

Maybe that's why there's more than a little anti-American sentiment baked into Canadian political culture. Either that, or we might just have a national inferiority complex. For Canadians, the United States is like the mean girl in high school, our very own Regina George. We hate her and love her and think she's terrible and sometimes she's not terrible to us, but she's frequently terrible to other people, but really, why won't she just pay attention to us? It hurts our feelings that she doesn't think we're cool.

But even the most Canadian-focused history class can't avoid talking about the influence of the United States. The United States has been a driver of Canadian politics, even from the very beginnings of the country. In the mid-nineteenth century the American doctrine of Manifest Destiny sought to expand the territorial claims of the United States throughout the entire continent, while the outbreak of the Civil War demonstrated the immense military power of the Union. Both threats, along with important internal factors, such as the political deadlock between Canada East and Canada West under the structure of government dictated by the 1840 Act of Union, drove political elites in Canada to seek to consolidate the provinces of British North America into a single dominion. A federal system gave control over important social arenas, such as education, to the provinces, but a strong national government was understood as a necessary corrective to the extensive, potentially rebellious powers claimed by American states.

The comparative history lesson was always clear: the United States emerged from the blood and war and Canada was founded through more civilized, though much less glorious, processes of negotiation and compromise. Evolution, instead of revolution, we were taught. At least in anglophone Canada, being Canadian is very much defined as being not-American.

There was also a racial logic embedded in the way we Canadians distinguished ourselves from Americans. To most anglophone Canadians, Canada was not-America. And in America, there was a long, indisputable history of anti-Black racism. And since Canada is not America, Canada cannot possibly be racist.

This seemed ludicrous to me, another aspect of multicultural gaslighting. And the ingrained anti-American sentiment of Canadian social life didn't quite hold up in my mind, either. America was a fabled place, where my ancestors were born and broken, where many of our cousins still lived, in the mythical Black enclaves of Philadelphia, Detroit, Harlem, and Chicago. I identified as Canadian to all those white people who asked me where I was from (because I couldn't possibly be from *here*). But, in all honesty, I thought of myself as Black (not African-Canadian and not only Canadian) and I thought of all Black people as connected to me, somehow. The Black-centered television sitcoms of the 1980s and 1990s that I watched to see someone, anyone, who looked like me—*227, Family Matters, The Cosby Show, A Different World*— shaped what I knew of African American culture. The substance and confines of all that I imagined Blackness could be emerged from the forms of popular culture deemed acceptable and respectable enough to make it to cable television. As the Only One, there weren't many other places where my ideas about Blackness could have come from.

I loved the Chicago Bulls of the 1990s, celebrated every Black victory wrested from the hands of white domination (even O. J. Simpson's acquittal, though we all know he was guilty as sin), felt fury at the Rodney King verdict, and wept when James Byrd Jr. was lynched by white supremacists in Texas. LeVar Burton thought reading was cool and so I did, too, and when I later discovered his role as a Black engineer on *Star Trek: The Next Generation,* it opened a world of possibility to pursue occupations in science and engineering that I had never considered. Maybe I wasn't bad at math like they said; after all, wasn't a 90 in calculus a decent grade? Any Black contestant in any game or competition instantly became my favorite. Lenny Kravitz was the greatest musician (and a Jew, my mother always pointed out) and Tracy Chapman's "Fast Car" was the best song of all time. Who cared about Nancy Kerrigan or Tonya Harding when Surya Bonaly could do a backflip on the ice?

I had an acute sense of what political scientist Michael Dawson has termed "linked fate," the idea that African-descended peoples experience and promote solidarity with other Black folks, that our individual fates are connected to the collective fortunes or failures of African Americans as a racial group. But mine was a continental, even global formulation of linked fate, and I felt a connection to African Americans through our common sense of history, folklore, imagined homeland, cultural symbols, experiences of subjugation, heroes, political commitments, and the intangible sense that, somehow, all our destinies were linked together.[4]

I think that the idea of Black linked fate was even more important to me because it provided a critical alternative to my existence as the Only One. Instead, I imagined I was part of a continental Blackness of *millions*. Canada might have been the Promised Land for my ancestors, but the United States was the place where Black people could feel like they belonged.

———

In hindsight, the idea that anyone could believe that racism magically stopped at the 49th parallel is ridiculous, especially given that Canada was founded as a white settler society. A more careful and systematic comparison between Canada and the United States reveals not the absence of racism but the ways that various formulations and intersections of individualized, structural, and institutional racism simply work differently, in ways that are sometimes harder to pinpoint. In covert ways that often stand in stark and sneaky contrast to the explicit history and contemporary manifestations of racism in the United States.

There is ample evidence of persistent socioeconomic disparities that plague Black communities, even long-standing ones. According to a series of reports published by Statistics Canada in 2019, between 2001 and 2016 unemployment rates among the Black population were higher than in the rest of the population, even at higher levels of education. Poverty rates are also higher and the wage gap between the Black and white groups is persistent and significant. A 2010 study comparing the economic status of Black and white populations in Canada and the United States found that wage gaps in the two countries are strikingly similar (controlling for the relative size of first-, second-, and third-generation immigrant groups). Black Canadians are twice as likely as non-Black counterparts to report that they have experienced discrimination in the workplace or have been treated unfairly. According to the Black Experience Project, two-thirds of respondents report that they frequently or occasionally experience anti-Black racism, and eight in ten report that they experience daily microaggressions, such as others assuming their work is inferior or being treated in a condescending way. Even second-generation Black Canadians, those born and bred in the country, report lower levels of feeling as though they truly belong.[5]

More troubling still is the way that Black Canadians most frequently experience Canadian democracy through their interactions with the coercive and punitive arm of the state. Numerous recent reports detail that Black people face rampant systemic racism in urban centers, are disproportionately stopped, carded, charged, arrested, and subjected to use of force by law enforcement, are overrepresented in the system of mass incarceration, and when incarcerated are much more likely to be put in "high risk" categories during their intake assessments, thereby limiting their visitation privileges, access to rehabilitation programs, and chances for parole.[6] According to CBC's Deadly Force database, Black and Indigenous people are overrepresented in fatal encounters with law enforcement compared to their share of the overall population; Black people have hovered around an average of

3 percent of the population over the past twenty years, but are 8.63 percent of fatalities.[7] Similar circumstances in the American context have launched a critical examination of what legal scholar Michelle Alexander has called the New Jim Crow,[8] but in Canada they barely register as newsworthy.

"So, you really think that you're a victim of racism? Come on. That's bullshit and you know it," white men would regularly challenge me. Why were they so angry at the mere thought that racism in Canada exists? "Tell me how racism has fucked up your life," they would demand.

Here's the thing about individualized racism. It's usually subtle and deniable. Sure, there were racial slurs hurled on the street, but it was much more common to experience some kind of racism that was difficult to prove. How did I *know* it was racism, and not something else? And, of course, many were convinced that racism could only operate at the level of racial slurs and nothing else, so the only discernible effects of racism, in their eyes, are hurt feelings.

Systemic racism is even harder to pinpoint because of the double denial of multiculturalism and the relational racial logic of anti-Americanism. When Obama was elected president of the United States in 2008, it got even worse. The triumph of a Black man in the White House—even though I lived in a different country—gave paradoxical fodder to the dismissiveness.

"There's a structural aspect to racism," I argued. I tried to explain how racism intersects with gender and other signifiers of identity. I am Black, but light-skinned, a cis-gendered straight woman but grew up poor, educated but still a first-generation university student. I stumbled in my attempts to explain the relationship between the open hostilities and microaggressions of the everyday and the more consequential ways that racialized power and privilege were built into political, social, and economic life.

White men, in response, would roll their eyes and either ignore or mock me for the rest of the conversation.

They always wanted concrete examples, but racism is protean, highly malleable, and able to adapt to different circumstances, absorbing its critiques and shifting forms to reinvent itself anew. It is purposeful exclusion and predatory inclusion, silences, subtle messaging, and shouted slurs, in- and hypervisibility. It is operationalized by differential effects of superficially universal laws and policies, the informalities and discretion built into systems of power, hidden entry points and overly emphasized exit ramps, and normalized patterns of behavior that are excused away because this is just the way things have always been done. It is, as I wrote in my first book, the various and sometimes conflicting legal, economic, political, and social distinctions that mark and maintain unequal access to prosperity, privacy, property, protection, and personhood.

Systemic racism can be state actions that deliberately limit movement, the accumulation of wealth, or access to opportunities, and it can be when governments choose not to act and instead let racist systems remain undisturbed. It is selective interest, sustained indifference, and messages of "personal choice" that naturalize racial inequality as the unavoidable consequence of individual failings. It is government protection and benefits that are hard to access or withdrawn without reason, or the co-optation of resurgent and radical demands in order to dilute, tame, simplify, and make them more palatable, marketable, consumable, and profitable. Systemic racism is anchored by ongoing constructions of mundane state practices that make racial classifications appear to be natural and normal, like in the census, and spectacles of government concern embellished in royal commissions, national inquiries, and official apologies, but with reparations that are materially shallow and recommendations that are quickly forgotten.

Racism is systemic in that there are multiple components of our social lives that work in layered and compounding ways to produce racially disparate outcomes. I was a high-achieving student and so seemed destined for university, but I nearly wasn't. What if my father's friend, my sixth-grade teacher, wasn't also the vice principal and wasn't able to keep the racism of others in check? I was able to attend a great university for my undergraduate degree (Carleton University in Ottawa, Ontario) and do well, but I nearly didn't. My parents could not contribute money to help pay for my undergraduate education, so I worked three part-time jobs during my degree and failed a few classes because there weren't enough hours in the day to study and work. I had never considered applying to do a PhD—it wasn't even in the realm of my imagination—but a political science professor (non-coincidentally, a woman of color) told me that I had the smarts and skills to make it, and I chose to believe her. I was admitted to one of the best universities in Canada for my doctoral degree, but I suspect that was because political theorist Joe Carens happened to be on the graduate admissions committee that year and saw great potential in research on race in Canada. When I illegally acquired and smoked cannabis with my friends, it was in someone's apartment in Toronto's student-infiltrated neighborhood of the Annex, not in Regent Park, where the police regularly harass Black folks for being in public spaces. When I applied for a postdoctoral fellowship, funded by the Social Science and Humanities Research Council of Canada, I was able to find a potential supervisor at Harvard University because my dissertation advisor, Jenny Nedelsky, made introductions for me.

And so, I can safely say even more clearly in hindsight than I could back then, that mine is not a story about individual perseverance against the odds of being the Only One, or having my achievements recognized in a race-neutral meritocracy, or one about working twice as hard and getting half as much. It is a story of luck, happenstance, being in the right place at the right time, having white allies who opened doors, benefiting from universal health care, state-subsidized tuition and academic scholarships, doing everything in my power to avoid any contact with the police, and having three kick-ass siblings to validate my experiences and counteract the gaslighting.

And it sure as hell isn't a story about the success of Canadian multiculturalism.

Before I moved to Boston in the summer of 2010, I had a conversation with Jenny, an American originally from Chicago, who has been living in Toronto for decades. We sat in her office in the University of Toronto law school, as we had done so many times over the years, surrounded by books and papers and the ether of decades of knowledge piled around us. I told her that I was excited to go to the United States in part to put my money where my mouth was. I had spent years trying to make the argument that there was racism and racial inequality in Canada, just as there was in the United States, and for years I had been told I was wrong. I had been told so often that there was nothing political about race or racism in Canada that I wrote an article on the subject so I would have something to hand to the mediocre white boys in my PhD program who told me, earnestly and sincerely, with only a hint of condescension and a dash of arrogance, that if I really wanted to know about race, I should just watch *The Wire*.

Jenny paused for a moment and kind of tilted her head. "That's so funny," she said. "One of the things that I find most compelling about your work is that you see race politics differently than American academics."

"Oh no," I said. I'd had enough of being different.

She laughed. "No, what I mean is that your work has turned many of my assumptions about race and racism upside down. I always thought that America was just racist. It was born racist back in the 1700s and it's still racist now. But your research . . . it asks not just why things are the way they are, but whether they have to be that way at all."

I listened, and knowing me, probably furrowed my brow, but didn't respond. I don't think quickly on my feet and I'm not good at taking compliments.

Jenny didn't mind. She gave me a hug and walked me to her office door one last time. "I hope you always retain the sense that things are odd," she said as we parted ways.

It was a perspective that came to define the next decade of my life in the United States.

CHAPTER 3

The Freedom Trail

(Boston, Massachusetts)

Harvard was not at all what I expected. It was like being thrown into the deep end of a pool, except in this case the pool was ancient, narcissistic, pompous, loaded with money—and utterly amazing. It's a place full of history, myth, and legend.

I had a one-year postdoctoral fellowship and the minute I arrived in the fall of 2010 I already felt behind and out of place. I was an immigrant to the United States, but an interloper and, I strongly suspected, an imposter at both Harvard and in my discipline of political science. I met with world-renowned faculty and brilliant graduate students, went to seminars and workshops hosted by the leaders of the discipline, and even sat in on a few statistics classes (still under the false impression that I was bad at math, of course). But I observed more than I participated, and I would have been soul-crushingly lonely were it not for the daily pleasantries I exchanged with the custodians who came around 5 p.m. each evening to empty the trash from my office in the Center for American Political Studies and the beautiful, kind women who worked in the café on the first floor of the Knafel Building.

On the weekends I sometimes took the Red Line train from my apartment near Porter Square into Boston. I'd wander around used bookstores and pretend I was a real scholar. I spent a lot of time reading in Boston Common or at pubs that had beer and lighting that were too dark for me. On the recommendation of an insightful bartender (because when you move as much as I do, you learn to make friends with the bartenders), I bought Howard Zinn's *A People's History of the United States*. It was my first introduction to American history, told from the bottom up, centering the point of view of those people that history so often excluded or forgot, whose contributions to the democratic experiment went uncelebrated. The stories weren't only of my enslaved ancestors, but also the Indigenous people that Columbus maimed, tortured, and murdered, the labor organizers who fought for a forty-hour workweek, and those who resisted the American impulse toward war and empire. In a country obsessed with the valorization of Great American Heroes who singularly conquer territory and enemies, it was a reminder of the risks taken and sacrifices made by people without wealth or power, who sought to create a better America, even as their efforts were frequently squashed and their accomplishments erased.

I spent hours walking around the city reading plaques. There are a million plaques and monuments in Boston, markers at the nexus of time and space, constantly shaping and reshaping landscapes and histories in spectacular, mundane, and half-hidden ways. The only monument to catch my eye for more than a minute was the Shaw Memorial, on the edge of Boston Common. It's a bronze sculpture that depicts Colonel Robert Gould Shaw, a white man sitting straight-backed on a horse, leading the African American soldiers of the 54th Massachusetts Volunteer Infantry Regiment to fight in the Civil War. An angel, or at least some kind of winged figure, floats above them. It had the tenor of white saviorism, but it was rare to see Black people in any kind of public commemoration in any form and so for that alone it was captivating. It was also haunting, this window into the past that depicted the free and previously enslaved Black people who wouldn't live to see emancipation. But it meant nothing. It was like eavesdropping on someone else's conversation or happening upon a stranger's funeral. I was interested and morbidly curious, but I didn't have any kind of emotional attachment to these soldiers' sacrifice in some foreign war.

Faneuil Hall felt haunted, though. Another famous Boston landmark, it was built by Peter Faneuil and funded by his profits in the slave trade. Some call it "the cradle of liberty" because it was the meeting place for revolutionaries and abolitionists. But before that it was a marketplace where people who looked like me were bought and sold on the bricks where I stood surrounded by swarms of tourists. In the cool breeze I could hear the screams of

The Robert Gould Shaw 54th Regiment Memorial in Boston Common.

mothers who saw their children ripped away. As a man dressed in colonial garb gesticulated enthusiastically to a group of uninterested high schoolers nearby, I imagined an elevated platform where a buyer forced open the jaws of Black men to examine their teeth and demanded to know whether the teenage girls were ready to bear children—more property, more profits. A market for the commodification of the human body. When those bodies inevitably broke under the weight of cruelty, violence, disdain, and torture, the buyers would simply purchase another. The cradle of liberty to some is a graveyard to others.

Boston, alongside other early metropolitan centers like Philadelphia and New York City, is considered the birthplace of American freedom. Even growing up in Canada I had heard of the Boston Tea Party, when American colonists outraged at the tax imposed in the Tea Act of 1773 dumped hundreds of crates of British tea into the harbor. Less often talked about is the hypocrisy of the white colonists who dressed as Mohawks (Kanien'kehá:ka) both as a disguise and to symbolize white colonists' struggle against imperial domination in the country they claimed as their own. The event is remembered as emblematic of the American revolutionary spirit, in which principled protest against taxation without representation was necessary to resist oppressive and dominating forces from across the sea.

This is the inheritance of white America: mob violence and property destruction committed in order to seize the freedom and respect one is owed by virtue of being white. The revolutionary ethic is embedded in the idea of the sanctity of life, the uncompromised exercise of liberty, and the individualized, relentless pursuit of happiness, no matter the cost.

The precondition for American independence, its revolutionary ideals, and the emergence of liberal democracy was the exploitation of Black labor and the expropriation of Indigenous lands. These systems of domination were not just an aberration of American democratic values, but a necessity for American liberty. Unfree Black labor was an integral part of the economic system of late eighteenth-century America. Slavery provided the promise of sustainable wealth that was needed to ensure that the colonies could operate free of British control. Territorial control of land was similarly crucial to the claims of American independence, and the desire to expand westward emerged as a fabled destiny of the American nation.

It was these dual imperatives, to steal labor and land, that enabled Anglo settlers of the thirteen colonies to create internal cohesion among themselves. The revolutionary generation began to see themselves as the natural masters of the continent, the real "natives" who sought to defend their land and lifestyles from despotic British overlords from the other side of the Atlantic Ocean. Their presence was mythologized as natural, inevitable, preordained, and permanent, the outcome of destiny, fate, God's grace, and honorable, righteous struggle. The liberty that the founding fathers spoke of so frequently was not just connected to the subordination of Black and Indigenous populations but was made possible by it.[1]

In this formulation, slavery is America's original sin. Americans understand slavery as an ugly scar on the otherwise uncompromised democratic values of the founding documents. Thomas Jefferson wrote the words of the Declaration of Independence— "we hold these truths to be self-evident, that all men are created equal, that they are endowed by their Creator with certain unalienable Rights"—even as he enslaved hundreds of human beings at Monticello and transmitted these composite contradictions throughout the thirteen original colonies, all of which allowed slavery in some form. The Constitution is revered as a grand compromise between the North, where slavery was much smaller in scale and was gradually abolished by 1804, and the slaveholding South, where the invention of the cotton gin in 1793 revolutionized the cotton industry and led to the growth and expansion of plantation-based slavery. The founding fathers are cast as mythical heroes who embedded slavery in the Constitution's three-fifths and fugitive slave clauses, but also sowed the seeds of the institution's demise—albeit in a provision that prohibited Congress from limiting America's participation in the international slave trade until 1808, twenty years after the Constitution had taken effect.

Slavery as original sin stands in contrast to the admirable ideals of the new nation. Slavery as sin binds and contains it, making it integral and evil, but also a moment, an act, a mistake, forgivable, something we can overlook and therefore overcome, an event in the past that we can together move past, an unfortunate aberration in an otherwise robust and healthy democracy.

Slavery as America's sin obscures the sheer magnitude of the transatlantic slave trade. It belies the European collaboration, conspiracy, and competition required to catalyze the emergence of capitalism and empire. It evades culpability for partaking in a globe-spanning economic system in which a small group of European nations plundered the rest of the world, funding the industrial revolution that catapulted Europe into a different century of economic and political development. It denies the intricate connection between the campaigns of terror that colonists wrought upon Indigenous peoples and how that stolen land then became labor and death camps for generations of stolen people. Slavery as original sin misses the triadic racial histories of Black peoples, Indigenous peoples, and white settlers, and the overlapping racial geographies that ripple out from, exceed, submerge, and push against the shifting territorial boundaries of the United States.

In this separation of American ideals from American

sin—what historian Edmund Morgan called the American paradox of American freedom and slavery[2]—we ignore the ways that understandings of American freedom are premised on the very existence of the unfree.

The original formulation of freedom and unfreedom in the seventeenth and early eighteenth centuries wasn't assigned according to or because of race. It's actually the exact opposite, and this is crucial: our modern understandings of race emerged from the institutionalization and routinization of slavery's exploitative and expropriative efforts, which frequently, usefully, and immorally required the differentiation between the free and unfree, the landowners and occupiers, the masters and wretched of the earth.

Though the first enslaved Africans arrived in British North America in 1619, systemic forms of racial discrimination began to curtail the basic rights of free Black people in the colonies beginning in the early eighteenth century, including laws that prohibited intermarriage, the ability to emancipate oneself through private manumission, the right to vote, and other legal protections. Racism *created* race, and the development of racial hierarchies was then used to justify the existence of racism. And because race is a relationship of power and not a biological or physiological marker of identity, these same efforts to draw distinctions between populations also created the grandest, most dangerous hoax of all—whiteness.

Whiteness isn't biological—it's a political status that distinguished citizens from slaves, a glass floor that guaranteed that even the poorest white person could not be classified as a slave (in contrast to free Blacks, who could be kidnapped or recaptured into slavery).[3] This political status—whiteness—emerged in the eighteenth century not because white people thought Black people were inferior, but because wealthy and powerful white elites feared that a multiracial, class-based coalition would develop and overthrow the colonial social order. In the nineteenth century, immigrants from Ireland or Italy gained the ability to whiten over time and gain access to the rights of citizenship, but as the United States Supreme Court ruled in the 1857 case *Dred Scott v. Sandford,* even free Blacks "are not included, and were not intended to be included, under the word 'citizens' in the Constitution and therefore claim none of the rights and privileges which that instrument provides for and secures to citizens of the United States."

By the time the Fourteenth Amendment of the United States Constitution was ratified in 1868, granting citizenship to "all persons born or naturalized in the United States, and subject to the jurisdiction thereof," including the formerly enslaved, Rebecca and Cornelius Thompson must have already decided not to return.

───────

My dad came to visit me in Boston once. It was after his first stroke, the one that shook him to his core, that ended his newfound love of jogging, a pastime he had started because of his unspoken fear that he would die before seeing the age of sixty, as his father had. If the racism doesn't get us, heart disease surely will.[4] The stroke took half the vision from his left eye and left him stranded at home and reliant on my mother, unable to drive for the first time in his adult life. Just get a taxi, I'd say. But it was outside the boundaries of his imagination, the idea of summoning transportation and paying for it. Growing up, he couldn't afford it; as an adult with a car, he didn't need it; as an elder, he couldn't fathom it.

My brother, Jon, came with him, under the auspices of wanting to visit, but really because my father couldn't travel alone.

I took the Red Line and then the bus to meet them at Logan

International Airport, because I similarly would never think to just call a cab. I remember telling them, on the way to their hotel, to watch out for Americans. "They're not what you think," I said. "They're *friendly*." And, sure enough, someone struck up a conversation with Dad while we were waiting in line to check in. People always say that Canadians are so *polite*, but what we actually are is passive-aggressive. Elevators are not for conversations with strangers; they're for staring silently at the glowing numbers above the door and avoiding eye contact. This was before the days of scrolling on one's phone and pretending to be otherwise occupied.

As we got off on the fourth floor to drop off some bags, the white couple who had shared the elevator with us, after having chatted with Dad for a full three minutes, cheerfully told us to enjoy our visit to Boston. My brother smiled at them and then turned to me and mouthed, in earnest and genuine bewilderment, "What the fuck?" I shrugged. Had I been in the elevator by myself, there's a not-insignificant chance that they would have politely asked me to send more towels to their room. That happens to me a lot.

We walked the Freedom Trail, a path through Boston that passes by landmarks significant to the American Revolution. It was, to be honest, underwhelming. We ate lobster ("This meal seems like an awful lot of work to me, Debra," said Dad, cracking an exoskeleton.) We crashed a public lecture that Canadian Supreme Court justice Rosalie Abella was giving at Harvard Law School. We went to Fenway Park; Dad liked that the best, I think, even though he had no opinions about the Red Sox, other than to note that they were the last pre-expansion Major League Baseball team to integrate in 1959, two years after Jackie Robinson had retired.

We walked through Boston Common and stopped at the Shaw Memorial. "Do you know about this?" Jon asked. "They were sent into an impossible battle. After Shaw was killed the Confederates buried him in a mass grave with his men and it was meant to be an insult. They said, 'We buried him with his niggers.'" My brother, the historian-turned-lawyer, starved for stories about anyone who looked like us, gazed at those bronzed faces and instead of seeing foot soldiers in someone else's war, saw our kin headed to their slaughter.

Jon and I met some friends one evening at a pub on Massachusetts Avenue. It was a weeknight and the bar was half-empty. My friends had to leave early, but Jon and I decided to stay a little longer to catch up. While getting what we thought were our last pints of beer at the bar, we struck up a conversation with two strangers who were the only other Black people there. I can't remember their names or anything about them, other than they were tall and fun and kind and had bright smiles. We talked for hours with them about being Black in America and being Black in Canada, compared notes, and laughed like we were old friends. One of them spoke better French than either of us, which I noted with embarrassment for not being more proficient in my second language, even after years of taking university-level classes. We made them explain the tradition of eating black-eyed peas and collard greens on New Year's Day and they were incredulous that we didn't already know.

Our talk turned to politics. It was early spring of 2011 and the white backlash against President Obama was well under way. The Democrats had managed to pass the Affordable Care Act in March 2010 but were then punished by the electorate in the November midterm elections, as the Republicans won a majority in the House of Representatives, flipped control of twenty state legislatures, and claimed the largest number of seats from Democrats since 1948.[5] The Tea Party had emerged as a formidable force within the Republican Party, pushing the mainstream core of the party further to the ideological right. Locally, Scott Brown had recently won the Senate seat that the late Ted Kennedy once held, becoming the first Republican to be elected to the Senate from Massachusetts in almost forty years. Political polarization was at levels previously unimaginable; the parties could agree on nothing. That evening the United States government was on the precipice of a legislative standoff that threatened to shut down the government.

"How is it possible that the government can shut down?" we asked.

They laughed. "Look," one of them said, "you know how your government makes plans for the next several years? Ours makes plans for, like, tomorrow and that's it."

When we parted ways one of them gave me a bear hug that lifted me off my feet. "So long, cuz," he said. They probably don't remember us at all, but I remember them for these crucial lessons of linked fate. That because of the expansive world of the African diaspora, we never need be the Only Ones. That generosity can be a form of resistance. That the history of the one-drop rule in America was designed to safeguard the boundaries of whiteness, but instead created the conditions for a Black America in which all shades of Blackness and even those with roots in the far-flung edges of the African diaspora can be brought into the fold. Like family.

It took the better part of a year, but I eventually found my people at Harvard. My comrades were never going to be in political science; much of the discipline is still hostile to research on race politics (at least, the way I think of race politics). So at some point in the spring of 2011, I invited myself to a conference hosted by the W. E. B. Du Bois Research Institute, Harvard's institutional home for its African American Studies program. During a break between presentations I was standing to the side of a table with coffee and baked goods, adding cream and sugar and wishing that I was baller enough to drink black coffee, when Henry Louis Gates Jr. saw me and came right over.

"And who are you?" he demanded, with a hint of a smile. I grinned. His tone was familiar. He sounded like the Black people I had met in Shrewsbury. The same intonations, the same gesticulations. I introduced myself.

"A postdoc!" he exclaimed. "Where have you been? You should be here." And from that moment on, Skip Gates, at that point not yet well-known among white audiences for his role as the host of the PBS program *Finding Your Roots*, decided that the Institute was where I really belonged.

Attending seminars and lectures from guest speakers every few weeks, I found myself in audiences comprised mostly of Black students and scholars, listening to research that was focused entirely on Black people. I was jubilant. I was thirty years old, and I had never before been in the presence of so many Black people to whom I was not related.

It was at this point that I discovered African American Studies, the same way that white people "discovered" America.* It had, of course, been there all along. I was annoyed to learn about it so late in the game, overwhelmed by all I knew I didn't yet know, and jealous, *so jealous*, of those who grew up haunted by the second sight of Toni Morrison, who already knew that Ella Baker was the architect of the civil rights movement, who understood the central

---

* I didn't plunder it, though.

tenets and nuances of the Black radical tradition, who had their sense of being measured in the weight of James Baldwin's words.

I had wasted decades being the Only One in Canada, disconnected from the legacies and insights of Black genius. No one had taught me about it. Ten years of failed attempts to learn French caused me, embarrassingly, to pronounce "Du Bois" as "do-bwaa"—it's actually "do-boys." In all the years of K–12 education, an additional decade in world-renowned institutions of higher learning, and three apparently useless degrees as measured by the knowledge acquired about my own goddamned history, I had only one Black teacher, a professor in my PhD, who co-taught a class with another professor. And now I was living in a city full of monuments, statues, and memorials about the origins of America, and yet still knew next to nothing about where I came from—only the white-imposed limitations of what I could be. I was pissed.

I was also confused. Incredulous, even. As I read more work written by and for Black people, I could see the invisible threads that held together the Black experience in the United States. Underlying the trauma and the terror, the hatred and the hauntings, the exhausting and endless fight to survive, there was an incredible, indelible love of American democracy.

On July 5, 1852, the abolitionist orator Frederick Douglass delivered his famous keynote address, "What to the Slave Is the Fourth of July?" He begins by stating his great admiration for the founding fathers, those "statesmen, patriots, and heroes" who signed the Declaration of Independence. But in the next breath he interrogates what the meaning of political freedom and natural justice could possibly be to those still enslaved. The celebration of American independence, Douglass argued, only "reveals the immeasurable distance between us. The blessings in which you, this day, rejoice, are not enjoyed in common. The rich inheritance of justice, liberty, prosperity and independence, bequeathed by your fathers, is shared by you, not by me." The Fourth of July, he assesses, belongs to white America, not Black Americans. And yet, Douglass was both a critic and a radical patriot who believed that the United States could live up to its democratic ideals.

Langston Hughes, a key figure in the Harlem Renaissance, wrote in his 1935 poem "Let America Be America Again" that America's treatment of the various parts of its underclass—African Americans, Native Americans, poor whites, and immigrants—means it is "the land that never has been yet." But by the end of the poem, he, too, offers hope: "America was never America to me / And yet I swear this oath—/ America will be!" Seventy-five years later, the idea that America is a great unfinished project, but that together Americans could strive to live up to the ideals set out in the Constitution, was also a standard part of Obama's speeches.

An even more recent example is the New York Times' 1619 Project, which argues that the moment of the nation's birth was not when ink was scratched on paper to create the Declaration of Independence in 1776, but rather in August 1619, when a ship arrived at Point Comfort in the colony of Virginia, carrying a cargo of twenty to thirty enslaved Africans. The central goal of the 1619 Project "is to reframe American history by considering what it would mean to regard 1619 as our nation's birth year. Doing so requires us to place the consequences of slavery and the contributions of Black Americans at the very center of the story we tell ourselves about who we are as a country."[6] The 1619 Project was wildly successful when it was first published in 2019 and is now a best-selling book.[7] The collection of essays argues for a renewed understanding of the centrality of slavery in the political development of the United States and the ways that the institution's legacy continues to shape modern American life in distinct ways, from traffic patterns in Atlanta to the perpetual failure of the United States to implement anything that comes close to a universal system of health care.

The project as a whole is also unabashedly patriotic. In an interview on MSNBC, Nikole Hannah-Jones, the creator of the 1619 Project, talked about her childhood ambivalence toward the American flag that her father hung in their front yard. A change of heart came as an adult.

"Through the years, and really in working on this project, I just came to understand our history in this country," Hannah-Jones confesses, sitting at a table with anchor David Gura and others. "Black people's role as truly believing in our founding ideals, and being willing to die again and again to make those founding ideals true for all Americans—there's no greater patriotism. And it's actually disrespectful to our ancestors not to claim this country and that flag, and to be able to claim our legacy here on these lands."[8]

Hannah-Jones opens the 1619 Project with a Pulitzer Prize–winning essay called "The Idea of America." Her central argument is that because Black Americans have been excluded from "We the people," they have had to believe in democratic ideas even more than white Americans. And it was the struggle for America to live up to those ideals, frequently spearheaded by African Americans for the benefit of all, that substantiated American democracy. When given the chance to leave America through various schemes (including those deceitfully crafted by the American Colonization Society in the decades leading up to the Civil War), they have not left; when excluded from the body politic, they have not checked out; when they struggled and won access to power, they have not oppressed others as has been done to them. African Americans, Hannah-Jones argues, have long been the "perfectors" of American democracy.

"Without the idealistic, strenuous and patriotic efforts of black Americans," she writes, "our democracy today would most likely look very different—it might not be a democracy at all."

This worship of American democracy gives me pause. In this formulation, ambivalence is un-American. And as one who is deeply ambivalent about all forms of nationalism, as one who has never felt a sense of belonging anywhere, I wonder: what good is the debate over whether America truly began in 1492, 1619, 1776, 1865, 1954, 1965, or 2008, when so many white citizens are unwilling or unable to empathize with Black loss, and so many settlers are unwilling or unable to imagine a decolonial politics? As James Baldwin once asked, is inclusion into existing political structures worth the price of the ticket?

At its core, democracy is actually about winning and losing. What matters is not who wins and who loses, but what the winners and losers do after they win or lose that divides democracies from dictatorships. In a democracy, those who win elections can't bar losers from participating in politics, from making decisions, or from exerting influence over politics in the future. Those who lose must respect the winner's right to make binding decisions. This is especially important when former winners become new losers; they must relinquish control. And we, the citizenry, must obey the decisions that come out of that free and fair competition, even if we don't like the outcome.[9]

Political theorist Danielle Allen calls the ability to accept inevitable losses *democratic sacrifice*. Why do we accept the outcome when we lose? Because we know that the determination of who wins and who loses is balanced and fair. Anyone can win, anyone can lose, and there are no systematic winners or losers. For democracies to remain stable, we all need to take turns being good losers.[10]

But, as Brown University political theorist Juliet Hooker has convincingly argued, democratic sacrifice is supposed to be shared equally among groups, made voluntarily, and honored by those who recognize the hardship of the sacrifice. This has, Hooker confirms, absolutely not been the case throughout American history. Rather, the weight of democratic sacrifice has never been fairly or equally shared, and African Americans are perpetual losers in American democracy. Whenever the polity has been presented with the choice between fighting for Black liberation or reifying existing racial hierarchies, it has chosen white supremacy. Maybe not every single time, but certainly more often than not. And in those rare circumstances when white interests have been put to the side in the name of Black equality, white people have certainly not lost graciously. Instead, when African Americans have struggled and won advances toward fuller participation in American democracy, they have been met with a disproportionate backlash in which white Americans have employed the power of the state, and sometimes the extralegal intimidation of white lynch mobs, to deliberately roll back these democratic gains.[11]

As Emory University historian Carol Anderson demonstrates, white backlash has been a consistent thread woven throughout American history.[12] The end of the Civil War and the failure (but actually the political sabotage, abandonment, betrayal, and dismantling) of Reconstruction was followed by Black Codes and Jim Crow. In the mid-twentieth century, white people first protested school desegregation and then left the public school system in droves rather than allow Black children to access the same quality of education. White southerners abandoned the Democratic Party over its support of civil rights legislation, catalyzing a political realignment of party politics that still stands today. Later, the civil unrest of the late 1960s, Black-led protests largely against police violence, and the assassination or exile of a generation of Black leadership became the justification for President Richard Nixon's emphasis on "law and order," and the subsequent decimation of Black communities in the War on Drugs. The election of Barack Obama was followed by a tidal wave of electoral backlash, most notably in the millions of Americans who voted for the overt racism of Donald Trump. In the summer of 2020, there were mass uprisings to protest the murder of George Floyd. Less than a year passed before voting rights, especially of racialized voters, were once again under attack and white American parents denounced critical race theory as the greatest threat facing the education system.

And yet: surprisingly, bizarrely, incredibly, tragically, African Americans continue to seek inclusion in a country that has, for more than four centuries, refused to love them back.

———

I didn't quite know how to articulate it then, during that first year living in the United States, but I recall having a great skepticism about this desire for democratic inclusion. It could have been that my introduction to the tension between democratic ideals and racial domination came from Indigenous scholars, such as Taiaiake Alfred, Kiera Ladner, John Borrows, Leanne Betasamosake Simpson, and Glen Coulthard. In their writings, they argue that Indigenous rights are not something that can be granted by the colonial state, that the British Crown failed to fulfill its treaty obligations, that Canadian sovereignty is a façade. Even the terminology of First Nations implies contested claims to sovereignty. *First* Nations implicates those who came first, long before others knew of the existence of lands across the ocean, present from time immemorial, and so all temporal claims to belonging or ownership must deal with the preeminence and preexistence of these original inhabitants. First *Nations* implicates a collective that is not an ethnicity, race, or any other kind of minority group, but instead is comprised of distinct nations, in the plural, often understood as a unitary group only because of colonial imaginaries that fail to comprehend the diversity among Indigenous cultures and languages.

This terminology is more than mere symbolism for Indigenous peoples, and it is not premised on a desire for more substantive inclusion into the Canadian polity. Rather, it is a demand for the revival of the nation-to-nation relationship between settlers and First Nations through decolonization. The question of land is central to these worldviews; in the words of Yellowknives Dene/University of British Columbia political theorist Glen Coulthard, Indigenous anticolonialism is "a struggle not only *for* land in the material sense, but also deeply *informed* by what the land *as system of reciprocal relations and obligations* can teach us about living our lives in relation to one another and the natural world in nondominating and nonexploitative terms . . ."[13] One of the most important lessons I took from these Indigenous thinkers, scholars, and creators was the knowledge that Canadian democracy was built on lies and maintained through coercion. There is violence at the core of state power. The historical record is quite clear that the same held true for America. I was unconvinced that embracing the same democratic institutions that were instrumental in upholding these asymmetrical power relations could lead to anything like equality, freedom, or justice.

Once my postdoctoral fellowship came to an end, I packed up my few belongings in a U-Haul and drove the 750 miles to Athens, Ohio, to start my first real faculty position as an assistant professor of political science at Ohio University. I traveled across this small piece of America the beautiful, being careful of where I stopped for gas and food because of the dangers of traveling through rural anywhere as a Black woman. The more time I spent in the United States, the clearer it seemed to me that there was nothing inevitable about the unsteady march toward racial progress. Though the arc of the moral universe is long, there was nothing that guaranteed it will ultimately bend toward justice.[14] In fact, I suspected, there was a good chance it wouldn't.

As I drove westward, the windows down and the horizon hazy, I thought about my last trip to Harvard University's Widener Library. There, I accidentally happened across a photograph called *The Soiling of Old Glory,* which was taken by Stanley Forman on April 5, 1976, for what was then the *Boston Herald American*. It captures a Boston teetering on the brink of an explosion, a city divided not simply by segregated neighborhoods but by court-mandated efforts to desegregate public schools by busing students between predominantly white and Black parts of the city. The Pulitzer Prize–winning photo is sufficiently horrifying that if you've seen it, you'd remember it. Forman captures the moment when a white teenager, Joseph Rakes, looks as though he is about to spear a Black civil rights attorney, Ted Landsmark, with a pole

The Soiling of Old Glory, by Stanley Forman, Pulitzer Prize, 1977.

bearing the American flag. Landsmark wasn't downtown with the intention of participating in a protest; he was just trying to go about his day. That's the part of the story I thought about then, driving once again toward a new unknown. He was just trying to live. To exist. Luckily, he was able to escape the situation with just a broken nose, but it could have been so much worse.

To me, the lesson is clear: African Americans' love of this country will be wielded as a weapon, whether we protest or do nothing, whether we are respectable or deviant, and that love will try to kill us in the end.

CHAPTER 4

Appalachian Elegies

(Athens, Ohio)

In May 1964, President Lyndon B. Johnson launched his vision for the creation of a Great Society. Standing outside the Memorial Auditorium of Ohio University, Johnson argued that with courage and compassion, America could create "a society where no child will go unfed, and no youngster will go unschooled." By the end of the summer Johnson directed fifteen separate task forces, working in secret, to study significant areas of American life—agriculture, education, the environment, the structure of government, health, urban affairs, natural resources, transportation. This research informed the significant number of policies put in place between 1964 and 1965, including civil rights legislation, immigration reform, education funding, Social Security expansion, and major spending programs such as Medicare, Medicaid, and Head Start. The centerpiece of the Johnson administration's policy agenda was the "War on Poverty."

The location for introducing this agenda was no coincidence. Athens, Ohio, is in the southeast corner of the state, nestled in the foothills of the Appalachian Mountains. It is far closer to West

United States president Lyndon B. Johnson outside Memorial Auditorium of Ohio University, May 7, 1964. According to Ohio University's archival records, this was the fourth of ten speeches he delivered that day, focusing on the "War on Poverty."

Virginia than it is to Columbus, Cincinnati, or Cleveland. The Hocking River, which snakes around the town before emptying into the Ohio River, floods every spring, and every seventeen years cicadas swarm the region, ensuring every step is marked by a cringe-worthy, squishy crunch. The town itself, like most places with a state university, is a Democratic stronghold, but the county and those that surround it are home to the Republican, rural, white poor.

Athens County itself is over 90 percent white and 26.6 percent of the population lives in poverty. The surrounding counties— Meigs, Morgan, Washington, Hocking, Vinton, Perry—are even less racially diverse (five of the six counties are something like 97 percent white) and much more conservative. Donald Trump won Ohio in 2016 and 2020, and after four years of "making America great again," he actually increased his support in this corner of the state, winning 76 percent of the vote in Meigs County, 74 percent in Morgan, 70 percent in Washington, 70 percent in Hocking, 77 percent in Vinton, and 74 percent in Perry. The original inhabitants of the region, the Shawnee, are all but erased from cultural memory, replaced by the Appalachians who ferociously center themselves and their culture as indigenous to the land.

Athens is a charming kind of place, in a "top ten most beautiful college towns you've never heard of" kind of way, which noncoincidentally doubles as a list of places where Black people are rare and unwelcome. It has redbrick streets, quaint two-story buildings that line Court Street, the main drag, and neighborhoods where many houses have a covered porch with a wooden swing that sways in the breeze. The few thousand people who live permanently in the town are greatly outnumbered by the 22,000-strong transient student population that lives in Athens from September to May, and during the academic year the bricks belong to the young.

Ohio University is a party school—it was even dubbed the "number one party school in the United States" by the *Princeton Review* in 2011 and *Playboy* in 2015. Thousands flock to Athens for the annual Halloween Block Party and every spring red Solo cups, beer pong battles, and kegs-and-eggs mornings are regular features of the dozen or so different "fests" each weekend in different parts of the town. Every and any occasion is an occasion to party. When the university cancelled classes because of an ice storm? FreezeFest. When the Hocking River flooded the south parking lot and residence buildings? FloodFest. When there was a shooting near campus grounds and classes were cancelled due to safety concerns? FugitiveFest. Drinking was a local pastime, in part because there was nothing else to do.

I have lived my entire life in majority-white spaces, but I had never been in a space with *this kind* of whiteness before. The contrast between the urban, lively, Northeast Corridor feel of Boston and this southern-tinged, insular Midwest town was striking. Here, in the heavy air of Appalachia, whiteness was in a constant battle against its own stereotypes. The region is a cornerstone of the mythological "white working class," those Americans purportedly forgotten or left behind by the slow death of extractive industries and manufacturing sectors. It is a population that was angered by Barack Obama's comments in 2008 that white working-class Americans were bitter and clinging to "guns or religion or antipathy toward people who aren't like them," and was infuriated by Hillary Clinton's generalization in 2016 that half of Trump supporters can be put into the "basket of deplorables."[1]

Appalachia is frequently positioned as the bedrock of the so-called conservative base, the last remnants of a white American culture built through resourcefulness and honest work, and yet the epicenter of America's opioid crisis and thus the litmus of how pride can quickly morph into hopelessness. The most direct engagement with the romanticism and abjection of the white working class of this territory is *Hillbilly Elegy,* J. D. Vance's best-selling memoir of growing up with Appalachian values in Middletown, Ohio—a town both bigger and more diverse than Athens. The book was called "a compassionate, discerning sociological analysis of the white underclass," by the *New York Times*, though it largely provides a skewed and simplistic catalog of pathological, self-destructive behaviors and beliefs of the white poor.[2]

The white people I met in Athens, those who were born and bred in the rolling hills, or even those who had adopted them as home, were quick to defend their culture. Appalachians are proud, you'll be told. There's community here, not like in the cities, where people don't give a fuck about their neighbors. We take care of each other. People would give you the shirts off their backs. There are Black Appalachians, too, you know. The people here are creative, generous, moral, and kind. Survivors, in the face of a national government that couldn't care less about the little people of Appalachia. The liberal media has it all wrong: the "drop-in journalists" of the *New York Times* and *Washington Post* don't spend enough time here to see the beauty of the region and its people. They're all just looking for more poverty porn. If you really want to know about *real* racism, Debra, just take a look at how the white people of this region are treated.

There's editing going on in both of these interpretations—the one that depicts Appalachia as impoverished and depraved, and the other, in which Appalachians are generous, proud, communally oriented survivors. At the same time, there's accuracy to both as well. Contradiction is in the nature of truth.

And so it's also true that in and around this tiny town in southeast Ohio, where the people were white and proud and poor, where fracking has brought the dying fossil-fuel industry back to life by poisoning the planet, the Confederate flag was everywhere—in windows, on bumper stickers, on T-shirts, flapping silently in the wind. As a Canadian who had lived in the United States for barely more than a year at the time, my knowledge of the Civil War was admittedly scarce. In my early days in Athens I stood frozen on the red bricks, looking quizzically at the differently arranged stars and stripes of red, white, and blue.

"Was . . . Ohio part of the Confederacy?" I asked Brandon, my colleague and one of my best friends, a white guy from Wisconsin who studies religion and democracy in northern Nigeria, and a sage consultant on the very important differences between the twelve main types of whiskey.

Brandon sighed. "No. No, it wasn't."

The Confederate flag is a symbol of many things. Its appearance here, in a place so far physically removed from its origins, also served as a warning. *I stand for southern pride, the Lost Cause, the war ignited to keep Black people as property, and if not that, then at least the endless struggle to keep them in their place*, the flag says. *You are not welcome here*, it warns. *The war isn't over.*

So, while it's true that Appalachia is gravely misrepresented in the rags-to-riches fantasy of *Hillbilly Elegy* and the moralistic paternalism of the Trump administration's four-year-long obsession with pandering to the needs, wants, desires, and tragedies of white Middle America (though not actually creating many policies that helped these communities), it's also true that there were parts of the surrounding area, outside the town limits of Athens, where *it was not safe for me to go*. Those small bars and restaurants along the highway where every single person stopped and stared when I entered the room. Those moments when I would sit at a table looking over a menu and a large white man would stand slightly too close to me but just out of my line of vision, silent, arms crossed. The time I went into a gas station and came back out to find someone had keyed my car. The subtle ways that the threat of violence always hung in the air.

There's a danger to generalizations here. Not all of rural America is white, and not all of the white working class lives in rural America. In fact, working-class Americans are racially diverse, especially compared to the near-total whiteness of the wealthiest 1 percent. Persistent, generational poverty is a problem everywhere in the United States, especially in urban areas. Rural economies are structured in much the same way as urban economies, and there are legitimate grievances about the paucity of services in rural areas.[3] Nevertheless, there is an important myth surrounding the idea of a virtuous white working class of rural America. These are the same white people who, in both the past and present, have been agents of racial terror.

The boundaries of whiteness have shifted over time, sometimes enlarging the category of who was considered white to bring in (at times, temporarily and conditionally) groups that had previously been excluded—the Irish, Italians, Jews, Hispanics.[4] Sometimes whiteness has been subject to caveats and footnotes for those who do not behave or perform according to its standards. That's why the phrasing of "white trash" implicitly carries the idea that white people *should* have access to wealth, *should* be individualistic and completely self-reliant, *should* look, act, and live in a particular way, and when they do not conform to these requirements their whiteness becomes contingent, though never thoroughly evacuated.

There are, in W. E. B. Du Bois's famous formulation, wages of whiteness that ensure that all white people, regardless of class position, immigrant status, or other markers of difference, are united by the unspoken universalism of whiteness. The benefits that come with the guarantee that all variants of whiteness exist at the apex of the racial order. There could be great inequality among white people, of course. But the wages of whiteness— psychological and material—ensured that all white people have access to political and economic opportunities that are racially exclusive.

Truth be known, the conservative white working class were the least of my troubles. My years in Athens were terrorized by a different manifestation of whiteness altogether.

Beware the white liberal.

You know them. You might even be them. I was once them. They are progressive, oh so progressive, but only insofar as their leftist politics don't require them to make changes, or give anything up, or speak against capitalism in any way, or recognize their active roles in perpetuating white supremacy. They vote

Democrat and *loved* Obama as if he was one of their own (because he was, in fact, one of their own). They like bilingualism—
but for their children, not as a broader public good or orientation.
They are woke/antiracist and will eagerly tell you so, because they
are, at base, desperate for a Black person's stamp of approval. Better yet if you can be their only Black friend so they can point to
you to demonstrate how not racist they are. They like diversity,
but only if the diversity is the kind I grew up with—a few token
people of color here and there. But not too many. Certainly not a
majority; that is unfathomable. They mean well. They have the
best of intentions. They believe that institutions are fair, because
the rules have been systematically skewed in their favor, ensuring that they have never really experienced unequal treatment at
the hands of those with power. They cannot and will not recognize the ways that they have fixed the game to ensure that they
win. When Donald Trump won the presidency in 2016, they
wore safety pins to show that they were not like those other white
people; they needed a way to diminish the chance that someone
might judge them by the color of their skin. Perish the thought.
When George Floyd was murdered and Minneapolis exploded,
they bought books. They admitted their white fragility and resolved to learn how to be antiracist, how to talk about race, how to
be less stupid about race, and why Black people might not want
to talk to them about it.[5]

There's a long history of the indifferent, unreliable white liberal. In his "Letter from Birmingham Jail," Dr. Martin Luther
King Jr. argued that the most significant stumbling block to Black
freedom wasn't the violent racism of the Ku Klux Klan, but was
rather the shallow understanding and lukewarm acceptance of
the white moderate. A white moderate, King argues, is one who is
"more devoted to 'order' than to justice . . . who constantly says: 'I
agree with you in the goal you seek, but I cannot agree with your

methods of direct action'; who paternalistically believes he can set a timetable for another man's freedom; who lives by a mythical concept of time and who constantly advises the Negro to wait for a 'more convenient season.'"[6] Both James Baldwin and Malcolm X, as well, warned about the danger of white people who seek to befriend in order to co-opt.

Whereas the psychological wages of whiteness for white conservatives are connected to protecting (in essence, *conserving*) the structures that maintain white advantage in politics, the economy, and society, the psychological wages of whiteness for this newest generation of white liberals are tied to virtue signaling. They want to be good people, and their morality is tied to giving the impression of their commitment to racial equality. But while their expressions of solidarity with people of color are perhaps sincere, they are still mostly hollow gestures, made largely with the intention of demonstrating that they are not racist, not one of *those* white people. And when those other white people are nearby, as was the case in Athens, the scramble to appear woke becomes all the more desperate, the performances more embellished, the hypocrisy harder to pinpoint.

It's tragically ironic, then, that while I was preoccupied with dodging the dangerous racial anxieties, resentments, and xenophobia of the conservative white poor, the white people who instigated the most harm to me were also those who claimed to be the most progressive. Universities are the breeding grounds for good white liberals. Like the white feminist who said I was too outspoken, didn't know my place, was too much like a bull in a china shop, who told this to anyone who would listen. Or the white political theorist who taught critical race theory and found ways to undermine my expertise to students. When he saw how much additional advising I was doing for Black students and other students of color, he didn't understand this as the extra, invisible labor that gets pinned on Black faculty because white faculty couldn't care less about the success of these students; instead, he decided that students sought me out because I had failed to maintain professional boundaries and reported this to the administration. The white-presenting but a little too adamantly self-identifying Latina who studied whiteness, who initially tried to connect with me by talking about "we women of color"; that is, until the department indicated she wasn't going to get tenure and she decided that I was the one undermining her. She, too, weaponized institutional rules and filed an official complaint against me. The newly hired Black head of the Division of Diversity, Equity, and Inclusion who thought I was stepping on her turf by creating a program to prevent Black students from dropping out and tried to rebrand the initiative as her idea. The dean who refused to step in when I brought my concerns about the institutional racism of the university to him, because the perpetrators "seem like they have enough problems right now; there's no need to rock the boat."

In my second year of teaching, the chair of the department, John, asked if I had a moment to chat, stepped into my office, and closed the door behind him.

"I'm sorry I haven't had you out to the house for dinner yet," he said. "We've been so busy."

"Oh, no worries," I replied. Brandon and another recent hire, a white woman, had been to John's house for dinner and drinks regularly and told me so. I just wasn't invited.

"So, we're having a small debate among the tenured faculty about the language in your letter of offer," he said. "Do you remember the sentence about what year we start counting your publications towards tenure?"

"Sure," I said, turning toward my desktop to pull up the document. Tenure regulations vary from place to place, and so while negotiating my contract (a strange middleman situation in which the chair negotiated with me on behalf of Ohio University, and then in turn negotiated with Ohio University on my behalf) I had asked for a guarantee that anything I published after 2009, when I signed my contract, would count toward my tenure requirements.

"Well," he said, "that stipulation is inconsistent with the other offers we made that year." He held his hands out, as if washing them of the whole debacle. "But it's up to you whether you'd like to keep that clause in. It really won't make a difference, in my opinion."

"Uh, okay," I said. "I'll get back to you." John left and I reread my letter a few times. Still confused, I walked to Brandon's office and asked to see his letter of offer.

There were some inconsistencies, all right. Brandon's letter was soaked with praise, was highly complimentary about his research, and exuded a genuine excitement at the prospect that he would consider joining the faculty. He was "the best fit" the department had ever seen. Mine was much more subdued. Like a contract. My starting salary was higher, though. I knew that women of color tend to undervalue our market value and had made that a focal point of my negotiations.

"Oh, so you're the one that got us that initial raise," Brandon said, skimming my letter as I read through his. "They told me that they started the three of us at the same salary out of equity concerns."

I raised an eyebrow. I negotiated better than my white colleagues and that raised "equity concerns"? I wondered whether I would have received the same equitable treatment had our positions been reversed.

Brandon's letter didn't reveal anything about why the extra clause in my letter was a problem, so I asked a senior faculty member in my department, Susan Burgess, what was going on. Susan was white, but had faced marginalization in the university and broader discipline long before I knew anything about either. She was thoughtful, joyful, and sharp as hell. And she had good politics, constantly using her seniority and clout to protect people of color. She published circles around everyone else in the department and some people hated her for it. I trusted her immensely.

"Our departmental norm is to count everything you've published towards tenure," Susan said. "No matter when you published it. You have enough out now that you could go up for tenure early, if you want to."

I slowly put the pieces together. "So, the clause in my letter of offer ends up discounting the stuff I published before 2009? Those articles would normally count?"

Susan nodded. "I take it John forgot to mention that during your negotiations."

"Yeah, he didn't mention that at all. In fact, this is the first I'm hearing any of this," I said grimly. I turned the situation over in my mind. "Why would John let me negotiate something into my contract that actually screwed me over?"

"Why indeed," Susan replied.

A year later, John was appointed to be an associate dean of the College of Arts and Sciences. Of course.

I have a hundred more examples, some more serious than others. In the midst of a later episode, the one that nearly broke me and shattered my perspective of the world and my role in it, the one about which I still can't talk easily and from which I have not yet fully recovered, I told Jenny Nedelsky and Joe Carens, my former advisors and forever friends, the details about what had happened. How there was nothing that could be done to stop the way that white people were able to use seemingly neutral institutional processes to punish me for existing. How I was a junior faculty member without tenure and felt the acute danger that my entire career was at stake just because some white colleagues thought I was too confident, too outspoken, and not nearly as grateful as they thought I should be for having an academic job in the first place. How I had to hire a lawyer and it was only under the threat of a lawsuit that the university relented. They were saddened, but not surprised.

"Every single Black academic we know has a story of professional sabotage," they said.

Like most white-collar industries, academia is teeming with highly consequential but never-said-aloud norms and expectations that are hidden in plain sight. For someone like me—a first-generation college student, Black, a woman, an immigrant, someone who grew up poor, now trying to fit into a predominantly white, elitist space—these rules were imperceptible until I stumbled over them.

Like the way that discussions must abide by the middle-class ethic of indirect communication, the sandwiching of criticisms with fake compliments, and the avoidance of conflict at all costs.

How people own workplace territories, and how frequently these turf wars are made more vicious by the fear that we are all, in fact, redundant.

That information is a kind of currency and it is possible to incur and be put on notice for having debt.

The valorization of overwork and its use as a determinant of a person's moral and professional worth.

How productivity is measured by publications and grants, and not by being a good teacher, mentor, advisor, colleague, or human.

The many ways that the university plays on the insecure yet narcissistic personality traits of so many faculty and administrators to solidify conflict and competition rather than solidarity.

The things that matter the most to ensure the success of

students of color—the hours spent on mentorship and advocacy, the development of an ethic of care and concern—are also the things that are detrimental to career advancement, tenure and promotion, and other opportunities.

The practice of being voluntold for tasks that you cannot refuse to do without seeming uncollegial.

The toxicity and ubiquity of the rumor mill.

The necessary and crucial labor of learning to work around incompetent or abusive colleagues.

The belief that academia is a meritocracy in spite of all the evidence to the contrary.

The moral credentialing that guarantees people who believe they are working toward justice are incapable of reflecting on how they uphold structures of domination with every fiber of their being.

The vast amount of invisible labor that falls disproportionately on Black, Indigenous, and faculty of color in part because we are so few and far between.

The problem of not knowing all that you don't know.

The literary prophet Toni Morrison once wrote, "The function, the very serious function of racism . . . is distraction. It keeps you from doing your work. It keeps you explaining, over and over again, your reason for being. Somebody says you have no language and so you spend twenty years proving that you do. . . ."[7]

Missteps are probably common among those who lack the class status or cultural fluency to survive like the fish out of water that we are. But how these violations of white liberal protocol are interpreted by the gatekeepers of what and who is acceptable— that's where institutional racism festers. Black folks in the Ivory Tower, and in many other white-collar professions, I'm sure, are given fewer chances, less benefit of the doubt, and take greater risks when we lean in because there is no safety net to catch us when we fall. These mistakes are taken as evidence that we truly do not belong, even as our workplaces rely on Black faces in order to appear to be diverse and multicultural. But the desired diversity of this kind of space is created in the service of whiteness, and so the hospitality is always conditional. Diversity needs to be commodifiable, marketable, and consumable, because its true aim is to improve the moral standing of liberal white people. It is intolerable when it steps out of line. Black women in particular can quickly move from pet to threat.[8]

The four years I spent in Athens weren't all terrible. Just mostly terrible. There were some beautiful moments, too. History is full of white allies and several of them, including Susan, spent some not-insignificant social capital to defend me from the worst of the barrage. I had spectacular students who made me love teaching before they went on to become spectacular people. I became friends with Marcus, the Bartending Philosopher, and our debates about morality and science fiction in an empty bar in the middle of weekday afternoons were a lifesaver. My best friend was Christy, a poet with a beautiful soul and an infectious laugh. She and I would go to half-price wine night every Tuesday at the fanciest restaurant in town. We would sit at the bar, chat with James, the gracious bartender, a talented violinist, and one of the only other Black people in Athens, and pretend we were in a big city. I spent hours jogging along the Hocking River and playing pickup soccer in a league organized by volunteers. I adopted a dog from the Athens County Dog Shelter and named him the Artful Dodger. He was abandoned and alone. And he had trust issues. Like me. He cried in the car when I took him home and so did I. In the last months of my time there I found my person; or, more accurately, he found me. The fireflies come out at dusk.

But those years took a toll. The last year I spent in Athens I focused all my energy on getting out. I applied to four positions, got four interviews, spent all of November 2014 flying across the country to present and defend my research, demonstrate my teaching abilities, and prove that I was a good "fit" during multiday interviews. I eventually had four job offers. I accepted a position in Northwestern University's African American Studies department. If I could just make it another few months, I could escape this enclave of white liberal resentment and treachery.

It was easier said than done. I was deeply depressed, traumatized by the years of professional sabotage, ruined by personal betrayals, irritated by the two years I wasted dating an exhausting, Peter Pan–like idiot, and full of self-loathing for not having known better. I smoked cigarettes to calm my nerves, weed to stop the nightmares, and sobbed nearly every day on the floor of my office. I couldn't shake a pervasive sense of shame, even though I had done nothing wrong. Internalized racism can really fuck you up as a person. And I was so, so angry. Rageful, in fact. If the town, the university, and everyone in it had gone up in flames, I would have danced with joy. I hate those people and I hate that place, even to this day. Susan, who had been through her own traumas of not belonging, understood better than anyone.

"The best revenge is a life well lived," she wisely advised.

I remember giving her a look. "I'm pretty sure the best revenge is revenge, Susan," I replied.

Is this what I had worked so hard and struggled for so long to be a part of? Is this what it meant to be integrated? To be trapped by this flattening of difference, this conditional tolerance, this imposition of pious woke whiteness? Was I supposed to be grateful? Would it always be this way?

White supremacy doesn't always make itself known in white hoods and a cop's knee on a Black man's neck. For people like me, who are surrounded by whiteness at every turn, who largely live an existence without the counterweight of Black folks to help combat the daily bombardment of messages that we are simply not smart, brave, disciplined, quick-witted, industrious, adventurous, capable, hardworking, professional, talented, alive, moral, *good* enough, we cannot help but absorb and internalize them. It's all so deceptively normal. The fish can't see the water.[9]

If this is what it meant to be Black in America, *why on earth would I want to be included in this?*

And yet, I still knew that the damage inflicted was so minimal, so negligible, compared to what was happening in Black communities throughout the United States. An entire generation was broken by the verdict of the Trayvon Martin case in 2013. They were broken in the summer of 2014 when Michael Brown was shot by police officer Darren Wilson and left to boil in his own blood for four hours in Ferguson, Missouri. And again, in November 2014, when Cleveland police officer Timothy Loehmann shot and killed twelve-year-old Tamir Rice within two seconds of arriving at the public park where Rice was playing with a toy gun. And again, in December 2014, when the grand jury refused to indict New York City police officer Daniel Pantaleo for using an illegal chokehold to squeeze the life from Eric Garner on Staten Island. And they were broken yet again by the murder of Freddie Gray in 2015 and the collusion that failed to convict his killers in Baltimore.

Broken, but then *awoken*.

CHAPTER 5

The Black Metropolis

(Chicago, Illinois)

It was in the aftermath of the Baltimore uprisings after Freddie Gray was killed by the Baltimore Police Department in April 2015 that Ta-Nehisi Coates's *Between the World and Me* was published. It was fortuitous timing, to have this slim, powerhouse meditation on race and racism in the United States emerge at precisely the same moment when we needed help to make sense of what was happening. What had happened to Coates, and the fury that was ignited, when his friend Prince Jones was murdered by the police. What kept happening, long after the murders of Michael Brown, Eric Garner, John Crawford III, and Tamir Rice. Akai Gurley. Gabriella Nevarez. Alton Sterling. Janisha Fonville. Samuel Dubose. Michelle Cusseaux. Stephon Clark. Sandra Bland. Botham Jean. Philando Castile. What we couldn't seem to stop from happening, all over the country.

Ostensibly writing a letter to his son, in the same tradition that James Baldwin wrote a letter to his nephew in *The Fire Next Time*, Coates poses a crucial question for Black folks everywhere: "How do I live free in this black body?" Throughout the book, he is fixated on matters of the corporeal: the vulnerability and violence that can at once extinguish Black bodies, lives, and lights, if we are not constantly vigilant against these dangers. And sometimes, even the greatest care and vigilance will still fail to protect our loved ones. Alongside this focus on Black bodies, the weight of history, and the social psychosis of being a Black American, Coates also considers other key questions that have occupied Black political thinkers for centuries: What is the cause of racial domination, and how does it intersect with class, gender, nationality, and sexuality? Who are our enemies, who are our friends, and can we—should we—form coalitions with other oppressed peoples? Are white people trustworthy as allies, and can they be convinced to abandon racism? What is the nature of America, and what stance should we take toward the American Dream?[1]

In some (Black) circles, Coates's nihilism was disquieting. It was an unabashedly atheist book, for starters. My peculiar form of Canadian Blackness had always manifested in a-religious terms, so Coates's dismissiveness toward religion barely registered, to be honest. But to some it was spiritual treason against the Christianity that they perceived to be the rightful and moral core of Black politics. More discussed within my professional circles was Coates's views of the intractable nature of white supremacy and the permanence of racial injustice. At the end of the day, he suggested, the struggle is all there is, futile though it may be. "Ideas like cosmic justice, collective hope, and national redemption had no meaning for me," he wrote in retrospect a few years later. "The truth was in the everything that came after atheism, after the amorality of the universe is taken not as a problem but as a given."[2]

It was a searing condemnation of the hopeful, postracial rhetoric that the previous seven years of the Obama presidency had encouraged. Coates also distanced himself from that central intuition of African American political life that I had found so confusing when I first moved to the United States—the unwavering love of American democracy, and the desire to be included in it as full members of the polity. The American Dream is not for us, Coates warned. The American Dream is delusion, distraction, and deception.

"The Dream rests on our backs," he wrote, "the bedding made from our bodies."[3]

It's easy to forget that in the early days of Black Lives Matter, most white people remained unconvinced that systemic racism in policing was a problem. "All lives matter" was still a common refrain among college-educated whites. When protestors took to the streets of Baltimore night after night, the media—and hence, liberal white people—could not see past the CVS that was looted and set ablaze. President Obama responded with his usual respectability politics–toned pandering, decrying the loss of human life with one breath and condemning property damage with the next. Baltimore City state's attorney Marilyn Mosby brought charges against each of the six officers involved in Gray's death and was momentarily heralded as an example of what Black faces in high places could do to substantiate the idea of accountability in policing.

But it was never going to be enough. One of the trials ended in a mistrial, two officers were found not guilty, and by July 2016 the remaining charges against the officers were dropped. Meanwhile, the Department of Justice's 2016 report on its investigation of the Baltimore Police Department revealed the intentional and disproportionate targeting of Black residents, finding that "racially disparate impact is present at every stage of [the] Baltimore Police Department's enforcement actions, from the initial decision to stop individuals on Baltimore streets to searches, arrests, and uses of force." The following year, eight Baltimore police officers who were members of the elite Gun Trace Task Force were indicted in a racketeering conspiracy that involved robbing people, filing false reports, extorting alleged drug dealers, illegal searches and seizures, and massive abuses of citizens' constitutional rights.

"This is not about aggressive policing," said U.S. attorney for Maryland Rod J. Rosenstein, "it is about a criminal conspiracy. . . . These are really simply robberies by people wearing police uniforms."

Police brutality, and by extension Gray's in-custody death, was only ever the tip of the iceberg of an inhumane, exploitative, rotten system. As Matt Taibbi wrote in *Rolling Stone* in May 2015, "Fix that little in-custody death problem, we're told, perhaps with the aid of 'better training' or body cameras (which Baltimore has already promised to install by the end of the year), and we can comfortably go back to ignoring poverty, race, abuse, all that depressing inner-city stuff. But body cameras won't fix it. You can't put body cameras on a system."[4]

———

As Baltimore boiled over, I made the move from Athens to Chicago. My aunt—my father's older sister, christened Carlotta but colloquially known as Auntie Gail (and even in my thirties I would never dare address her without the prefix)—was inexplicably proud.

"Debra made it to Chicago," she told my father. "She made it *home*."

I think she had only ever been to Chicago a handful of times. We had cousins who lived there, of course. All Black folks have cousins who live in Chicago. I don't know why she thought it was home and I didn't get the chance to ask her before the throat cancer took her voice and then her life. But the idea of home is like that—it's a construct, an imaginary, a field of vision. It doesn't necessarily require physical presence. Sometimes just a feeling is enough.

And Chicago felt like home. Chicago, the traditional territory of the Council of Three Fires—the Ojibwe, Odawa, and Bodéwadmi peoples—and still home to more than 100,000 tribal members throughout Illinois. Chicago, founded in the 1780s by Jean Baptiste Point du Sable, a Black trader, fortified before the War of 1812, forcibly surrendered by Indigenous peoples through settler colonial violence and coercion. Chicago, the city of gangsters, corrupt politicians, world-class universities, and an unmistakable skyline. Chicago, its radical roots extending from Mother Jones to the Haymarket Square riot, the 1910 garment workers' strike, and beyond. Chicago, the Black enclave of art, history, rebellion, and genius because of the Great Migration, when thousands of Blacks fled the tyranny of the Jim Crow South and the terror of white lynch mobs beginning in the early twentieth century. Chicago, where more than 500,000 African Americans from southern states such as Alabama and Mississippi landed between 1940 and 1960, remaking the South Side into what it is today. Chicago, that great Black Metropolis, where the legacies of Ida B. Wells, Emmett Till, Fred Hampton, and Michelle Obama collide.[5]

I *loved* Chicago. I didn't have the same time or level of freedom as I did in Boston, to just wander and meet strangers and observe the city life. But there was a pulse to the city, a tone, a tenor, that made it feel alive. It might have been the lake; there's something about a city on the edge of water that breathes life. It could have been the size and diversity of the city itself. After four years of small-town life, where white liberals' surveillance of me and my deviant Blackness was wrapped in the auspices of neighborly concern, it felt freeing to be invisible. But the real magic of Chicago was the Black people.

For the first time since I moved to the United States, I was in a place with a Black community. And while the Black community of Chicago isn't necessarily indicative of other kinds of Blackness in the United States—it was born out of a particular historical moment and space, has morphed and reshaped itself over time, and is more contradictory and pluralistic than it appears to be from the outside, just like everything else—it still meant that I could abandon my albatross of being the Only One for a time. After thirty-some-odd years of being in majority-white spaces, I was in a world where there were people who looked like me. Black folks in Chicago were even from a similar ancestral legacy. The Black Refugees to Canada and the Great Migration to Chicago (alongside other cities like Detroit, Baltimore, New York, Los Angeles, and Philadelphia) weren't so different, at the end of the day. We are a people descended from freedom-seeking movement.

The thing I treasured the most were the everyday moments of shared humanity; a smile and a nod on the CTA red line; exuberant laughter from a front porch in Englewood; chicken and waffles at 5 Loaves; that instant when my eyes would lock with an immeasurably patient Black server dealing with the arrogant Karen in line in front of me, always but a nanosecond away from demanding to speak to the manager.

There was also the danger of being in a city like Chicago. My friends and family would hear about the "deadly summers" and the gun violence and were constantly worried for my safety. But when my brother came to visit and we walked to the local diner for breakfast, I told him about the single most important act of Black self-preservation in Chicago: "Don't make eye contact with the cops."

Jon laughed. "You're joking, right?" I wasn't. Freddie Gray had made eye contact, before he ran.

I also finally, *finally* had access to a Black community in my professional life. I was a faculty member in the African American Studies department at Northwestern University, with scholars who researched Black religious traditions, Black art and culture, Black urban politics, Black history, Black women's health, Black literature, Black political thought. I had never had Black colleagues in my department before. Ever. It was a dream, to be welcomed to this atmosphere of Black talent and imagination. It was an honor, to find myself in the same department where my mentor Richard Iton had once taught.

Richard was one of the members of my dissertation committee during my doctorate. He was trained as a political scientist but had left the discipline long ago for the broader, life-giving air of African American Studies, like me. He was absolutely brilliant, the epitome of still waters running deep. Tall, bald, and soft-spoken, he had a slow, distinct kind of saunter, wore a black leather jacket, and always slung his backpack over one shoulder. Whenever we spoke, he would always sit back in his chair, cross his arms, and give me this puzzled look, as if he couldn't quite figure out why I wanted to talk to *him*. A Black Canadian who was born and raised in Montreal, he spent most of his career living in the United States. At times it seemed he felt the pull of home and family. In 2008 he returned to teach at the University of Toronto, where he had held a tenure-track position in the 1990s. He originally left because the political science department at Toronto was, at the time, according to him and some others in the department, incredibly racist. A small group of professors and students successfully recruited him back; we told Richard things had changed. I went to see him during his office hours and asked him how it was going.

"Eight months," he said with a wry smile and a sigh.

"Eight months until what?" I asked.

"Until I can leave," he replied.

It was September 14.

Richard, who once told me his first book—award-winning, but also the one he thought he had to write to be recognizable in a discipline whose main function is, of course, to discipline—was no better than a paperweight. Richard, whose second book starts with the familiar dilemma of how those who are excluded from politics seek to engage with it nevertheless, and then details what he calls the Black fantastic—"the minor-key sensibilities generated from the experiences of the underground, the vagabond, and those constituencies marked as deviant—notions of being that are aligned within, in conversation with, against, and articulated beyond the boundaries of the modern."[6] Richard, who said to me, the first time I met him at a conference in Chicago, that instead of feeling that I didn't belong anywhere, I should insist that I belong *everywhere*, and that I needed to claim all sites, spaces, successes as my own.

He was a kindred spirit. I was heartbroken when he passed away in April 2013. He had been sick for a decade and hadn't told anyone. Leukemia. Not even his closest friends knew. It was very like him. He was a fiercely private person. In the last article he published, hauntingly titled "Still Life," in which the last section was appropriately, tragically titled "Love You to the End," Richard calls for an appreciation of the power of ambiguity, uncertainty, and incoherence in this thing we call politics, this undecided designation of Blackness. The idea that there is a kind of generative genius that comes from being a project—and, I've always hoped, a person—in flux.

He meant more to me than I did to him, of course, but that's just the way of intellectual giants and we who try, desperately, to follow in their footsteps. I liked to think he would have at least been pleased that I was at Northwestern momentarily, but certainly long enough for his legacy to become my moral compass. Long enough to feel at home and haunted at the same time. Not because he loved Chicago—a mutual friend told me years later that he hated it, actually; cops harassed him constantly and it wore him down. But the idea of home is like that—it's what we desire it to be, the fantastical, a projection. It doesn't necessarily require accuracy or truth. Sometimes just a feeling is enough.

Most of all, Chicago was extraordinary because it was where my daughter was born. I don't think I loved anyone or anything, until her. To be perfectly honest, I didn't think I was capable of love, until her.

It was a strange thing, just three days after her birth, to finally make it to the pediatrician's office, bleary-eyed and racked with exhaustion, walking slowly so I didn't rip the stiches from my emergency C-section, still getting to know the squinty, wrinkly, beautiful little gremlin sleeping in her car seat, and to be asked to identify her race on an official medical form.[7] It was a tragedy to have just twelve weeks of parental leave, only available to me by the good graces of the provost's office since I didn't qualify for the limited unpaid leave available under the Family and Medical Leave Act. It was a personal calamity to return to a job that required me to write and think and teach coherently while trying to function on rare and segmented sleep, trying to heal from massive bodily trauma, trying to become accustomed to a new city, new relationship, new situation, newborn, newfound life.

It was a psychological blow to have to deal so immediately with the casual racism of white neighbors. In online forums, it was passive. "I hate to have to post this," one woman wrote on a neighborhood "moms" group, "but if this was MY nanny, I'd want to know." She posted a picture of an older Black woman sitting on a park bench, her eyes closed, her hand on a stroller in which a toddler also slept. The comments were a chorus of gratitude for this Good Samaritan who was keeping white children safe through her surveillance of Black caretaking. I had learned long ago the pointlessness of arguing with white women about their racism on Facebook, but I stayed in the group in case my picture appeared one day.

In person, the racism was plausibly deniable. More than a few of these innocent, would-never-ever-consider-themselves-racist liberal white women stopped me as I walked through the park with my white-looking, blue-eyed, tornado-haired child to ask about how much I charged as a nanny. "I'm her parent," I would say.

"Oh, sorry," they replied, always embarrassed. I would just look at them until they walked away. The problem wasn't the accusation that I was a nanny—it's a ridiculously hard job, and it's a massive policy failure that universal child care isn't the norm. But I also didn't like the assumption that I was a nanny because of my race and gender, nor did I like the presumption that being a nanny was somehow less admirable or less worthy than any other job.

But let's talk about parenthood and child care for a second, and therefore, money.

I had gotten a decent salary increase in the move from Ohio University to Northwestern University, but I was still an assistant professor and had three years to go before I could go up for tenure and promotion. Because academics are on nine-month contracts my last paycheck from Ohio was issued in mid-June and I didn't get my first check from Northwestern until October 1. Our rent in the north end of the city was absurd and we were locked into a two-year lease because we were desperate, had a fifty-pound dog, and our landlord was a crook. Even with good health insurance, the bills from my daughter's birth were several thousand dollars. And we had severely miscalculated the cost of child care, which was in the neighborhood of a staggering two thousand dollars per month at the local YMCA.

And these were just the bills that came with how we were living at the time—I also had a decade of debt from student loans and living in an expensive city on a measly grad school stipend, a car loan to pay every month, and zero savings from four years of being underpaid in my first job. Without those decades that I benefitted from the Canadian social safety net—meaning, I was not in massive debt for the invariably futile attempts to diagnose and manage my autoimmune condition or for the medical care required to save my father's life after his strokes—I would have likely been impoverished. But I still worried about money nearly every minute of every day. It was only years later that I came to realize the psychological freedom attached to having a financial cushion. That's what having money does—it gives you the space, time, privilege, and leisure to think about things that aren't money. But in those days, we were constantly one check-engine-light away from financial ruin. I felt like I was already failing my daughter in the very first months of her life.

I wasn't alone.

One of the most consequential outcomes of the civil rights movement and the legal protections against discrimination in housing, employment, and education born from that struggle was the emergence of the Black middle class. And while the fabled American middle class is constantly under threat, life in the Black middle class and white middle class are not at all the same. According to landmark research by my Northwestern colleague sociologist Mary Pattillo, Black middle-class neighborhoods are characterized by "more poverty, higher crime, worse schools, and fewer services than white middle-class neighborhoods."[8] Life in the Black middle class is, in a word, precarious. Income, occupation, home

ownership, and education are usually telltale signs of class position, but wealth—the difference in value between what you own
and what you owe—matters far more.

And so, while white people's wealth begets intergenerational
white wealth, African Americans' ability to accumulate wealth and
transmit it to future generations was sabotaged by the purposeful
destruction of Black property by white mobs (for example, during
the Tulsa Massacre of 1921), redlining, and devalued neighborhoods and housing markets. As Richard Rothstein details in his
book on racial residential segregation, *The Color of Law*, an entire
constellation of racially explicit laws, regulations, and practices at
all three levels of government (federal, state, and local) combined
with the private discrimination of real estate agents, banks, and
homeowners associations to create a nationwide system of under-
served urban neighborhoods that are predominantly Black surrounded by wealthy suburbs that are predominantly white.[9] Black
Americans were also locked out of some of the most important
components of the social safety net and mechanisms of generating
wealth, including home ownership, in both the New Deal of the
1930s and the GI Bill of the postwar era.

In the twenty-first century, skyrocketing student debt, depressed wages, college degrees that couldn't guarantee social
mobility, a couple of devastating financial crises that ravaged
Black communities through foreclosures and depleted retirement
funds, family imprisonment, and the lack of affordable housing
have compounded stark and enduring racial disparities. In 2016
the median net wealth of white families was $171,000, compared
to $17,000 for Black families. The difference between the mean
household net worth of white households compared to Black
households is close to $800,000. Altogether, Black people hold
less than 3 percent of the nation's wealth. Some economists have

recently argued that when wealth is used as an indicator of one's class position, we have good reason to question whether a Black middle class exists in America at all.[10]

I *loved* Chicago. But in Chicago, I was Black, middle class, an educated professional in my mid-thirties, a professor at one of the best universities in the United States, and totally, completely broke.

The money problems were punctuated by endless and acute anxieties of being a Black parent. I at once realized that the foundational, central horror of slavery wasn't the unfreedom, the forced labor, the confinement, the ravaged and broken bodies, the sexual violence, the erasure of the names of our kin, our culture, and our gods, the commodification of lives or the dehumanization of being, but the unrivaled evil of ripping children away from those who bore them, who fought to keep them, who loved them still, always, forevermore, unconditionally and without fail. I could feel the generations of fear. Pacing the long, dark hallway with my infant daughter as she cried at 3 a.m., I heard the gravity of my father's voice as he explained to me, on the day I got my driver's license at sixteen years old, that when I was pulled over (not *if*, but *when*), I was to keep my hands at ten-and-two. Pushing her stroller through the park, I recalled the story of the day my grandfather found out my father ran home from his neighborhood school in Toronto every day in the 1950s and raged at him for the infraction of white comfort in white public spaces.

"Are you mad? Don't *run*," my father recalled him yelling. "They'll think you stole something and then how will I keep you safe?"

It didn't matter that my daughter was lighter-skinned—and how to make my white-looking child understand the richness and beauty of Black culture and Black history is another set of anxieties altogether. The trauma was mine, my father's, my grandmother's, her grandmother's. I went looking for ghosts in America and I found them, haunting me as I laid my hands on my daughter's chest in ritual night after night after night to make sure she was still breathing as she slept.

Being a parent is to be in a constant state of fear and worry, especially in those early weeks of haze and nocturnal quiet punctuated by heart-piercing pterodactyl-like cries, when children are tiny and squishy and squinty and helpless. It is also full of the deepest kind of love there is—irrepressible, infinite, I-will-burn-down-this-entire-city-if-you-are-harmed love. I didn't know that the love and fear were tied together so tightly. I don't know how to love other than through fear. Neither did my father, or his parents, or their parents, or theirs. Those who came before me also didn't know how to show care and concern other than through

"Black Lives Matter is an ideological and political intervention in a world where Black lives are systematically and intentionally targeted for demise. It is an affirmation of Black folks' contributions to this society, our humanity, and our resilience in the face of deadly oppression." Alicia Garza, "A Herstory of the #BlackLivesMatter Movement," *The Feminist Wire*, October 7, 2014.

threats, yelling, switches, belts, and rampages, and I will not—*I will fucking not*—repeat these intergenerational mistakes. And while I can't quite forgive them for the violence, I now understand the way that love and fear are exhaled in the same shaky breath. Black people love fiercely because we are afraid.

And we have good reason to be afraid.

A few months before I moved to Chicago, journalist Spencer Ackerman wrote a series of articles in the *Guardian* beginning in February 2015 that revealed the Chicago Police Department's use of a former Sears warehouse in Homan Square, on the city's West Side, as an off-the-books interrogation compound. Between August 2004 and June 2015, Chicago police "disappeared" more than 7,000 people, more than 6,000 of whom were Black.[11]

Less than a month before I moved to the city, Chicago police officer Dante Servin was cleared of involuntary manslaughter in the death of Rekia Boyd. At 1 a.m. on March 21, 2012, Servin—off-duty at the time—was driving in the alley next to his home on the West Side when he encountered two men and two women walking to a nearby store. According to Servin, the group was being loud and when he asked them to quiet down, one of the men swore at him. According to one of the young men, Antonio Cross, he waved Servin away, thinking that Servin was trying to buy drugs. Servin claimed that he saw Cross reach toward his waistband for a gun—it was actually a cell phone—and as Servin turned his car in the opposite direction, he pointed his unregistered gun across his body and fired at least five times. One of the shots hit Cross in the hand, and one hit twenty-two-year-old Rekia Boyd in the back of the head, killing her.

Cook County state's attorney Anita Alvarez waited ten months to gather evidence in the case, including an interview of Servin, and finally filed charges of involuntary manslaughter and reckless discharge of a weapon against Servin in November 2013. On April 20, 2015, Judge Dennis Porter told Boyd's family that they were in "a court of law, not a court of emotion," and then found Servin not guilty. The rationale for Porter's decision? Servin had been undercharged by the prosecutor's office. What Servin had done was intentional and therefore "so dangerous it is beyond reckless," Porter said; "the crime, if any there be, is first-degree murder."[12]

Two months after my daughter was born, the city of Chicago was forced to release the video of the murder of Laquan McDonald. According to the police, seventeen-year-old Laquan McDonald was suspected of attempting to break into cars on the southwest side of Chicago; he lunged at police officers with a knife and was fatally shot in the chest. For more than a year, Chicago officials refused to release the footage from the dashboard camera of one of the police cars on the scene and turned a blind eye when eighty-six minutes of additional surveillance footage from a nearby Burger King was mysteriously erased after five Chicago police officers gained access to its video equipment. The Chicago Police Department also denied more than a dozen Freedom of Information Act requests for the video.

Journalist Brandon Smith eventually filed a lawsuit for its release. The video became public on November 24, 2015, and clearly demonstrated that McDonald was walking away from the police when he was shot by Chicago police officer Jason Van Dyke, who paused after McDonald fell to the ground from the first shot and then fired an additional fifteen shots at the teenager. Van Dyke was in the process of reloading his gun when another officer told him to hold his fire.

"Sixteen shots and a cover-up" became a rallying cry among Black activists in the city.

The dashcam video of Chicago police officer Jason Van Dyke shooting teenager Laquan McDonald sixteen times in thirty seconds was finally released on November 24, 2015, by court order and a full thirteen months after McDonald was murdered. There were protests in the days that followed, including on Friday, November 26, when hundreds of demonstrators marched down the middle of North Michigan Avenue, Chicago's "Magnificent Mile" shopping district, blocking access to stores on one of the busiest shopping days of the year.

In the winter of 2016 I incorporated a week on Black Lives Matter into my sophomore-level course on Black Social and Political Life. It wasn't nearly good enough—there was too much to discuss and not enough time.[13]

The next semester I designed a new course called Black Lives Matter and the Struggle for American Democracy. It was a freshman seminar, full of mostly Black students, though there were a handful of white students as well. There was Ruby, the aspiring journalist who grew up in New York City and thought that Chicago paled in comparison; Najma, Black, Muslim, hijabed, soft-spoken, and brilliant; Barret, a six-foot-ten freshman on the Northwestern basketball team; Eric, a white guy on the Northwestern football team who wanted to be able to understand more about what his Black teammates were telling him; and at least ten others with their own reasons for taking the class. Every

Monday and Wednesday morning, we came together in a hard-to-find room in the depths of the library stacks to talk about what American democracy had promised African Americans, whether it had kept those promises, and what Black Lives Matter was now demanding in return.

It should be clear by now that Black Lives Matter is not simply a reincarnation of the civil rights movement. It was instead founded on a bedrock of Black feminist politics in the age of social media. In the words of Chicago organizer Charlene Carruthers, it is unapologetically Black, intent on rectifying the marginalization of LGBTQ folks within Black communities. It conceptualizes deviance as resistance, fugitivity as liberation, and rejects all forms of respectability politics that seek to achieve racial justice through the appeasement of white discomfort and lessening of white guilt. In her brilliant book *Reckoning: Black Lives Matter and the Democratic Necessity of Social Movements*, political scientist Deva Woodly argues that the radical Black feminist pragmatism of the movement involves the activation of a unique politics of care, which, among other things, understands racial oppression as a source of psychological trauma, sees joy as a political resource, and looks to restorative forms of justice rather than punishment to address harm. In recognition of the power and necessity of local, grassroots activism, Black Lives Matter has a decentralized organizational structure that has, at times, led to serious fractures over vision, funding, ideological orientation, and political strategies between national leadership and local chapters.

Black Lives Matter emerged in 2013 when George Zimmerman was acquitted for the murder of Trayvon Martin. I had heard rumblings about the case coming out of Florida, whose "stand your ground" law seemed to be designed to protect those whose fear of Black people was contrived, historic, and pungent.

It certainly had failed to protect Marissa Alexander, who, in May 2012, was found guilty of aggravated assault with a lethal weapon. She fired a warning shot, with her licensed gun, at her estranged husband to prevent him from harming her. No one was hurt. She was nevertheless sentenced to twenty years in prison. But it was the Trayvon Martin case that made national headlines, sparking Black-led protests that were the largest mass mobilizations in my lifetime. We—Black folks across the country—wore hoodies to demonstrate how easily it could have been any of us. We pushed back against the Fox News narrative that Trayvon was somehow responsible for his own death. It didn't change the outcome of the trial in July 2013—Zimmerman was acquitted—but something had shifted. Something in the air felt heavier, denser, more volatile.

And then, on August 9, 2014, unarmed teenager Michael Brown was shot and killed by police officer Darren Wilson in Ferguson, Missouri, a suburb of St. Louis. The city exploded. At first, no one really knew what had happened. There were conflicting eyewitness accounts. For a time, we were told that Brown died with his hands in the air; protestors yelled "hands up, don't shoot!" in agonizing tribute. The Ferguson Police Department initially refused to release the name of the officer involved in the shooting. Images of mostly white police officers in military-grade vehicles and riot gear and armed with weapons, tear gas, and rubber bullets clashing with mostly young Black protestors splashed across the front pages of national newspapers. There were smashed car windows and lootings and a convenience store that burned. Curfews were imposed; on August 18, Missouri governor Jay Nixon called in the National Guard. The murky, disjointed information about the actual shooting was sharpened and subsumed by real-time confrontations between the police and protestors, streamed and shared on social media. On August 24, a *New York Times* profile on Michael Brown declared that he was "no angel"—and we knew that just like Trayvon in his hoodie, we would all somehow be found responsible for our own murders.

The police closed ranks, as they always do. Policing is a dangerous job, the unions cried, and officers are the thin blue line that separates civilization from chaos. Officers around the country began wearing wristbands that read "I AM DARREN WILSON." Predictably, Wilson claimed that Brown had attacked him and reached for his gun. In his deposition before the grand jury, Wilson said that Brown was so big it made Wilson feel "like a five-year-old holding onto Hulk Hogan," and that he feared for his life: "I felt that another one of those punches in my face could knock me out or worse," he claimed. "I mean . . . he's obviously bigger than I was and stronger and . . . I've already taken two to the face I didn't think I would, the third one could be fatal if he hit me right." He said that Michael Brown did have his hands in the air, but that it was in an act of aggression. "The only way I can describe it, it looks like a demon, that's how angry he looked. He comes back towards me again with his hands up." According to Wilson, Brown was ready to run through the ten gunshots that Wilson fired at him, "like it was making him mad that I'm shooting at him. And the face that he had was looking straight through me, like I wasn't even there, I was even anything in his way." But the shots did stop Brown, in the end. Six of them.

In his defense, Michael Brown said nothing; the dead cannot speak.

On November 24, 2014, a St. Louis grand jury declined to indict Wilson in the death of Michael Brown. The decision came in the wake of yet another police killing—this time it was twelve-year-old Tamir Rice, who was shot by Cleveland police officer Timothy Loehmann while playing with a toy gun in a public park.

That one hit close to home. I was still in Ohio at the time, and so many Ohio University students came from Cuyahoga County. The Black students walked around campus with a weight on their shoulders those days; how many of them had siblings that age? Less than two weeks later, a grand jury decided not to indict New York police officer Daniel Pantaleo in the chokehold killing of Eric Garner. We took to the streets again. It wouldn't be the last time.

It wasn't clear at first what was unleashed, that summer in Ferguson. "You can never see the end from the beginning," my father used to say. It was a moment of pure possibility, but also of intense backlash. Policing is a revered profession in North America. I grew up watching *Law & Order* with my father. It was an era when popular culture routinely presented the police as righteous, honorable, and objective seekers of truth, protectors of the social order, guardians of democratic rule. Television taught me that police catch bad guys. At home, my father told me to avoid the police at all costs, even if it meant running away. It's not that the times had changed from when my grandfather told my father not to run; rather, my dad knew that the police will be violent whether we run or not.

The Civil Rights Division of the Department of Justice released the findings of its investigation into the Ferguson Police Department in March 2015. The scathing report revealed that the police department was more akin to pirates than protectors, intensely focused on revenue generation rather than public safety. The predation was endemic and shocking: the city of Ferguson routinely pressured the police department to generate more revenue; police officer evaluations and promotions depended on their "productivity" in issuing tickets; officers "expect and demand compliance even when they lack legal authority," leading to a pattern of illegal stops, arrests, searches, and seizures, the use of excessive force, and retaliation against anyone who exercised free speech rights; police leadership was unresponsive to complaints of officers' misconduct; the municipal court system used its authority to compel payment of fines and fees imposed by its own racketeering; and both the policing and municipal court system were saturated with intentional racial bias against—and which disproportionately harmed—the city's African American population. It was never "one bad apple." The entire orchard was rotten.

The idea that maybe, *just maybe*, the police might be the problem was always going to be a hard sell for white people. There are long-standing divisions in how white and Black people view the police. For example, in a survey conducted shortly after the Ferguson uprisings, 71 percent of whites expressed a great deal or fair amount of confidence that the local police treat Black and white people equally, compared to 36 percent of Blacks.[14] The brewing backlash against efforts to hold the police accountable intensified after two New York police officers were murdered in their patrol car in an unprovoked attack in December 2014. Patrick Lynch, the president of New York City's largest police union, the Patrolmen's Benevolent Association (now called the Police Benevolent Association), placed blame squarely on Mayor Bill de Blasio, who had spoken candidly about the warnings he gave to his mixed-race son to "take special care" in encounters with the police.

"There's blood on many hands tonight," Lynch said. "That blood on the hands starts at the steps of City Hall and in the office of the mayor."

When de Blasio spoke at the funerals of the officers, the rank and file in attendance turned their backs in silent protest. A not-so-silent protest happened in the weeks following the murders, as arrests for crimes and ticket infractions went down around the city, though union officials denied that the work slowdown was an organized response.

The idea that maybe, *just maybe*, democracy didn't work in the same way for Black citizens as it did for white citizens was an even harder sell. The "all lives matter" crowd felt that Black Lives Matter activists were the ones unnecessarily using the race card to get special treatment. Dr. King's dream of a world where we would be judged by the content of our characters and not the color of our skin was launched like a grenade by precisely those same good white liberals who voted for Obama and imagined themselves as being on the right side of history, but who would have refused to march with King then, as they refused to join in the struggle now.

And yet, the call that Black Lives Matter still resonated around the world, uncontained by imaginary lines of national borders. The movement conceptualized racial formations and structures as global in nature and emancipation as a worldwide struggle that implicates us all.

It was the process of teaching and learning with these students that served as my entry point to a more radical understanding of Black politics. Though Black Lives Matter most obviously confronts unaccountable, persistent patterns and practices of police violence, it is also a movement aimed at revealing the systemic devaluation of Black lives in all spheres of public life. The naysayers will insist that slavery ended centuries ago, but the logic that justified Black enslavement persists. The connection between Blackness and criminality was born from coerced, exploited labor of chain gangs and convict leasing after the fall of Reconstruction, reified through popular culture and the mythology of the Lost Cause, and given a veneer of scientific legitimacy in the use of racial statistics to confirm narratives that Black people were inherently degenerate and bound for self-destruction.

During the long civil rights movement, Black activists insisted on their divine humanity. In fact, Harvard historian Evelyn Higginbotham's original use of the idea of "respectability politics" was never meant to refer to the ways the Black middle class tries to conform to and uphold white cultural norms. Instead, it describes the way that low-income Black women used their religious beliefs to defiantly insist that they had lives worthy of respect. With an acute understanding of what America sought to project on the world stage in the global struggle with communism ("Freedom! Individual rights! Equality!"), Black people took their demands to the international arena, laying bare the hypocrisy of democracy's broken promises.[15]

Nevertheless, the connection between Blackness and criminality persisted. As political scientist Naomi Murakawa argues, the opponents of civil rights in Congress claimed that crime was a consequence of demands for Black civil rights that had gone too far, and segregation was a more harmonious social order. The proponents of civil rights argued that it was the lack of rights that bred crime by sustaining racial inequality and leading Black people to distrust the law. But both, Murakawa demonstrates, connected Blackness to criminality. The War on Drugs, an effort spearheaded in the 1980s by the Reagan presidency to criminalize illegal drug use with harsh penalties, exploded the incarcerated population. By the time of the 1994 Crime Bill, signed into law by Democratic president Bill Clinton and making "tough on crime" discourses a source of bipartisan agreement, Americans had centuries of laws, policies, beliefs, and cultural priming that made Black people seem dangerous, unworthy, and unhuman.[16]

Police violence isn't new, but Black Lives Matter shone a spotlight on how pervasive it is. Barack Obama was the first Black president but he was also a white liberal, a centrist, and above all, a politician who mourned the lost era of bipartisan compromise, which had long since passed. He didn't seem to understand why Black Lives Matter activists wouldn't come to the table, *his table*, just to talk and smile for pictures and be co-opted into the mainstream of the Democratic Party and have nothing ever change.

Still, his administration was responsible for a far more consequential maneuver, made by the Department of Justice, headed by Eric Holder Jr. until 2015 and then Loretta Lynch. Using section 14141 of the U.S. Code, the Civil Rights Division launched investigations into police departments across the country. In cases where a pattern or practice of constitutional violations of citizens' rights were found, the Department of Justice then entered into "consent decrees"—agreements with local governments on policing reforms, monitored by the courts. Reading through the Department of Justice investigations of police departments across the country—Chicago, Baltimore, Philadelphia, Ferguson, and more—it's clear that the spectacle of police murders captured on video and amplified in a viral circuit of overlapping tragedies at once implicates and masks the endemic racism of a system that calls itself "justice" but so rarely embodies that ideal.

As my students and I dug deeper into the facets of this system, there were horrors at every turn: police killings that are underreported by more than half; the obscene militarization of law enforcement agencies, including the SWAT teams and the tanks that occupy city streets during Black protests; civil forfeitures that allow the police to seize and then keep or sell any cash and property that they allege is involved in a crime, like pirates; police oversight boards that mostly employ former cops; police unions that maintain crimes committed by the police are legal and justified; overworked and underpaid public defenders with mere minutes to spend preparing for each case; mostly white prosecutors who overcharge defendants in order to coerce plea deals; the racialized legacy of the War on Drugs; mandatory minimum sentences and three-strikes laws that incarcerate nonviolent offenders for decades; the cash bail system; administrative fines and court fees that target and then imprison the poor when they cannot pay; peremptory strikes that all but guarantee Black defendants are tried by mostly white juries; the barriers to prisoner reentry to society when the label "felon" can be used to deny access to public housing, private rental markets, food stamps, jobs, professional licenses, travel, and more. *The fact that we as a society think it is appropriate to put human beings in cages.* We condemn ourselves in our complicity with the cruelty of the carceral state. Abolition is the only way forward.[17]

I didn't used to think this way. My students made this radical turn possible. You cannot be a decent teacher without a reservoir of hope for what the future holds and for those who will bring it into being. Police and prison abolition is just a single star in the constellation of Black radical politics that asks us to imagine a different kind of reality. We rage against the calamity of the present because we know, believe, dream that the world can be better than it is now. By the end of the semester, I realized that the central lesson wasn't about the ways that agents of the state worked to hasten Black death, but instead about the forces that ensured resilience and perseverance of Black life.

We have good reason to be afraid, and yet we love fiercely, unwaveringly, audaciously, nevertheless. It is not a love for American democracy; it is a love for Black people. For Black art, Black culture, Black hymns, and Black prayers. For the ancestors we honor, the archives we keep, the futures we dream. For resilience in the face of deadly, torturous oppression. For the curiosity and wonder of childhood; for Black boy joy and Black girl magic. It is, as Richard Iton wrote, an understanding of love as a public good and loving as a political act, especially for us, who are so often, so callously deemed to be unworthy of tenderness or respect, and incapable of deep, lasting commitment.

Built into the core messaging of Black Lives Matter is a simple, central idea—that despite the psychological weight and corporeal brutality of white supremacy, the exploitative schemes of racial capitalism, the toxic barometer of heteronormativity, Black life and Black livingness are sacred, immensely joyful, full of love and pride and resilience and wonder. It is home, because the idea of home is no more and no less than what we are willing to make it, what we are able to dream into existence. And that feeling is more than enough.

It was a necessary armor for what would come next: smack in the middle of the academic semester, on November 8, 2016, Donald Trump was elected president of the United States.

CHAPTER 6

The Western Frontier

(Eugene, Oregon)

In the summer of 2017, we made a cross-continent move. I had accepted a position at the University of Oregon, partially because I was recruited with tenure and the promise that I would be able to help build a new Black Studies program, and partially because administrators at Northwestern University, assuming I wouldn't leave for a lower-ranked university, lowballed my retention offer.

"You can't eat prestige," my father replied when I told him about the move.

At the time, Oregon was a state about which I knew next to nothing, including whether it was pronounced "Ore-gone" or "Ore-gun." It is a breathtakingly beautiful place. Crossing the border with Idaho from the east and heading toward the coast means passing through dramatically different terrains, like transversing invisible thresholds that separate one world from the next. Barren scrublands, beautiful in their strength and resilience, turn into the Cascade Mountain range, deemed ancient only by our limited human metrics, covered in blinding snow, either by storm or sunlight.

On the west side of the mountains is the Willamette Valley, the anglicized version of *whilamut,* a Kalapuya word that means "where the river ripples and runs fast." Here the seasons are only two—dry and wet—and life is everywhere, in discrete, symbiotic layers, and on everything. Each tree giant (my Oregon-born son's first words) has its own ecosystem growing on, out, beneath, from it—moss, ferns, lichen, mushrooms, insects, birds, beasts of all kinds. Head farther west still and solid walls of evergreen mountains enclose winding roads. The western edge of the continent is an unforgiving coastline, with sand dunes that muffle the roar of the ocean; that is, until you've crossed the precipice, and then the temperature suddenly drops ten degrees, the wind batters your face, and the endless ocean is before you, majestic and uncompromising and a reminder of how infinitely small and temporary we are.

The ideological divisions in the state mimic these discordant environments. The rural parts of the state, especially those in eastern Oregon, are notoriously conservative, even bordering on libertarian. Think of the story from 2016 that made international headlines, about the Malheur National Wildlife Refuge takeover by an armed white militia, led by Ammon Bundy. The more populous, coastline cities are known for their progressive, liberal politics. The television show *Portlandia* is far more accurate than anyone wants to admit. There are also overlapping strands of the left-wing politics of environmentalists, "social justice warriors," and drum-circle hippies. At times, those on the extremes of left and right make strange bedfellows, agreeing on the undesirability of "unwarranted" government interference such as putting fluoride in the drinking water or mandating vaccinations for children.

And, of course, there's a fascinating history of fascist and antifascist organizing and violent clashes between them. Portland, Oregon, has been an epicenter of white supremacist organizing since at least the 1970s. Neo-Nazi groups such as the now-defunct White Aryan Resistance (WAR) have been replaced by a multiheaded monster that includes the Proud Boys (founded by Canadian Gavin McInnes), Three Percenters, Oath Keepers, Patriot Prayer, and the umbrella Patriot Movement, which comprises more than 566 antigovernment groups and militias that were active in the United States in 2020. In response to the growing neo-Nazi presence, activists formed Rose City Antifa in 2007, the first officially recognized antifascist organization in the United States. Whenever white supremacists rally, antifascists counterprotest, and in recent years these ideological conflicts have inevitably turned into riotous, and sometimes deadly, street brawls.[1]

I lived about one hundred miles south of Portland in Eugene, Oregon, nicknamed "Track Town USA," population something like 165,000. The north and south ends of the city are marked by two buttes, Skinner and Spencer, easy to climb and worth it for the glorious view from the top. The Willamette and McKenzie Rivers run through the town, and during football season the footbridges are packed with jubilant students crossing from the main campus to 54,000-seat Autzen Stadium, unmistakably stamped with an enormous yellow-on-green "O." Every Saturday a market takes over the downtown core, featuring locally grown fruits and vegetables, food trucks, and a drum circle populated entirely by white people with dreadlocks. A 2017 city ordinance banned dogs from downtown streets, a thinly veiled attempt to drive the large, mostly white homeless population out of the city and make way for million-dollar revitalization projects.

I once again found myself in a predominantly, exceptionally white space that white people could only see as quaint or charming, and not hostile or dangerous. My white students at the University of Oregon often entered my class on the politics of race and immediately confessed that they had grown up in the suburbs of Portland, or in a small town in Northern California, and so had never really had to think about race, even as their racially homogeneous upbringings were, of course, by design.

Long before Oregon became a state, diseases brought by Europeans caused epidemics that killed between 70 and 90 percent of the Indigenous population of the region, the Kalapuya. Those who survived the "Indian Wars" that followed throughout the nineteenth century were shuttered onto tiny reserves while their territory was given away to white homesteaders. In Oregon Territory, acts were passed that outlawed slavery but required that Blacks leave the territory within three years (1843) or they would "be whipped twice a year until he or she shall quit the territory" (1844). When Oregon joined the Union in 1859, a clause that prohibited Black people from settling within the state was written

The Ku Klux Klan in Portland, Oregon, circa 1922.

into its constitution. It was, quite literally, founded as a white ethno-state.

By the summer of 2017 some of our worst fears about a Trump presidency were beginning to be realized. In his first months in office, Trump had already announced a plan to restrict legal immigration, proposed to bar transgender people from serving in the military, launched a barrage of attacks on journalists and the media, and revised Title IX protocols for investigating sexual assaults on college campuses. These were just the tip of a very big, unavoidable iceberg. But many of my friends in political science were still confident that the strength of democratic norms, the counterbalancing effects of a free and independent press, and the limits on executive power in a presidential system would prevail. Political institutions are kind of sticky and slow to change, they said. There are checks and balances that protect against exactly this kind of situation, they advised. A one-term president can't do that much damage, they promised.

Oh boy. Were they ever wrong.

A force that had previously been invisible to white liberals came hurtling into public view that summer, violent, blinding, and undeniable. It was a potent fury that African Americans had long known was embedded in the core of the country, a basic lesson that permeated every piece of advice from our elders, every work of Black ingenuity, every Black history lesson sanitized by white teachers.

White supremacy has never been conquered. Instead, it has always been reconjured, into indiscernible, rhizomatic formulations.[2] Like the supernatural duppy of Jamaican folklore—a malevolent spirit that escapes the body between death and burial—white supremacy was not abolished with slavery, but instead lives on, spectral and sanctioned, infiltrating and irrepressible. It wasn't just Trump that we needed to worry about. It was the conditions that enabled Trump to come to power and those who were emboldened by his victory.

Oregon was an early battleground for this most recent iteration of America's immortal white supremacy. In May 2017, Jeremy Christian, a self-proclaimed white nationalist, verbally accosted two Black teenagers, one of whom was wearing a hijab, while on the light rail train in Portland. When bystanders intervened, Christian stabbed three men, murdering two of them. Just nine days after the attacks, Joey Gibson, the founder of Patriot Prayer, led a Trump Free Speech Rally in Portland. It was still easy, at this point, to think of this situation as unique to Portland, America's whitest big city, or as attributable to a few unstable, volatile, racist individuals.

But then, a few months later, the Unite the Right Rally descended on Charlottesville, Virginia. The tiki torch light revealed not the expected image of aging neo-Nazis from rural America living in a dream world of their own, but rather bankers, lawyers, software designers, police officers, young people who literally lived next door and were willing to fight, tooth and nail, to preserve something as mundane as a monument to the Lost Cause. They marched for two days, screaming "Blood and soil!" and "Jews will not replace us!" while Charlottesville police were instructed not to intervene in fights except in cases of "extreme violence." On August 12, 2017, a white supremacist, twenty-year-old James Alex Fields Jr., deliberately drove his car into a crowd of protestors, killing thirty-two-year-old Heather Heyer and injuring dozens of others. President Trump responded by saying there was blame and very fine people on both sides.

It was a watershed moment, but many more would follow.

Watershed moments were declared every week, as the press trumpeted that this time, *this time* Trump's rhetoric had led to something truly outrageous. Pipe bombs were mailed to Democratic leaders in late October 2018, around the same time that an anti-Semitic white nationalist murdered eleven worshippers at the Tree of Life synagogue in Pittsburgh. In August 2019, a twenty-one-year-old white man killed twenty-three people at a Walmart in El Paso, Texas; in a racist screed online he echoed Trump's language and warned of a "Hispanic invasion" before specifically targeting Mexicans in the mass shooting. Two people were murdered and one wounded at a Black Lives Matter protest in Kenosha, Wisconsin, in August 2020 by white teenager Kyle Rittenhouse, who had joined a group of armed men and traveled to Wisconsin from Illinois with a semiautomatic, AR-15–style rifle to help "protect Kenosha businesses." The ultimate watershed of all watersheds culminated in the violent insurrection of the U.S. Capitol on January 6, 2021, after Trump claimed the 2020 election had been stolen.

It was all unfathomable, until it happened. Then again, as historian Jefferson Cowie writes, the undercurrent that has consistently wound its way through the heart of American freedom for centuries is a core belief that freedom for white people means the freedom to violently dominate racialized others.[3]

"It's just astounding to me that white liberals are like, 'Oh my God, I cannot believe this is our country, this isn't who we are,' when this is exactly who Americans are, doing as America has always done," I complained to my colleague Joe Lowndes sometime in the spring of 2018. We were supposed to be meeting to plan a conference, but for twenty years or more, Joe has been researching the intersection of the Republican Party, populists, and the radical right, so instead of working I was peppering him with questions about his experiences doing ethnographic research at white supremacist demonstrations and militia meetings.

"How is this possible?" I continued, exasperated. I was refer-
ring to Trump, but I meant all of it. Everything. Living on the West
Coast during the Trump presidency meant waking up to bad news
that had already been happening on East Coast time for hours.
Every day the headlines screamed, "Trump did something terrible, again!" It wasn't shocking anymore. It was just exhausting.

Joe leaned back in his chair and crossed his arms. "Yeah, Trump
may be new, but something like Trumpism has been with us for a
long time. Since the 1960s there have been these, like, right-wing
moments of insurgency within the Republican Party. Trump just
helped move far-right radicals toward the Republican Party and
the Republican voter base toward far-right radicalization."

I thought for a moment. "So . . . this is much worse than
people realize, isn't it? Everyone is focused on Trump as a char-
ismatic leader—I mean, the guy's an idiot and a narcissist but
apparently some people like that—but what you're saying is that
Trumpism is going to outlast Trump?"

"Yeah," Joe said. "Look, I've been to Trump rallies. And
they're *wild*. But the most interesting thing isn't so much that
Trump is leading his supporters, but it's the crowd that's kind of
urging him in certain directions. So sometimes he says things and
they fall flat, so he tries something different and that gets him a
bunch of cheers. And that's what drives a lot of what he says about
a number of things like immigration, the police, Black Lives Matter. It's a kind of politics that has its own momentum."[4]

Under Trump, this momentum was visible and emboldened
white supremacy. It made anonymous racism less amorphous;
instead of colorblind racism we had visceral fascism, even in a
quaint, charming place like Eugene. There was still an occasional
Confederate flag on the back of a pickup truck around town, but
now there were also neo-Nazis. In my classroom. In a state in
which a license is not required to carry guns openly and that has

very few restrictions on carrying a concealed weapon. At a university where I was one of around a dozen Black faculty members.

Maybe a month after that conversation with Joe, I attended a workshop during a Canadian political science conference in Edmonton, Alberta. I was a panelist on a roundtable tasked with discussing experiences of women in political science. During the Q&A session, a younger white woman asked the panel for advice about hostile students. She was teaching in Great Britain in the aftermath of Brexit and said that some of her pro-Brexit students were argumentative in class and intimidating during office hours. Especially white men.

"I don't know how to handle this," she confessed in a shaky voice. "Have any of you encountered this? Do you have any advice?"

I immediately volunteered to answer the question. "Here's what I do," I said to her and started listing the processes I had put in place to keep myself safe. "If you have teaching assistants, require them to attend class so that you have backup if you need it. Have a plan to deal with violent students that doesn't involve calling the campus police, because if there's an altercation between, like, me and a white person, campus police are much more likely to shoot me. Schedule office hours at the same time as a white colleague who is comfortable intervening if you need it. Don't post your office hours online. Have a doorstop in your office and prop your door open during office hours; don't ever allow a student to close your door . . . unless it's a student that needs your help because they've been sexually assaulted. Arrange a code word with the admin staff so you can call them to interrupt a meeting. If you're going to do media, give a heads-up to your department chair so they know why people are calling for you to be fired. Don't answer your office phone—just let everything go to voice mail so you have a record of the death threats . . ."

I trailed off as I realized the looks of horror I was getting from my Canadian colleagues.

"Deb, oh my God," one of the other panelists said. "Are you serious? That is terrifying."

Her comments stopped me in my tracks. I hadn't thought of it as terrifying before. It was just my life. Until that moment, I hadn't realized how my ideas of normal had shifted. Maybe I was becoming an American, after all.

For the three years we were in Oregon, we lived in Kalapuya Ilihi, the newest residence hall at the University of Oregon at the time. My colleagues thought I was absurd—their exact words were "insane," actually—for accepting a position to live on campus, among freshmen. But Kalapuya Ilihi means the homeland of the Kalapuya people, part of the Confederated Tribes of the Grand Ronde and the Confederated Tribes of Siletz Indians, and though slavery is often cast as America's original sin, the country was si-multaneously founded through the dispossession of Indigenous peoples. The common thread between the two is the way that both land and people were turned into property, and therefore subject to narrow European conceptualizations of ownership. These en-tanglements are not uncomplicated. American history is marked by Indigenous slaveholding, even after the conclusion of the Civil War, and Black participation in the massacre of Indigenous peo-ple and the encroachment of their traditional territories as Buffalo Soldiers. And there were always, *always*, various kinds of govern-ment intervention that pitted one group against the other to erode Indigenous sovereignty and exploit Black labor.[5]

And so it meant something, at least to me, to continue my decades-long struggle with the idea of home alongside young people who were away from home for the first time. It seemed

Kalapuya Ilihi Residence Hall at the University of Oregon. The statue in front of Kalapuya Ilihi is a bronze casting of the sculpture *From the Mad River to the Little Salmon River, or The Responsibility of Raising a Child*, by Rick Bartow (1946–2016), a member of the Wiyot tribe of Northern California.

like a moral responsibility, at least to me, to live among students who were looking to forge new connections on the traditional territory of those who had been there since time immemorial and were forcibly displaced from their home, and to teach these young adults that this was now our home only through the legacy of theft, coercion, deceit, and death. It seemed important, at least to me, to contend with and against ideas of home in the discomfort of this unearned inheritance, as an immigrant, as a foreigner, as a descendant of stolen people exploited on stolen land, to think about what kind of community we could build with those just beginning to learn more about the world around them. It was absurd. It was an honor.

Because I had an official role with University Housing as the faculty-in-residence, I was able to arrange to teach my Black Lives Matter class in the auditorium on the first floor of

Kalapuya Ilihi. On the very first day of class, I started with a land acknowledgment—these are now commonplace throughout Canada, especially at academic conferences and political events. And, truth be told, they had become superficial lip service, much more about a performance to confirm the status as a "good white person/benevolent white organization" than a genuine commitment to decolonial politics. But land acknowledgments are exceedingly rare in the United States and so the students were surprised when I started a class on Black Lives Matter by talking about the meaning of our presence on Indigenous land.

"I wanted to have this class here," I began, "because I live here, and I know a bunch of you do as well. This place is our home. And even if you don't live in Kalapuya Ilihi, maybe you think of this university as your home. I wanted to have this class here so we could think, every single time we meet, about how our homes were built on the destruction of the homelands of others. And to think, every single time we meet, about how we are all complicit. We cannot just write ourselves out of the systems of domination that have created the modern world."

I asked them, in those first moments together, to think about what it means to be in that particular space, to take up space, to make a space into a home, to honor space. To think about the tensions between home and habitat, malleability and mobility, the intimately familiar and the extraneously alien, roots and routes, discovery and displacement. To think of land not as something we possess, but rather the ways that ideas of property ownership are tied up with beliefs, sometimes embedded in law, about who could own property, who could be dispossessed of their property, and who could be bought and sold as property. That the idea of possessing and being possessed means we are all haunted by that which was supposed to have been destroyed, displaced, long gone, but is actually still here, in the room with us.

Being reflexive about Black politics requires facing the realities of settler colonialism in North America. Black people are not quite settlers, but instead are *arrivants*. It's a term, coined by Indigenous scholar Jodi Byrd, that recognizes that we did not come here by choice, and yet are complicit in and benefit from settler colonialism as a violent, continuing structure of the social, political, and legal order that erases and dispossesses Indigenous people, at times precisely because our search for home, inclusion, and belonging frequently imagines this territory and nation as belonging, unproblematically, to us. Black freedom cannot, will never, be won through Indigenous displacement.[6]

In Oregon, I wasn't the Only One, but I was one of the Very Few. It reminded me of spending my adolescence trapped in Oshawa, Ontario, except this time I was armed with a better understanding of my Blackness, in all its intersections and complications and mutations and privileges and nuances and peculiarities.

It was a sense of Black identity that germinated from the isolation of growing up as the Only One in a racially homogeneous place and time while Canada crowed about its multicultural character. It was saturated with the implicit messaging of white supremacy, respectability politics, and the precariously but poisonously fragile whiteness of my mother's Jewishness (a long story for a therapist and another day). It was geographically detached from the potential kinship of other Black communities in Canada, including newer ones that had markedly different cultural intonations and traditions than those of the American-descended branches of my family tree. It yearned for the imaginary, false coherence of Black America, momentarily glimpsed at schoolhouse reunions and mined from incomplete visions of popular culture. It crystallized only once I came to the United States and found more than I had bargained for in the realization that Blackness only appears monolithic because of the difference-collapsing protocols of white supremacy, which reasons that a singular Blackness is easier to dominate, control, manipulate, exterminate. It cowered in the arbitrariness of Black death, and reveled in the struggle for Black life and the strange, incredible connectedness of Black people, as my children say, neverwhere and everyhere.

I know it might not make sense. It doesn't have to make sense. I am not particularly interested in coherent story lines, parsimonious explanations, or happy endings that confirm the resilience of Black folks in the face of unrelenting state violence and exclusion. If there is a moral arc to the universe, I don't know if it bends toward justice, or if I'm smart enough to make proclamations about the moment we are in, and how it relates to either those moments that have passed or that have yet to come. This shit is complicated and sitting in the presence and discomfort of those complications without trying to resolve them is analytically, politically, morally necessary.

On a day like any other sometime during our first two years in Oregon, my daughter and I were playing outside when she told me, point-blank, "Mama, I don't want to be Black." She was not quite four years old.

My heart dropped. "What makes you say that?" I asked.

She skipped away, her curls bobbing behind her, and joined a group of students sitting on the lawn. She's like that—evasive, precocious but fierce, hard to pin down, somehow a butterfly and tiger combined. I let it be, for the moment. Parenting isn't about one talk, one lesson, one grand gesture; it is instead the long game of all the small moments, each and every day, delicately connected like an infinite string of Christmas lights. I would have a thousand more chances to open her mind to the joy and beauty of being a Black person, day in, day out, in word and deed.

But this three-second conversation was a flickering light that threatened to extinguish countless others, and it made me realize how many of my discussions with her about Blackness in these white spaces were warnings of danger, or stories of struggle. I realized how badly we needed to build a life in which she didn't hate her gorgeous curly hair or didn't see me as the Only One. I will be damned if I hand this trauma down to another generation. I will not let my children be tricked into hating themselves.

I found out through the usual channels that McGill University's political science department was hiring in the subfield of Canadian politics, which was still a major focus of my research even though I had been in the United States for nearly a decade. I debated whether to apply for what seemed like a very long time. A job at McGill would mean leaving the United States, probably for good.

But all signs pointed to Trump winning a second term. The idea seemed unfathomable to many, but I was, at that point, sure of it. The reason is simple: white middle-class life in America hadn't changed all that much under Trump.

Don't get me wrong. Trump's presidency was a shitshow from beginning to end. He almost started a nuclear war with North Korea, remember that? But if you were protected by class privilege in America, as I was, then all that mattered was that the economy was strong. If I weren't Black and an immigrant, if I didn't care about transgender people's rights or families that relied on food stamps to survive or children in cages at the southern border or any of the other vulnerable people who bore the brunt of Trump's policy changes, his administration would not have impacted my day-to-day existence at all. Other than the pervasive sense of impending doom that hung in the air, that is.

I also knew that the real changes were happening in the realm of political institutions—minor shifts to rules and regulations that were less discernible, harder to pinpoint, and therefore so much, much more consequential and dangerous to American democracy. As Harvard University political scientists Daniel Ziblatt and Steven Levitsky argued in their 2018 book, *How Democracies Die*, democracies often become authoritarian regimes through the actions of those elected to lead. Their book clearly identified warning signs that they saw in the first years of the Trump presidency, especially the erosion of the norms that had long served as the "guardrails" of democracy.[7] Trump the spectacle, Trump the accident, Trump the demagogue, Trump the aberration of American values, Trump the culmination of American white nationalism—all of this mattered less than the way Trump as the leader of the executive branch stretched the norms of what was acceptable behavior and action in a democratic regime.

Personally, I was much more worried about the Supreme Court. Trump had already appointed Neil Gorsuch in January 2017 to succeed Antonin Scalia, whose seat had become a partisan political battle during Obama's last year in office. Justice Anthony Kennedy, who had long been a pivotal swing vote on the ideologically divided court, announced in June 2018 that he was planning to retire. Trump then nominated U.S. Court of Appeals for the District of Columbia Circuit judge Brett Kavanaugh. He was confirmed to the U.S. Supreme Court in October 2018, despite the credible accusation of sexual assault by Dr. Christine Blasey Ford, who put herself in the middle of a painful, traumatic firestorm with nothing to gain.

It felt like a double blow to democracy. The first was that the Kavanaugh hearings occurred in the middle of the cultural reckoning wrought by the #MeToo movement, and Christine Blasey Ford was a compelling, expert witness, able to draw on her PhD in psychology to explain why she could remember some details from the assault and not others. And yet, not even this clear, un-equivocal condemnation before Congress could prevent the nomination from moving forward. Even Dr. Blasey Ford knew the odds she was up against, telling the *Washington Post* in September that she had struggled with whether to come forward. "Why suffer through the annihilation if it's not going to matter?" she asked. In the end, she felt that her civic responsibility outweighed her anguish and terror.[8] If only the Senate had shown the same dedication to the moral core of democracy.

The second blow emerged from the knowledge that Supreme Court judges are appointed for *life*. It was now a court dominated by conservatives. And if the unthinkable happened to either eighty-five-year-old Ruth Bader Ginsburg or eighty-year-old Stephen Breyer—two of the court's four remaining liberals—Trump would be able to appoint a full third of the Supreme Court during his presidency.[9] A much more liberal Supreme Court had already gutted the Voting Rights Act in 2013; *Roe v. Wade* was hanging on by a thread. This court could skew American politics to the right, without recourse or remedy, for a generation. My children's generation.

I threw my hat in the ring at McGill. I was invited to an interview on campus. I flew across the continent six weeks after giving birth to my son and somehow was able to sound coherent while presenting my research to my potential future colleagues, who were generous and enthusiastic. I got the job.

"Are you, like, *sure* sure?" I asked my partner. By that point, we had had several hundred conversations about a potential move to Montreal. I was far more worried about it than he was. "You'll be unemployable because you aren't bilingual," I warned.

"So I'll learn French," he said with a grin. "How many people get the opportunity to learn another language as an adult? To live in another language as an adult? This sounds amazing," he replied. He's always up for an adventure. It's annoying and I am so incredibly fortunate, it boggles my mind sometimes.

My colleagues at the University of Oregon were kind and understanding of our decision to leave. "Can we come, too?" they joked.

But I had mixed feelings. It was clearly a good move, especially for my children. They would have the chance to grow up in Montreal. All my friends who grew up in Montreal still love the city; neither my partner nor I could say anything like that about our hometowns. The move to a world-class institution like McGill was clearly a good career opportunity for me. And yet, I couldn't shake the feeling of disappointment. I had come to America to vindicate, to absolve, to atone, to claim a debt of blood and bondage and here I was, just like Rebecca and Cornelius, fleeing to Canada. I felt like I was letting them down, somehow.

I was still processing these complicated emotions and trying to manage the crushing anxiety of planning a cross-continent, international move with an American partner, who required legal immigrant status in Canada, two small children, both of whom needed proof of their Canadian citizenship, and a dog, whom we would have to drive to Montreal because of his anxiety issues, when someone from the University of Oregon's Museum of Natural and Cultural History reached out. The Eugene museum used a monthly pub talk featuring faculty at the university as a fundraiser; would I be interested in presenting my research at its "Ideas on Tap" series in February 2020?

I wrote to Lauren, the academic programs coordinator, and said I'd be happy to, but my current research on Black Lives Matter was not yet ready to be presented to an audience. "But," I wrote, "I'm moving back to Canada and I've got a lot of feelings about it. Could I present on that?"

Sure, she wrote back. Whatever you want.

That February night was the last gathering I went to before the world stopped a month later, in March 2020. The event was held at a brewery a couple of miles from the university; it was a huge, open space with a gorgeous wood-crafted bar in the front room, and a large back room where polished wooden tables had been pushed against the walls, the center of the room now featuring neat rows of chairs. At the front of the room there was a small stage, a screen, and a podium that I sighed upon seeing, since I'm much shorter than most realize. I'd have to find a stool to stand on during my presentation. COVID was looming on the horizon, but it hadn't hit yet and the room was packed. At least a third of the audience was comprised of my colleagues, my students, and my friends, but the rest were total strangers. I wondered why they'd come.

Lauren welcomed the audience and provided a brief background about the "Ideas on Tap" series before giving me a generous introduction, during which I tried not to squirm. The audience clapped politely as I stepped up to the microphone—my friends who worked in Residence Life in the Department of University Housing, sitting in the back corner, cheered. My first slide displayed a picture of railroad tracks that dissolved into birds flying against a blue sky under the title of my presentation: *Return: Some Probably Incoherent Thoughts on Race, Democracy, and the Boundaries of Belonging*. I took a deep breath and looked at my students seated in the front rows as I began.

"A few weeks ago I was talking with my father, and he said, 'You know, Debra, your daughter was the first Thompson born in the United States since Cornelius Thompson escaped slavery. It's been over a hundred and fifty years, and some days, I think we came back too soon.'"

I paused. "I've been thinking about those words ever since."

CHAPTER 7

Borderlands

(Neither Here nor There, Nowhere and Everywhere)

Y ou're Canadian? Are you going to become an American citizen?"

The question, not unlike when Canadians asked me where I was really from, usually came from a well-meaning stranger or acquaintance who had just found out how long I had been in the United States. This time it came from a group of wide-eyed, refreshingly earnest freshmen, sitting across the counter from me in the community kitchen of the Kalapuya Ilihi residence hall at the University of Oregon. Not unlike that common Canadian question, this one was similarly loaded. Usually, I would demur or avoid answering. I'm exceptional at changing the subject. And I didn't have a lot of answers at this particular moment—a move to Montreal was in the realm of possibility, but was not yet certain. But I'm a teacher at heart, and teachers teach, even when the questions don't have easy (or any) answers.

"Do *you* think I should get American citizenship?" I asked. It was a Sunday morning, and my partner and I were making pancakes for anyone who wanted them, as we did every week. Our portable speaker was playing NPR in the background, though one of the resident assistants had deemed it "too nerdy" and took over with a playlist of her own. Another group of students were playing "the floor is lava" with our daughter, cheering and clapping whenever she triumphantly jumped from one couch to the next and taking turns giving her piggyback rides to safety.

"Of course you should get American citizenship," one student replied confidently. I think her name was Lauren. She was in the College Republicans, and every Tuesday night she would carry a giant American flag out of the building and take it . . . somewhere. She disagreed with everything I said, but always, always wanted to talk to me about politics. "Don't you want to vote? I thought you were a political science professor?"

"But how much does voting even matter, really?" asked Jeremy, a student in the "academic residential community" for those interested in law and social justice. "We could vote in every single election for the rest of our lives and we still wouldn't have even a fraction of the power of the Koch brothers." The other students nodded.

"I love how you refuse to be cynical and hopeless about the state of American politics, Jeremy," I teased.

He laughed along with the others, though he was, of course, right—and many, including me, were pessimistic about the fate of American democracy. It was 2018 and the naïve optimism of "hope" and "change" of the Obama years had long disappeared. Instead, we wondered if the Trump presidency was the beginning of the end, if it would be impossible to repair what had already been damaged, if this was how the world's longest-standing democracy would die.

"So, if I got citizenship, I could vote, even though it would apparently be a waste of time," I summarized. "Are there any other reasons why I should think about getting citizenship?"

They stared at me thoughtfully. After a few moments, my partner, wearing our infant son in a baby carrier and flipping pancakes on the other end of the long counter, said, "Well . . . not that this is all about me, but if you were deported, that would be pretty bad for me."

"They can't deport you, you're married to an American!" A student named Joy had just walked into the kitchen in plaid pajamas, fuzzy slippers, and impeccable makeup. She gestured at my partner. She paused. "Wait. You're American, right?"

"I am," he replied, "but we're not married."

This scandal required several minutes of discussion—half of the students were shocked, and the other half thought we were heroes for destroying the patriarchy. All agreed that we should have a giant "unwedding" party on the quad and invite the entire residence hall. I tactfully steered the conversation back to citizenship.

"Besides," I said loudly over the din, "being married to an American wouldn't save me from being deported."

"So citizenship gives you the right to stay," Joy said. She took a seat at the counter and grinned at my daughter, who had just climbed into the empty seat beside her. "That seems important."

"I think the better question is whether you *want* to be an American," said Dani, a student from Austin, Texas, who would eventually become an honorary member of our family. She reached over to grab a chocolate chip pancake from the tray to give to my daughter. It was her fourth pancake of the morning. "Like, honestly, when Trump was elected everyone said they wanted to move to Canada. Things here are so screwed up right now. Do you *want* to be part of this mess?"

"Ah, well, that's the question, isn't it?" I grinned. They looked at me blankly. Even cynical Americans have a hard time imagining that not everyone would choose to be a citizen. "Look," I said. "You're all students at the University of Oregon. So, let's pretend you're citizens. You're members of this community. You have certain rights and certain obligations. Are there still things about the way this community operates that you don't like? Are there things that, say, President Schill's office is doing that you're not cool with?"

"Umm, is there anything Schill *is* doing that we're cool with?" someone muttered. There was a pause, made more dramatic by the dissonance between the pensive looks on the students' faces and the new Drake album playing in the background—a song called "Portland" by a Black Canadian in America. Fitting.

My partner broke the ice. "Well, we moved in here weeks before you all came, and the university used prison labor to make the furniture in your rooms, and to move all of it into the hall. Are you cool with that?"

His intervention did the trick. Soon the students were listing grievances, large and small: out-of-state tuition fees were absurdly high; campus police carried guns; Nike cofounder Phil Knight and his million-dollar donations left duck-shaped footprints all over the university; there was an explicitly racist mural in the main stairwell of the library that the university refused to remove; first-year students were required to live on campus, even though living off campus was much less expensive; students who had protested a speech by the university president were charged with "disruption of university" and "failure to comply" under the student code of conduct; President Michael Schill responded to the interruption by publishing an op-ed in the *New York Times*, a venue students couldn't dream of accessing with their own rejoinder.[1]

"Okay," I said. "But you're here. You're part of this community. You're all Oregon Ducks and you mostly love being Ducks, right? And so all this"—I gestured widely—"including all the stuff that you don't like, all the stuff that you find morally repulsive—that's part of the deal, too. Being here makes us all complicit. And yet, here we are. The question is whether you can live with the injustice built into the bones of community, whether you want to use your membership to make it better for everyone, or whether it's possible to wash your hands of it altogether."

"This is boring," announced my daughter. "Can I have another pancake?"

In many ways, the struggle for citizenship has been the defining feature of the African American demands on American democracy since the founding. It's only from the vantage point provided by the obscene privilege of having a Canadian passport that I could even entertain a skepticism of anyone's devotion to and longing for inclusion in the American Dream, regardless of how caveated that inclusion has been.

It's a laudable goal. Who can argue against the quest for citizenship in a world where so many would risk everything for the chance to attain its protection? Is there anyone who isn't haunted by the image of three-year-old Alan Kurdi, forever asleep in his bright red T-shirt on the Turkish shore, or Oscar Alberto Martínez Ramírez and his not-quite-two-year-old daughter Valeria, locked in a final embrace among the reeds of the Rio Grande?

"You have to understand," writes Somali-British poet Warsan Shire, "no one puts their children in a boat unless the water is safer than the land."[2] People literally die for the chance to access American citizenship. It's a gateway to build a life in which security and safety are all but guaranteed—at least, on paper. So, while immigration conjures the specter of walls, borders, and detention centers, citizenship, its palatable epilogue, is the realm of oaths and allegiance, rights and responsibilities, ceremonies and celebrations. The triumph of the latter smudges out the trauma of the former.

In the social sciences, we often think of naturalization—the long, time-consuming, and often expensive process of becoming a citizen—as an indicator of a migrant's successful integration into a political community. It's supposed to be a good thing. According to the Obama-era Task Force on New Americans, civic, economic, and linguistic integration of new Americans is fundamental to the individual success of immigrants and refugees and the collective well-being of America, the "nation of immigrants."[3] We rarely focus on what immigrants give up when they become new citizens. We don't speak about what it means to ask non-white people to "integrate" into predominantly white spaces; we never question whether integration is a harmful or violent process. The legend of American generosity, American benevolence, American "give me your tired, your poor, your huddled masses yearning to breathe free" magnanimity, cannot exist without the intimation that immigrants—and especially immigrants of color—are permanently in debt. Our successes are because of the American Dream; our failures are our own doing. We should be grateful. Immigrants can never truly repay that which we are presumed to owe.

But for those lucky enough to be born in Canada or the United States, citizenship is more a matter of happenstance than anything else. "I was born into three citizenships: American because I was born there, Canadian because of my parents, and Greek because of my grandparents," Anastasia, a student in my honors seminar at McGill University, once told our class. "And I've never had to prove I'm worthy of any of them at all."

Citizenship, University of Toronto law professor Ayelet Shachar argues, is like a birthright lottery—we are born into privilege or precarity by chance. There but for the grace of God go I, my father would say. Though lotteries are often synonymous with

fairness—selection is random, and everyone has an equal, but mi-
nuscule, chance of winning—the lottery of birthright citizenship
is inherently unfair. Shachar suggests that it's not altogether unlike property inheritance, because it allows a small group of recip-
ients to pass down their unearned privilege to their heirs, and in
doing so, we perpetuate vast, life-chance-defining, compounding
forms of inequality on a global scale. Citizenship is worth something because not everyone can have it. Its exclusivity raises its
value, and, by consequence, its moral dubiousness.[4]

Democracy literally, and somewhat unhelpfully, means rule by
the people, but the precise composition of "the people" isn't always clear. The *demos* has always been exclusive in one way or
another, whether the restrictions limit access according to race,
gender, age, immigration status, ability, language, or wealth.[5]
Whether or not we are included in the idea of the people, citizenship is also a legal category. It is official membership in a political
community, the possessor of "the right to have rights," as political
theorist Hannah Arendt put it, and this status is granted by the
state.[6]

But even—and perhaps especially—without citizenship,
you still must engage with the state. It just happens in distinct,
anxiety-producing ways. Biometrics, photographs, complicated
paperwork, administrative fees, medical exams, hostile questions
or interviews at ports of entry, nonresident tax compliance systems, appointments at the U.S. consulate, immigration status
verification systems, more complicated paperwork and more administrative fees, forced departures to reset a visa or get a new
entry stamp in your passport, providing documentation that your
spouse and children are in fact your spouse and children, and

entire ecosystems of state surveillance are part and parcel of the bureaucratic labyrinth of legal immigration. Even the pathway to a work visa is far more difficult than most imagine—you have to have the time, money, and ability to move mountains to make it happen,[7] and even then it could all be left up to the discretion of a finicky border agent at the Wild Horse Port of Entry outside Havre, Montana, population 9,715.

U.S. Citizenship and Immigration Services (USCIS)—the agency responsible for administering the immigration system—is meant to be the friendlier, gentler arm of immigration enforcement. It's not supposed to invoke terror in the name of protected borders and national security, like its parent agency, the Department of Homeland Security, or its close collaborators, U.S. Immigration and Customs Enforcement (ICE) and U.S. Customs and Border Protection. Most of my interactions with the people who work at USCIS were quite pleasant, actually. I don't know how many of the platitudes were a direct result of the guillotine the agency held over my legal status in the country. Anytime I needed to speak with a representative, engage a border agent, or visit any of the field offices, I was always, without fail, well dressed, punctual, polite, and deferential. It wasn't just a code-switching exercise to fit into white society; it was a tactic of survival, a purposeful use of respectability politics to ensure my ability to continue working and living in the United States.

At border crossings when I travelled by car, I found that it was necessary to fudge the details of my research interests. "What do you do?" they'd ask.

"I'm a professor at the University of Oregon," I'd say.

"What do you teach?"

"Political science."

"What kind of political science?"

This is where it was tricky. Answering "the politics of race" would sometimes land me in the little processing building off to the side so the officers could "check my documents." Responding with something like "I teach about democracy" was much safer. Sometimes I could head off talk about politics—always a dangerous topic when you can't discern the partisan leanings of the person holding your green card—by redirecting the conversation to football.

"The Oregon Ducks?" the agents would ask.

"You bet!" I'd say. Sometimes I even made sure I was wearing some kind of green-and-yellow University of Oregon paraphernalia to prove I was really and truly a member of the community.

"Scooooo Ducks!" they'd respond.

I hate college football. I've never even seen a game and won't until colleges start paying the Black athletes that generate millions of dollars with their unpaid, body-wrecking, brain-traumatizing unpaid labor.[8] But border agents love college football. It was a foolproof tactic. After all, school spirit is kind of like nationalism. It requires the same kind of unearned, unwavering loyalty.

In my mind's eye I anthropomorphized USCIS as though it had a personality that I encountered on a regular basis—it was huge, cold, unforgiving, and intimidating. Slightly sociopathic, perhaps, in the sense that it could go from being kind and gentle one minute to threatening your life and livelihood the next. Unpredictability and uncertainty are part of the danger, the menace. Dealing with the monster required the kind of survival skills one only develops after having had emotionally abusive relationships: to tiptoe quietly around its constantly changing rules, do anything to avoid setting it off, anticipate what it wants in any given moment, be constantly on guard in case some tiny mistake ignites its disproportionate wrath. It followed me everywhere I went, this silent system of surveillance that wanted to know exactly where I lived, that needed to be updated every time I moved, that was in cahoots with the human resources office anywhere I worked with tentacles that stretched across all my other interactions with the state—especially border agents, the police, and the Internal Revenue Service. Being invisible is another crucial survival strategy. My ancestors who fled to Canada knew it just as well as I did. The fewer interactions with the monster, the better.

The massive system of paperwork and USCIS state surveillance is a one-way street of a lot of responsibility and few rights. As a legal immigrant, I had the right to stay and work in the United States, temporarily. Because my initial immigration status as a visa holder was dependent on my continued employment, it meant that my employer at the time, Ohio University, where the institutional racism nearly broke me, held an extraordinary amount of power over my ability to remain in the United States. Quitting wasn't an option, if I wanted to stay in America. And I was lucky, so *unworthily fortunate*, to be among the most privileged class of immigrants: English is my first and only language, I am educated, I had the money (or, at least, the room on my credit card) to hire a lawyer if I needed to, I am Canadian, I have the socioeconomic privilege and reputational deference that comes with a white-collar job in the professoriate. I was eventually able to get a green card, also known as permanent residency, which was an even more secure migrant status. It gave me the freedom to leave that toxic job and environment and move to Chicago and Northwestern University, both of which were so much better for my career, my sanity, and my soul.

Most immigrants are not positioned so securely. Between the worlds of legal and unauthorized immigration, there is an entire spectrum of those with precarious migratory status. There are, sociologist Luin Goldring and her coauthors argue, multiple dimensions of and pathways to this precarity, which is marked by an absence of work authorization, residence permit, or the right to remain permanently in the country, the right to remain in a host country independent of a third party's (for example, sponsoring spouse or employer) sanction, and social citizenship rights, such as health care and education. In effect, migrants who are authorized to be in a country temporarily may still be exploited, vulnerable, and marginalized.[9]

And this is nothing compared to the hardships and challenges of being undocumented. Citizenship is something that you never even think about when you have it, and that keeps you awake at night when you don't.

I could, of course, pass as American-born, and while I was welcomed into the various African American communities that I encountered, I was still an immigrant. A noncitizen. I was able to conceal my status not just because of the cultural similarities between Canada and the United States, but more importantly because the feigned bogeyman of American immigration politics is from Mexico or Latin America. I am not what most people think of when they imagine an immigrant to America. But then again, what most people think of when they imagine undocumented people—if they think about them at all—is probably wrong. There are the admirable, hardworking, Americanized DREAMers, for sure, but there are also "day laborers, housekeepers, construction workers, dog walkers, deliverymen, people who don't inspire hashtags or T-shirts," as well as young, brilliant people like Karla Cornejo Villavicencio, who watched her migrant parents pursue the American Dream, and who bore witness as it broke them and others with equal parts vitriol and neglect.[10]

"Speak English!" an old white man once spat at me at an airport.

I stared at him, shocked and momentarily speechless—not by the hostility, but because it wasn't the kind of hatred I was used to.

"That's . . . literally the only language I can speak," I said, in a voice much too small.

How odd, I thought, that I've always been so ashamed that I come from a bilingual country and can only speak English. That I'd tried for years—*decades*, in fact—to learn French and failed miserably each time. How strange, I thought, that this racist white man was so angry at the very thought of bilingualism, when bilingualism and even trilingualism is the norm in most of the world. How funny, I thought, that the blows don't land as hard when they're not meant for you.

They still land, though.

Even as the vast majority—77 percent, to be precise—of the more than 40 million foreign-born people living in the United States are lawful immigrants, it is the 10 million "unauthorized immigrants," and more specifically the estimated 8.1 million of them from Latin America, that capture the public's imagination and shape the terms of political debate.[11] Unnoticed are the 100,000 Canadians that constituted the largest nationality of visa overstays in 2017 and the fact that Canadians and Europeans combined represent nearly half of all U.S. immigration overstay violations, though they are rarely detained or charged.

As migrant justice activist Harsha Walia argues, the so-called "migrant crisis" is politically contrived. Mass migration is the outcome of multiple and intersecting global crises, including exploitative relationships within the global capitalist system, unequal power relations of economic and political conquest between the Global North and Global South, and the disastrous and worsening effects of climate change. But the political distortion of a worsening "migrant crisis" positions Western nations as victims of unwanted, unauthorized, unrelenting migration, even as our settler-colonial countries were founded by the millions of Europeans who were also unwanted, unauthorized, unrelenting in their efforts to commit to the destruction of Indigenous peoples and the outright theft of their lands.

"No one is illegal on stolen land," writes the Red Nation coalition for Indigenous liberation, "except those who stole it."[12]

After being a lawfully admitted permanent resident for five years, I could apply for American citizenship. I would have been eligible after three years if my partner and I had just gotten married, but we've got children, and so we don't need the state to validate our commitment to each other. The application asked me questions, such as whether I'd ever been a member of the Communist Party, or if I was a habitual drunkard. I had to list every single time in the past five years that I had left the country, where I went, and for how long I was gone. It cost about $725 to file. When the COVID-19 pandemic added an additional eight months to my application's processing time, I also had to apply for a travel document that would allow me to leave the country and travel to Montreal without surrendering my green card. That cost an additional $660, and the fate of my green card was still up to the discretion of border agents, travel document or not.

Borders are not just physical barriers; they are also bureaucratic ones. Borders are often paperwork labyrinths where boundary crossings can only happen if your circumstances fit the predetermined categories of a dropdown menu. Sometimes borders are more about the passage of time than passing through space. When an immigrant overstays their visa, for example, their legal status shifts from documented/legal to undocumented/illegal not because they crossed a territorial boundary, but because a temporal boundary crossed them.[13] In this world of bureaucratic borders that encircle a community and guard access to its membership, whether it's the USCIS or the University of Oregon, the administrative burden of time, money, and expertise is always high, processes are always opaque, exceptions are always punished, and consequences are always dire.

For the record, Canadian immigration regulations aren't any easier to navigate. Nor is Canada's immigration regime any more benevolent, fair, or efficient than what exists in the United States. Canada's "points system" gives the impression of neutral and objective metrics that are then applied equally to all would-be immigrants. But the policy gives preference to "economic" immigrants—those who are self-sufficient, highly educated, can speak English or French, and can fill an established need in the country's labor market. The economic immigrant category is more than double the size of the targets set for the family reunification stream, and the number of economic immigrants admitted in a given year is greater than family reunification immigrants, refugees and protected persons, and humanitarian and compassionate admissions *combined*. A more troubling ethical issue concerns those who come to Canada through the Temporary Foreign Worker Program, especially agricultural workers and live-in domestic caregivers, who are often, though not exclusively, racialized minorities and must contend with unscrupulous recruitment practices, exploitative working conditions, employment mobility restrictions, insecurity throughout the labor migration cycle, and limited protection from human rights abuses.[14] My interactions with Immigration, Refugees and Citizenship Canada were fairly straightforward—I sponsored my American partner for permanent residency and obtained proof of citizenship for my American-born children—and the process was still lengthy, costly, and chock-full of errors that could have ruined *everything* if I hadn't had money, friends who speak French, access to legal advice, and the rights and privileges of a Canadian citizen.

I debated for a long time about whether to get American citizenship. The timing of it all got especially tricky when I accepted the position at McGill University. It was supposed to start in July 2020. If I left the country before getting citizenship, I would have to surrender my green card; if I wanted to work or live in the United States again, I'd be back at the beginning of a long, costly, burdensome, not easily accessed immigration process. And Trump's presidency made it clear that the ability for foreign nationals to immigrate to the United States wasn't a foregone conclusion. Everything seemed much more uncertain. At the end of the day, my reasons for becoming an American citizen were pragmatic, personal, and political.

In pragmatic terms, Donald Trump was elected in November 2016 on a platform openly hostile to undocumented migrants, but it soon became apparent that his administration's priority, under the careful watch of comic book villain Stephen Miller, was to slow all legal immigration to a trickle as well. The Trump administration's ability to radically change so much of the American immigration paradigm in such a short time would actually be impressive, if it weren't so purposefully harmful to so many people. There was the Muslim travel ban, the dramatic reduction of refugee admissions, the revocation of the Deferred Action for Childhood Arrivals and Temporary Protected Status programs, increased rejections for visa and asylum applications, the proposed reduction to the family reunification stream of immigrants, and new "public charge" inadmissibility criteria that denied visas and green cards to immigrants who had ever used a public benefit or *might one day use them.* Trump also launched a controversial, likely unconstitutional attack on birthright citizenship and nearly hijacked the 2020 census by insisting it include a question on citizenship status. For a presidency marked by chaos from beginning to end, Trump's agenda to transform the policy realms of immigration and citizenship was notably, undeniably coherent. As *The Atlantic*'s Adam Serwer has written, the cruelty was, in fact, the point.[15]

In personal terms, my partner and children are American. In February 2018, the United States Supreme Court ruled that immigrants—including permanent residents, like me—do not have the right to periodic bond hearings and could be held by United States immigration officials indefinitely.[16] *Indefinitely.* The word scared the shit out of me. Was I just supposed to trust the state to be benevolent? That keeping my head down and following all the rules would be enough to protect me from indefinite detention, without cause, for any reason? Was I willing to bet my freedom on it?

Citizenship isn't perfect, but it offered greater protection against the indefinite. More importantly, if the unimaginable happens, I want to be put in the same pen as my children. I need to be able to go where they go, whether voluntary or forced. This might sound dramatic, but the legacy of slavery haunts me. It lives in my bones. Whatever you think you know about slavery—the horrors that Black people were subjected to—remember that it was, without a doubt, at least a thousand times worse than what you can imagine. Slavery was cruel and inhumane in many ways, but most especially because it ripped children away from parents. The institution was economically invested in and fundamentally predicated on our powerlessness to protect our children from harm. Citizenship gives me the ability to keep my children safe— at least, in some ways. For many Black parents, citizenship cannot even guarantee safe passage to the corner store.

In political terms, this is my ancestors' legacy. My kin were owed a debt for their centuries of forced labor. But as an immigrant, I have no legal claim to citizenship on these terms. The principles of family reunification in immigration policy—what Republicans sometimes call "chain migration"—do not have a clause that accounts for the blood debt of the nation. But Black folk know of debts and forced repayments. When enslaved Haitians revolted and won their freedom, France responded by demanding $150 million for "lost property"—the property being the formerly enslaved. It was the Haitians who were once property that were forced to pay reparations to their oppressors. This demand was, University of Virginia professor Marlene Daut writes, "the greatest heist in history," plummeting the first Black republic into debt, the echoes of which reveal themselves in Haiti's status as the poorest country in the Western Hemisphere.[17]

Black people know of debts, bad checks, and promissory notes defaulted. The Fourteenth Amendment granted citizenship to the formerly enslaved. I would collect.

The morning of my citizenship interview I woke up early to go over the study guide one last time. It covered one hundred questions on principles of American democracy, the system of government, rights and responsibilities of citizens, and American history, geography, symbols, and holidays. The answers were straightforward, simplistic, and begging for further explanation. But editorializing beyond the answers provided in the guide was obviously a terrible idea.

"Although USCIS is aware that there may be additional correct answers to the 100 civics questions," the guide admonished, "you are encouraged to respond to the civics questions using the answers provided in this pocket study guide." Tempting as it was,

I knew I shouldn't launch into an explanation about the academic consensus on the centrality of slavery as a cause of the Civil War and the way that "states' rights" was used as an ad hoc justification to maintain the economic trade in human lives, or how the study guide's definition of the rule of law as "no one is above the law" does a great disservice to one of the most fundamental concepts in democratic rule: that laws should be applied universally to all people, regardless of power, wealth, or status, and so citizenship is, at least in theory, the great equalizer among all those who possess it.

As a political science professor, I didn't really need to study. I teach university-level classes on these civics lessons. But I'm a nerd and I've never not studied for a test, so I silently quizzed myself over my morning coffee before heading to the USCIS building in Portland, Oregon.

I walked in fifteen minutes before my 10:30 a.m. appointment time, as per the instructions in the letter I carried with me. The security guard asked to see my letter and sent my bag, coat, and boots through a TSA-like security screening. I walked through a metal detector, gathered my things, and headed to the second floor. The large waiting room was silent, sterile, and nearly deserted. There were only five other people, each clutching a file folder of documents that could summarize, justify, legalize their place in this country. Usually I would bring a book with me to any waiting room, but the only book I brought on the trip was the one I had assigned to discuss in my graduate seminar the following Monday: Jason De León's *The Land of Open Graves*, a haunting ethnography about the thousands of undocumented migrants who cross the Sonoran Desert of Arizona—those who make it and those who don't. I left it in my hotel room. Impertinence is only safe for white people. Agents appeared from a set of open double doors and called a name; the others who had arrived before me stood as each name was eventually called, and followed the officers down the hall.

At 10:45 a.m., an older, white officer in a red and blue checkered shirt appeared and called a name. Raphael, or something. No one answered. He turned to go, and then stopped, looked back at me and the other woman left in the waiting room, and said, "Debra isn't here either, right?"

"I'm Debra!" I said, probably too quickly.

"Oh!" he said. "We thought you weren't going to show up because your address was in Canada. Hold on, let me get your file. I'll be right back."

Oh. My. God, I thought. What if he hadn't thought to ask if I was there?

A few minutes later I followed him through a locked door and down a short hallway to his office. He stood on one side of a Plexiglas divider and asked me to raise my right hand. "Do you promise to tell the whole truth, to the best of your ability?"

"I do," I said.

We settled in. He took my passport, green card, and Oregon driver's license. I realized it was a good thing I hadn't gotten around to getting my Quebec driver's license yet. When you transfer a license from one state to another, sometimes the DMV will punch a hole in your old one to render it invalid. Quebec would probably confiscate it or something.[18] I hadn't even thought of that.

"We thought for sure you weren't coming," he said.

"The last time I talked to someone at the National Service Center they basically said I couldn't reschedule the interview to an office closer to Montreal, so I got on a plane." I smiled, hoping that the sentiment would come through in my tone since I was wearing a face mask.

"Yeah, we can't switch your file to a different field office. It's supposed to stay with the one closest to where you live. In America," he added, almost as an afterthought.

"Sure, that makes sense." I nodded. It didn't necessarily make sense. What if someone moves in the middle of their application?

"Don't worry," he said. "Someone would have noticed you in the waiting room sooner or later."

I nodded and smiled behind my mask.

"There are two parts to this stage of the naturalization process: an interview and a test," the agent explained. "Let's start with the test. You will be asked up to ten questions on U.S. history and you must correctly answer six. What is freedom of religion?"

The abrupt change from instruction to question caught me off guard.

"Sorry?" I said.

"What is freedom of religion?" he repeated.

"Oh. It's the ability to practice your religion, or to not practice your religion, free of state interference."

He typed my answer. "What is the highest court in the United States?"

"The Supreme Court."

"What ocean is on the East Coast of the United States?"

"The Atlantic Ocean."

"The Federalist Papers supported the passage of the U.S. Constitution. Name one of the writers."

Alexander Hamilton, I sang in my head. "James Madison," I answered out loud, to prove something I can't quite articulate.

"Name one state that borders Mexico."

"Arizona," I said, thinking about the book I didn't bring.

"There were thirteen original states. Name three."

"New York, Massachusetts, and Virginia."

"Okay, so you have six correct answers, and that's it for that portion of the interview!" the agent said.

"Oh, okay. Great!" I said. I was just starting to get into the swing of things. I like tests. Academic ones, at least.

The next part of the interview involved going over the answers I had provided in my N-400 application for naturalization. The agent read the application's questions to me, and I confirmed my answers; mundane biographical information about my mailing address, nationality, employment, and children's names. "I'm in Montreal for the year," I told the agent. It wasn't untrue. I was still technically an employee of the University of Oregon—I took a year of leave without pay instead of resigning my position outright.

"Oh, like a sabbatical?" he said. "I know academics do that all the time. Go to other universities for a little while."

"Exactly," I confirmed. My intentions are none of the government's business, I thought to myself. It was very American of me.

The yes/no questions in part 12 of the application ("Additional Information About You"), which the agent read out to me, tell the story of some of America's greatest anxieties. Have you EVER claimed to be a U.S. citizen? Have you EVER registered to vote in any federal, state, or local election in the United States? Have you EVER voted in any federal, state, or local election in the United States? Do you now have, or have you EVER had, a hereditary title or an order of nobility in any foreign country? Have you EVER been declared legally incompetent or been confined to a mental institution? Do you owe any overdue federal, state, or local taxes? Have you EVER not filed a federal, state, or local tax return since you became a lawful permanent resident? Have you EVER been a member of, or in any way associated (either directly or indirectly) with the Communist Party, any other totalitarian party, or a terrorist organization? Have you EVER advocated (either directly or indirectly) for the overthrow of any government by force or violence? Have you EVER persecuted (either directly or indirectly) any person because of race, religion, national origin, membership in a particular social group, or political opinion? Did you EVER receive any type of military, paramilitary, or weapons training? Have you EVER committed, assisted in committing, or attempted to commit, a crime or offense for which you were NOT arrested? Have you EVER been arrested, cited, or detained by any law enforcement officer for any reason? Have you EVER been convicted of a crime? Have you EVER been removed, excluded, or deported from the United States? Have you EVER hurt anyone?

I dutifully answered no to each question, though that last one gave me pause. What adult human hasn't been hurtful to someone at some point? I was mean to a girl named Melissa in grade two, and I still think about it. And how ironic that a country in which the police disproportionately murder Black people, and an administration puts children in cages along the southern border, would demand to know if I had ever harmed anyone. The hurt I assume I caused to a terrible ex-boyfriend or two pales in comparison to the violent depths of state power.

The agent tappity-tap-tapped his keyboard and furrowed his brow. "Okay," he said. "Here's the problem. You live in Canada and the system will only accept a current mailing address that's in the U.S. I'm going to have to get approval for this."

"Oh," I said. "I tried to get all this sorted while we were still in Eugene, and everything was on track to be processed before we left, but then COVID hit, and everything was delayed."

"Yeah, that really threw our case processing times for a loop," he said. "Don't worry, I think this will be fine. But I've got to go get this approved by my manager and I can't leave you alone in my office, so let me take you back to the waiting room."

I followed him back to the waiting room. The five others had also returned, each holding a miniature American flag and a large white envelope. They each received some kind of certificate from an agent and left, one by one. Proud new Americans. I sat down and thought about how I left all my anxiety medication back in Montreal, like an idiot.

The agent came to get me after about ten minutes of waiting. He gave me a quick thumbs-up. "We're good to go!"

"Oh, thank goodness," I said. "Do you think that the naturalization ceremony will be scheduled soon? I read online that sometimes it can be scheduled for the next day, but maybe I can change my flight if there's a chance it can happen early next week."

He shook his head. "I'm going to swear you in right now," he said. "We used to have ceremonies, and some people really liked that because they could invite their families, but now with COVID, we're just doing them after the interviews."

We sat back in his office, the Plexiglas between us once more.

"So, here's the thing," he said. "I'm just going to put on this form that you live in Eugene, since it was your last American place of residence. That's what it will say on your Certificate of Naturalization."

"Okay," I said. "So, will any correspondence get sent to Eugene? I can give you my in-laws' address in Chicago, if that's the case."

"No, no. It's fine," he said and smiled. "Look, after this meeting you'll be a citizen. So, you're moving out of the jurisdiction of USCIS. There's no reason you'll ever have to talk to us or hear from us again. It doesn't really matter what address we have on file for you, because after today your file will be closed. As a U.S. citizen, you can live wherever you want, even if that's Canada."

"Great!" I said, but my mind was whirring. How interesting that where I lived could be so problematic as a green card holder and applicant for naturalization, but completely fine as a citizen. Citizenship is a legal status, and so it's a kind of administrative border in itself. Before my interview, I was on the side of the border where an unusual circumstance, like a sabbatical in Canada, was a problem, but I was about to cross over to the side where none of that matters. Citizenship grants the freedom to be unorthodox.

"The only complication is getting back here once you leave," he explained. "I'm going to have to take your green card, since you're no longer a permanent resident. You'll get a Certificate of Naturalization once we're done here, and you can use that to apply for a passport. So, you'll be able to get back to Canada on your Canadian passport, but if you want to come back to the United States, you'll need an American passport. I'm not sure how you apply for those from Canada, but I'm sure it's possible."

I handed him my green card. It made me a little sad to give it up. It was a fixture in my legal existence in the United States for five years. I was legally required to carry it with me at all times. I had grown attached to it.

A few minutes later, I repeated the Oath of Allegiance.

I hereby declare, on oath, that I absolutely and entirely renounce and abjure all allegiance and fidelity to any foreign prince, potentate, state, or sovereignty of whom or which I have heretofore been a subject or citizen; that I will support and defend the Constitution and laws of the United States of America against all enemies, foreign and domestic; that I will bear true faith and allegiance to the same; that I will bear arms on behalf of the United States when required by the law; that I will perform noncombatant services in the Armed Forces of the United States when required by the law; that I will perform work of national importance under civilian direction when required by the law; and that I take this obligation freely without any mental reservation or purpose of evasion; so help me God.

The Oath of Allegiance is highly problematic, to put it mildly. What does it mean to renounce and abjure all allegiance and fidelity to another sovereign when dual citizenships are permissible? How can I support and defend the Constitution when the Fourth Amendment lets killer cops walk free on the regular and when Black Lives Matter, labeled as "Black identity extremists" by the FBI, is considered a national security threat?[19] The requirement that naturalized citizens will bear arms on behalf of the United States was a great subject of debate among those in the Canadians-in-America Facebook groups I belonged to. That, and the lifelong tax obligations that are bizarrely based on citizenship and not residency.

The agent gave me a big white envelope with my naturalization certificate and a letter from President Donald Trump and a miniature American flag. And that was that.

It's a strange thing, to walk into a building as an immigrant and walk out a citizen. It was anticlimactic. It wasn't quite reparations, and it wasn't justice for my ancestors. But I think it was something.

―――――

Citizenship is imperfect. Black people know this.

Citizenship can be predatory. Indigenous peoples teach us this.

Citizenship is exclusive by nature. Migrants breathe this.

And so, Black freedom dreams are not reducible to the struggle for citizenship. They never have been. They never will be. Citizenship simply cannot sustain our aspirations for freedom and belonging, hope and connection. I loved living in the United

The letter from President Donald Trump, in which he writes, "The United States is now your homeland, and all Americans are now your brothers and sisters. You have pledged your heart to America. And when you give your love and loyalty to America, she returns her love and loyalty to you." Is it? Are they? Have I? And as to America's capacity to return love and loyalty, I have some questions.

States not because I was enamored with all that America could offer, nor because I was drawn in by the promise of American democracy or the moral imperative of American citizenship, but because of Black America. Because of the durable, resilient ways that Black Americans exist in excess of America's democratic moorings. The struggle, the grief, the joy, the culture, the kinship. The aunties who sneak crisp bills into your pocket, the street corner camaraderie, the political positions shaped, styled, and swept away on the floors of barbershops and beauty salons, the moral battery of anger and hope in every protest, the aesthetic of bright yellow clothes on smooth brown skin, the art and ethos of storytelling and tall tales. The moments of recognition that came when I passed another Black person on the street and we nodded to one another—the age-old message, I see you, I know you, I recognize you, we are here, in this hostile space, together, and that alone is a strength that they do not know and a power they cannot take. The central, inalienable belief that we as individuals and as a people are part of something larger, bigger than, beyond, through, and in spite of the nation-state. This, and not citizenship, is the crux of Black freedom dreams.

Our diasporic, dreamscape politics cannot be resolved by inclusion into the nation-state that has been the source of our oppression, and thus our quest for liberation does not end at citizenship. But this liminal space of being and becoming, of fugitivity as flight, can be powerful, perhaps even revolutionary. Because inasmuch as the act of moving is often done alone, there have always been communal efforts to create spaces of sanctuary that harbor and protect those who flee. It is this ethic of care and concealment, resistance and refuge, secrecy, safety, and survival, that shapes a transformative politics.

Cornelius and Rebecca knew implicitly what took me decades to learn. As fugitives we generate new possibilities, alternative horizons for racial justice, and different kinds of relationships, coalitions, and practices to defy established boundaries and breathe life into new, emancipatory spaces.[20] Fugitivity is freedom, but escape has its costs. Remember, Shrewsbury was full of people who were trying to hide.

CHAPTER 8

Je reviendrai parmi vous

(Montreal, Quebec)

Montreal is haunted.[1]

Montreal is haunted in the way all old cities are haunted. It is a place that bleeds history, a sedimented past that began long before our Eurocentric ideas of discoveries and foundings and records. What we now call Montreal has been known by many names and the land has been the site of wars, trade, enslavement, rebellions, and riots. The twenty-first-century cosmopolitan feel of the city can't hide the sense that it is a strange, unique kind of place, where old and new intermingle sometimes seamlessly, and other times with purposeful or unavoidable discord. That's what a haunting is, really. A psychological presence and material absence, something recognizable and familiar, but just beyond our field of vision. That which has equal potential to be malevolent and helpful, guiding and misleading, protective and hazardous.

Montreal is also haunted with the ghosts of my past: my ex-husband lives somewhere in the city. I don't know which neighborhood, but my siblings do, the traitors.

The global pandemic amplified the feelings of hauntedness. It might have been the way that playgrounds were empty, normally bustling streets were silent, and people were increasingly wary of each other—anyone could unknowingly spread the virus. More likely it was the thousands of people in North America who had died in a matter of months. There was something so strange about walking through a very quiet and calm version of O'Hare International Airport in Chicago and boarding a flight to Montreal. There were only five people on the plane, including me and my two children. When we landed at Pierre Trudeau International Airport, it was also empty and eerily silent.

I approached the customs agent to submit the mountain of paperwork involved in moving back to Canada. He was a young white guy, maybe in his late twenties, masked and perfectly bilingual. He was reading legal scholar Michelle Alexander's *The New Jim Crow*, a book that was published back in 2010. It was an instant classic, playing a large role in changing public perceptions of the racial inequities built into the system of mass incarceration in the United States. Now it was the summer of 2020, just two months after George Floyd had been murdered by the Minneapolis police. Tens of thousands of people marched through the streets of downtown Montreal in protest. Some carried signs of Black Montrealers who were recently killed by the Service de Police de la Ville de Montréal (SPVM)—Pierre Coriolan and Nicholas Gibbs. A few years earlier, the SPVM had also killed Black residents Alain Magloire, René Gallant, and Bony Jean-Pierre. After the march had ended, the police used tear gas to disperse the remaining protestors.[2]

The agent put the book aside to accept my documents. We exchanged some pleasantries—him, probably out of boredom, me, because border agents scare me and are nicer when I am politely conversational. My eyes kept sliding over to the familiar cover—I had assigned the book in class for several years—and I decided to broach the topic.

"What do you think of that book?" I asked him.

"Oh, have you read it? It's just so terrible," he said. "I can't believe they treat people like this. I had no idea."

My smile was frozen under my mask. Who was the "they" he was talking about? The police, the state, the prison-industrial complex, Americans writ large? And how was it that he didn't consider himself, an agent of the Canada Border Services Agency, part of that "they"?

The Canadian–American border has always issued its own kind of violence toward Black migrants, including the hundreds of Black asylum-seekers who risked life and limb to flee the Trump administration.[3] Jon, who you know by now is my brother, worked at the Canada Border Services Agency years ago, and he and I used to spend hours discussing how officers' uniforms had changed over the years and what the change was meant to imply. According to Jon, officers wore blue collared shirts and khakis in the 1990s; now their attire mimicked the navy uniforms of the police, complete with badges, name tags, walkie-talkies, handcuffs, Kevlar vests, guns, batons, and drug-sniffing dogs. Maybe the shift was just symbolic—in the years he worked at Toronto Pearson Airport, Jon rarely put anyone in handcuffs, and only got into a physical altercation once. But the symbolism of an armed police force at ports of entry was important. Welcome/ Stay out.

"Yeah," I said. "I think a lot of people have the same reaction to that book as you." I paused, trying to decide how far down the rabbit hole I wanted to go. I thought about asking his opinion on which part of the book he found the most interesting, or why he picked it up in the first place, or if he knew about the disproportionate rates of Black and Indigenous incarceration in Canada, but then decided not to. "My students seem to, at least." I ended, cautiously.

"That's great that they're learning about this in school," he said, nodding approvingly. "I just feel like we really need to educate ourselves on this. Things won't change otherwise." He finished stamping my documents and gave me instructions on how to get my goods released from customs after we finished our mandatory two-week quarantine to ensure we weren't bringing COVID-19 back to Canada with us. "Welcome home," he said.

Welcome. Home?

As if to punctuate the emotional and bureaucratic complexity of returning to Canada, we quarantined in a cute little cottage in Oka, Quebec, a village just northwest of Montreal on the north bank of the Ottawa River. The quarantine requirements meant that we couldn't leave the property for two weeks—not even to walk the dog—and so I found this place on Airbnb and booked it because it was situated on a few acres of woodland. We only had our luggage and what my partner brought with him as he drove across the continent with Dodger. And so, we quarantined. For two weeks. In a cottage with no phone signal and Wi-Fi that didn't work. With two children under five, and *none of their toys*. It wasn't terrible, but my god, we played a lot of hide-and-seek. Like, *a lot*.

It felt odd to come back to Canada, and to spend my first weeks on Canadian soil in Oka. In 1990 a dispute over a proposed golf course expansion onto Kanesatake land led to a violent, seventy-eight-day standoff between the Quebec police, the Royal Canadian Mounted Police, the Canadian military, and Indigenous protestors. The dispute, of course, was about much more than a golf course expansion, and Kanien'kehá:ka resistance to colonial domination can be traced much further back than the 1990s and continues to this day.[4] Nevertheless, the so-called "Oka

Crisis" led to the creation of the Royal Commission on Aboriginal Peoples (RCAP), which culminated in a four-thousand-page report and 440 recommendations, most of which have never been implemented. RCAP was supposed to be the beginnings of reconciliation between Canada and Indigenous peoples.

Thirty years after the Kanesatake Resistance, almost twenty-five years after RCAP, five years after the Truth and Reconciliation Commission of Canada, a year after the National Inquiry into Missing and Murdered Indigenous Women and Girls, and the government of Canada had bureaucratized the issue to death. How many more reports did we need to record the violence of settler colonialism, not just in the past, but in the here and now?

A homecoming for me was simultaneously an intrusion in Tiohtià:ke, what we now call Montreal. As a Canadian citizen, I had the right to move and settle anywhere in the country, but in order for my American partner to come with me, we had to have the permission of both the federal government and the government of Quebec. But we didn't have to ask the Kanien'kehá:ka Nation. One person's homecoming is another's colonial invasion.

Just a few months shy of the anniversary of my first year back in Canada, a gut-wrenching announcement came from an investigation of the grounds surrounding the Kamloops Indian Residential School in British Columbia, which revealed 215 unmarked graves of Indigenous children. Over the next month came more revelations from across the country of more dead children, including 751 unmarked graves near the former site of the Marieval Indian Residential School in Saskatchewan. The sheer horror was difficult to comprehend. And it was just the beginning. In the months that followed, more grave sites were found, more dead babies were mourned. I thought, again, of the parallels between slavery and the genocide of Indigenous people; the way both used children to coerce some to cede title to lands and others to continue to submit to forced labor. The ways that both Black and Indigenous peoples struggle to protect our children from harm. Just imagine—your children, and every other child in your community suddenly vanishes, stolen by a malevolent power intent on your destruction. It is the apocalyptic, dystopian landscape often depicted in future-oriented science fiction, but premised on what has already happened to Black and Indigenous people in the not-so-distant past. What would those thousands have grown up to be, to change, to dream, had they not been murdered by the church and state?

My partner and I brought our children to a gathering in Parc Jeanne-Mance to mourn the little ones. This one was smaller, more intimate than the thousands of people who would show up to protest the following week on Canada Day. We were in a crowd of about a hundred, listening to the drum circle. A young Indigenous man with a beautiful smile approached an Indigenous woman close to us and offered her the tiny bowl of smoking herbs. She drew the smoke toward her face with her hands and said something I didn't quite catch.

My daughter watched intently, her eyes wide. "Que faites-vous? What are you doing?" she asked, in both languages, because that's how she talks to strangers now.

He came right over, knelt down, and smiled at her. "We believe that our prayers travel to our ancestors through the smoke," he explained. "Do you want to try?"

She nodded and mimicked his actions. "Can my little brother do it, too?" she asked earnestly. The man nodded encouragingly, and she repeated the motions once more, because older sisters always speak and act on behalf of their little brothers.

"Thank you," she said solemnly. Then, a heartbeat. "I'm sorry that your children died."

The man smiled gently at her. "Me too," he said.

If Montreal is haunted, then all of Canada is a graveyard.[5]

————

My return to Canada in the summer of 2020 happened during a particular moment. Some called it a racial reckoning, harkened and accentuated by death, substantiated through struggle, haunted by the conceptual space between what was imaginable and what was possible. We didn't know then what had come crashing into the public sphere, full of chaos and passion, fury and rapture, and later, predictably, dilution and co-optation. Even now, two years removed from the uprisings, there isn't a coherent narrative that can explain why the world stopped to protest, to grieve, to rage, to rebel, to mourn, together.

Perhaps it was no coincidence that these global uprisings occurred during another unforeseen, unprecedented moment, when COVID-19 was still relatively unknown and seemingly uncontainable. The protests might have been the result of a common, mass realization of the similarities between these two different yet interlocking existential threats, both of which feast on fear, degradation, and vulnerability, both demonstrating the precarious nature of human life. In this collision of forces, individual isolation, loneliness, and depression wrought by the virus gave way to collective grief, collective action, and collective hope.

But the epidemic did not affect us all equally and time revealed other devastating facts about the intersection of racism and COVID-19, these two pandemics: that COVID-19 killed disproportionate numbers of Black people; that public health is the marrow of systemic racism, and the dismissiveness, cruelty, and racist abuse that Joyce Echaquan, an Atikamekw woman, faced in her last moments of life were not exceptional; that anti-Asian hate in Canada was so common that one out of every two people of Asian descent reported being the target of racism in 2020; that increased police powers under the pretext of protecting public health enabled law enforcement to suppress and violently remove unhomed populations from public spaces; that a predominantly racialized essential workforce was, ironically, deemed socially disposable.[6]

Perhaps the uprisings of 2020 were just another story about the racial politics of the Trump era, much more about whiteness than anything else. Adhering to COVID-19 protocols and attending protests against racial injustice were both a kind of action that allowed white liberals to distinguish themselves from those *other* white people, the "real" racists, the ones who put Trump in power in the first place.

The virtue-signaling environment of social media proved to be the perfect breeding grounds to add to the archive of temporary cultural fads of middle-class pandemic life: home office decor and Zoom room ratings; Netflix's *Tiger King*; baking bread and trading sourdough starters; board (bored?) game revivals; pandemic puppies; Zoom hangouts; Timbaland and Swizz Beatz's *Verzuz* series; D-Nice's Instagram dance parties; K-pop fans' sabotage of Trump rallies; home gardening; the explosion of TikTok; the formation of school pods of privilege. When the people of Minneapolis took to the streets, it captivated an already captive, bored, and isolated middle-class audience with nothing better to do. Racial justice was just the latest COVID-19 trend, to some. This isn't to say that white liberal motivations weren't genuine, but time has proven that they certainly weren't permanent.

I returned to Canada during this fleeting time, at precisely the same moment that many people were looking for insight into what we mean when we talk about anti-Black racism, a topic that is emotional, fraught, uncomfortable, and dominated by uninformed opinions. Many people wanted to start having difficult conversations about race, police brutality, racial inequality, white guilt, and more, but simply didn't have the vocabulary. I was surprised to find that my research expertise on race and racism in Canada was in high demand. It was a far cry from years prior, when I landed a job interview at my alma mater, the University of Toronto, and during my research presentation a senior faculty member raised her hand to ask a question, but instead announced that "there's nothing original or interesting about this work whatsoever." Perhaps my work is better now than it was back then. Or perhaps timing is everything.

Or perhaps, in the summer of 2020, the needle hadn't shifted all that far. There were politicians kneeling at protests, political platitudes, a tidal wave of principled statements denouncing anti-Black racism and promising to do better, and corporate commitments to "EDI," but so much of it seemed like the same performative virtue signaling of white liberals. Would anything be different in a year?[7] Ten years? I wasn't convinced.

Nevertheless, I started talking to people in government agencies, nonprofits, even some private sector organizations about the dimensions and durability of Canadian racism, the ways that we all unintentionally reify power and privilege, and how we, collectively, can work to dismantle racist social structures. I didn't want to join the equity, diversity, and inclusion hustle because it seemed kind of gross to me, that my presence could give these organizations a reason to pat themselves on the back for having done all they could do to solve racism.

The compromise I made with my conscience was to refuse to soft-pedal anything. I didn't pull any punches. I tried to lay out, as clearly and often as I could, the systemic, compounding, institutionalized nature of racism, and especially the ways that it is embedded in law, policies, and everyday practices. I wanted people to be able to make the connection between the racism of police brutality and the racism in health care, in school discipline, in hiring and promotion practices, in the K–12 curriculum, in standardized testing, in graduate school admissions, in the welfare office and foster care system, the way that Black folks' interactions with the state are frequently violent and coercive, in residential patterns and the availability of public services, in literally every facet of social, political, and economic life. How this is the situation not in the distant past or somewhere else, but here, in Canada, and now, in these first decades of the twenty-first century. The way our most cherished egalitarian and redistributive policies—the welfare state, universal health care, a race-neutral immigration system, official multiculturalism—have largely failed to eradicate racial economic inequality because that's not what they were designed to do.[8] The racism of Canadian denials about Canadian racism.

The Black Lives Matter marches across Canada during this moment were never simply in protest of anti-Black racism and police violence in the United States. They were an effort to bring to light the similarities of the racism that Black people face *here*, in *this* country. Black activists, organizers, and communities in Montreal have been combatting rampant police brutality for more than a century. It is they, and not white liberals, who have carried this heavy burden across time and space. In this moment, activists once again asked the broader public to think about the myriad ways that Canadian racism is pervasive, systemic, harmful, and homegrown.[9] Canadians were asked to reconsider the unflappable levels of trust they have in law enforcement, with around 90 percent reporting in 2019 that they had either a great deal or some confidence in the police.[10] In Montreal, the Defund the Police Coalition issued a list of ten demands, including calls to defund, disarm, demilitarize, and decolonize the police force and reinvest that funding in programs created and designed by communities to prevent harm, the creation of an unarmed service to address mental health and drug-related crises, and more social programming in vulnerable and overpoliced communities.[11]

It didn't take me long to realize that there is something quite peculiar about race and racism in Quebec that I simply hadn't noticed when I lived in Ontario for all those years. Don't get me wrong; Montreal is an amazing city. In the summer, public life happens outside. Outdoor spaces are full of people gathered in groups, drinking wine and smoking weed, playing sports, dancing, singing, talking rapidly and loudly in a French-English-sometimes a third language mélange. We moved into a tiny rental apartment in the Plateau and our neighbors' children immediately taught my daughter how to play street hockey in the ruelle behind our connected triplexes. In the winter, Montrealers just continue living their lives, as if it's not minus 40 degrees Celsius, and the system of snow removal is a marvel of modern municipal policy coordination. I struggled through everyday interactions with my very rusty French, but eventually figured out enough to get by and vowed to get better.

It wasn't all romance, bagels, and bilingualism, of course.* Much was all too familiar. In August 2008, police officers of the SPVM happened upon several young men playing dice in a park in Montréal Nord, one of the poorest urban postal codes in Canada. The officers called the group over to their cruiser, including Dany and Fredy Villanueva, brothers who had immigrated to Montreal from Honduras in 1998. When Dany Villanueva tried to walk away, Officer Jean-Loup Lapointe followed and wrestled him to the ground. Other young men in the group moved closer to the scuffle and Lapointe fired four shots at them, killing

---

* Team St. Viateur!

the younger Villanueva brother, eighteen-year-old Fredy, and wounding two others. A lengthy coroner's inquest found that the shooting was legally justified, but preventable.

The moment was important in the collective memory of communities of color in the city in part because it was yet another iteration of a macabre ritual—the police defy their own rules, disregard their own training and protocols, act in ways that make situations even more dangerous, cause the death of an innocent teenager (usually a person of color), and then have their own recklessness dismissed from the moral calculation of what is justifiable under the law. It was the same cold rationalism that failed to hold officers accountable in the deaths of Rekia Boyd, Michael Brown, Tamir Rice, and so many others. It failed to hold Constable Allan Gosset responsible for the shooting of nineteen-year-old Anthony Griffin, unarmed and complying with Gosset's commands, outside the Notre-Dame-de-Grâce police station in Montreal on November 11, 1987. And again, when SWAT team leader Michel Tremblay was exonerated for shooting twenty-four-year-old Marcellus Francois in the head while he was in his car waiting at an intersection for the light to change in July 1991—a case, the Montreal police claimed, of "mistaken identity." The rule of law—the central, fundamental democratic premise that stipulates we are subject to the same laws, applied in the same way, regardless of our position in society—has never held police, or the wealthy, or the powerful to the same standards as the rest of us.

And just like in Chicago, Ferguson, New York, and other cities across the United States, Black people in Montreal are far more likely to encounter the police while just trying to live their lives. Between 2014 and 2017, Indigenous and Black people were four to five times more likely than white people to be stopped by SPVM. In 2019, under the moral panic rhetoric (inflected, of course, with anti-Black racism) of "gun violence," the SPVM launched a new anti-gun squad, which then proceeded to disproportionately charge Black people in the northeast of Montreal for nongun infractions—75 percent of those charged by the gun squad in its first six months were Black, and less than 30 percent of the charges involved guns.[12] In 2018, activists collected 20,000 signatures from people throughout the city, which compelled the city of Montreal to hold public hearings on systemic racism and discrimination within its municipal jurisdiction.[13] In June 2020, at the height of the George Floyd protests, the Report of the Office de consultation publique de Montréal outlined the failures of the city of Montreal to recognize systemic racism and discrimination, especially in jurisdictions such as employment and promotion practices in the city, policing, access to cultural institutions, housing, and urban planning.

Some forms of racism are as predictable in Montreal as they are elsewhere: in 2019, years of student protests finally forced McGill to rename its men's varsity sports teams from the undeniably racist "Redmen" to the vague and inoffensive "Redbirds," even as alumni made noise about "ruining tradition."

Other incidents had a distinctly maple-flavored tinge of denial, arrogance, and deflection. In 2014, the Théâtre du Rideau Vert used a white actor in blackface to portray beloved Montreal Canadiens hockey player P. K. Subban. The artistic director, Denise Filiatrault, responded to criticism by saying, "I had no idea people were so sick and petty. I've had it. It's terrible. . . . We won't have any more black characters. It's done. Either people don't have the same sense of humour, or I am too old."[14] A few years later, director Robert Lepage, a Quebec icon, cast mostly white performers singing African American slave hymns in his play *SLĀV,* later admitting to "clumsiness and misjudgment" after the show was cancelled amid accusations of cultural appropriation. In each case, many in the French-language media claimed that freedom of artistic expression was far more important than the overblown, American-imported accusations of racism.

Quebec as a political entity adds a layer of complexity to these dynamics. While the rest of the country celebrates the race-neutral platitudes of Canadian diversity, Quebec governments have consistently viewed the official multiculturalism policy as an underhanded attempt to destroy Quebec nationalism. Prime Minister Pierre Trudeau, who introduced Canada's official multiculturalism policy in the House of Commons in 1971, was himself fiercely opposed to the political demands coming out of the Quiet Revolution. This, in addition to the nearly twenty years of constitutional crises that would follow during the last two decades of the twentieth century, added to a long history of mistrust. The province rejects multiculturalism and instead employs a model of interculturalism, which recognizes French as the common language of public life and the need to protect Quebec's majority culture, but seeks to protect fundamental civic values, including minority rights. It means that secularism is understood as part of Quebec culture—though it is actually a fairly *recent* addition to white francophone Quebec culture—but so too are the remaining artifacts of Catholicism, such as the giant cross atop Mount Royal. It also plays out in interesting ways in education—access to English schools is an inherited right of parents who received their education in English in Canada (redeemable with some not uncomplicated paperwork and permissions), but immigrants and a large majority of Canadian citizens who are francophone must enroll their children in the French system.

It wasn't even a question for me and my partner, about whether we were going to send our children to a French or an English school. Of course we wanted them to go to the French public system. We live in Montreal, and it's a bilingual city. They need to be bilingual as well. And while the private school system is heavily subsidized in Quebec, we believe education is a public good. Allowing those who can afford it to opt out of the public system creates vast and often downplayed inequalities, especially between white middle- and upper-class Quebecers who can afford private school tuition and lower-income new immigrants and people of color who can't.

We brought our five-year-old daughter to her new school for the first day of the "classe d'accueil" program in September 2020, where she would be placed in a classroom with other new immigrants in her grade, learning French for the first time. She was dressed in a red-and-white striped dress, had a Band-Aid on one knee from a tumble she had taken the previous day while learning to skateboard, and was totally unfazed by the prospect of going to a new school in a new language. She began to run toward the steps of the school, oblivious to the giant statue of Jesus parked right in front of the entrance.

My partner, in contrast, stared up at it, a look of horror frozen on his face. He looked at me, incredulously. "What the actual fuck," he said. "How is this appropriate?"

I shrugged. "It's part of Quebec culture," I replied.

"It's a statue of *Jesus*," he said, "outside a public school that's called Jean-Baptiste-Meilleur."

"Does this strike you as odd because you're American and you believe in the separation of church and state or because you hate the Catholic Church?" I asked. It wasn't an insult. He had abandoned Catholicism a long time ago. The only thing he still carried with him was the guilt and the nagging feeling that he didn't really deserve happiness.

"Both," he replied grimly, as we followed our daughter into the school.

By the time I left Canada in 2010, the central question of Quebec sovereignty had given way to political debates about secularism, the definition and limits of the "reasonable accommodation" of minority cultural practices, and whether public servants should be permitted to wear religious symbols. On occasion the conversation included concerns about racism, Islamophobia, and whether white supremacists should be considered "domestic terrorists," especially in the months following the murder of six men at the Quebec City Islamic Cultural Centre in January 2017.[15] But for the most part, the debates occurred within certain convictional confines, which have, for the entirety of Quebec history, refused to acknowledge or understand the intersection of systemic racism with other racial formations like Islamophobia, the attack on minority cultures, and the danger of the radical right.[16] There is widespread agreement across the political spectrum: francophones are a "founding race" of Confederation, Quebec is a nation within Canada, and Quebec has the right, especially given the ways Canadian federalism works, to do what it deems necessary to protect French language and culture.

There are many in Quebec—and especially in the francophone media, in spite of some important and at times heated internal debates[17]—who would tell you that the efforts to protect Quebec's distinctiveness are necessary. The Québécois are a national minority in a mostly anglophone country, and a linguistic minority faced with repelling the cultural behemoth of American media and popular culture. They will also tell you that these efforts have nothing—*absolutely nothing, how dare you suggest that*—to do with race. The denials are of a different tenor than the usual Canadian sort, which tend to include the knee-jerk response, "But *multiculturalism!*" In Quebec, it's not the typical Canadian platitudes of "racism exists, but not here." It's much more convoluted, more like, "There is no such thing as race or racism, except for the racism faced by white Quebecers, because it's racist to imply that Quebec is racist." Confusing, I know.

But race has always had a lot to do with Quebec, long before Quebec became a province of Canada. Corrie Scott, a professor of feminist and gender studies at the University of Ottawa, argues that there are clear racial dimensions to the ways that English colonizers thought of and described French colonizers throughout the nineteenth century. French Canadians, Lord Durham and others wrote, were an inferior, backward, not-quite-white people. And yet, throughout Canadian history there has also been a clear line drawn that separates the British and French Canadians, the two peoples capable of civilization and destined to create the country, from other, non-white people. Whiteness doesn't require that all white people are treated equally. It does, however, create a glass floor that separates white people from non-white people— transparent but solid, so white people are able to see who lies below them, but are guaranteed the safety of never falling to that level.

The most famous invocation of race in Quebec is Pierre Vallières's 1968 manifesto, *Nègres blancs d'Amérique*, translated as "White Niggers of America."[18] It was a wildly popular book, truly a landmark treatise published at the height of the Quiet Revolution.[19] The central argument equates the discrimination and exploitation faced by French-speaking Québécois to that of Black Americans. And yet, in adding an adjective to turn an offensive word into an oxymoronic phrase—"nègres blancs"—Vallières acknowledges that francophone Québécois, as a white population, should not be subjected to the same treatment, the same dismissal, the same disgust as Black people. Vallières makes this clear, Corrie Scott contends, "when he writes 'je ne puis supporter d'être un nègre,' declaring himself a 'nègre' primarily to express that he doesn't want to be one after all." White people, in effect, are entitled to better treatment.[20]

No matter how much kinship Vallières and Québécois nation-
alists of the 1960s felt with other colonized peoples struggling for
freedom around the world, the use here of "nègres blancs" is a dys-
functional appropriation of Black freedom struggles. France was
an active participant in and benefactor of the transatlantic slave
trade, and white Quebecers—francophones and anglophones—
enslaved Black and Indigenous people. Black people's fight for
citizenship rights in North America or to overthrow colonial rule
in Africa is simply not in the same category of social phenomenon
as francophone challenges to anglophone dominance in Quebec.
To imply otherwise is a purposeful misremembrance, co-optation,
and dismissal. The analogy also casts French Québécois as a colonized people, and in doing so erases the historic and ongoing
violence of settler colonialism toward Indigenous peoples. It intersects and enables other kinds of settler-derived moves to innocence, which allow settler populations to ignore Indigenous claims
to self-determination that might compete with others—including
both Quebec and Canadian sovereignty.[21]

It doesn't matter how frequently we are told that French
colonialism was more peaceful and trade-oriented than British
colonialism—it wasn't, and all colonialism is violent. Nor does
it matter, as a senior white francophone male scholar once found
it necessary to interrupt my conference presentation to angrily
insist, that Pierre Vallières was highly sympathetic to the Black
Power movement and "had many Black friends." And while Vallières claimed that Quebec had no "black problem"—meaning
no Black people—there were, in fact, many actual Black people
in Montreal—francophone and anglophone—fighting against
rampant and frequently violent racism, and without access to any
kind of public platform to challenge Vallières's claims.[22]

This history strikes at some core contradictions of what Corrie Scott calls "doing things with race in Quebec." Race doesn't

matter, unless we're talking about how Quebecers are oppressed by anglophones. White francophone Québécois can refer to their history using the language of Black freedom struggles, but not acknowledge the actual history of Black freedom struggles in Quebec. The cultural importance and state support of laïcité, a term that describes the French tradition of a strict separation of religion and the state, does not necessarily apply to the Catholic religious symbology of public schools, street names, or the cross that used to hang in the provincial legislature. White francophone Québécois have a difficult time seeing themselves as both victims of one form of domination and the perpetrators of domination toward others.

These contradictions continued, even in the so-called moment of racial reckoning.

On June 1, 2020, Quebec premier François Legault said in response to the murder of George Floyd that there is work to be done to fight racism and racial profiling in Quebec, but added—in English, curiously enough—that there was no systemic racism in the province. He maintained this stance even after the tragic, preventable death in September 2020 of Joyce Echaquan, an Indigenous woman who was mistreated and mocked by hospital workers in Joliette. A few weeks later, on October 14, 2020, Legault contended that his role as the premier of Quebec was to fight racism, not divide Quebecers further by conceding to the demands of antiracist activists.

When the coroner's public inquiry into Echaquan's death was published in October 2021, the first recommendation was that the Quebec government "recognize the existence of systemic racism within our institutions and make a commitment to help eliminate it." Legault didn't budge. In fact, just a few weeks earlier he disparagingly called a member of the opposition party, Gabriel Nadeau-Dubois, "a woke." The next day, Legault clarified what he meant: "For me, a woke is someone who wants to make us feel guilty about defending the Quebec nation, of defending its values as we did with Bill 21, of defending our jurisdictions . . . a woke is someone who sees discrimination everywhere."

It's hard to tell whether these views are representative of the Quebec population. There's a tendency in the rest of Canada to think of Quebec as a particularly racist part of the country. It's a perception—perhaps even a stereotype—that isn't necessarily based on empirical evidence, though research by political scientists Luc Turgeon and Antoine Bilodeau demonstrates that those who "strongly support" Quebec sovereignty are less enthusiastic about immigration. However, they caution, public opinion toward immigration in Quebec certainly isn't negative; there's no real "backlash" against immigration in Quebec in the same way there is in some European countries. Other political scientists have argued that French-speaking Quebecers hold unfavorable views toward religious accommodation because of their low levels of religiosity and not because they are more racist than the rest of the country.[23]

But then again, there's Bill 21, also called the Laicity Act. The 2019 legislation, passed by the Coalition Avenir Québec (CAQ) government, bans public servants "in a position of authority"— teachers, police officers, prosecutors, judges, and the like—from wearing religious symbols while at work and requires those receiving services of the provincial government to do so with their faces uncovered. Bill 21 is a classic example of a law that seems like it applies equally to everyone but doesn't, really. The explanatory notes of the law contain a caveat for Christian dominance, stating that "the bill may not be interpreted as affecting the emblematic or toponymic elements of Québec's cultural heritage that testify to its history." More to the point, Christian religious practices aren't impacted by this law, while the practices of other religions most certainly are. As lawyer Supriya Dwivedi argues in an essay on the decade-long history of the debate over the rights of religious minorities in Quebec, "Bill 21 has the practical effect of targeting only minority faiths, such as Judaism, Sikhism, and Islam, in which adherents are required to wear certain garb or symbols. This isn't a question of simply removing religious symbols—it interferes with the actual practice of religion."[24]

Let's be crystal clear: the law is deeply discriminatory. It violates the fundamental rights laid out in the Canadian Charter of Rights and Freedoms, especially freedom of religion guaranteed in section 2(a) and the equality rights of section 15. The Legault government's preemptive use of the notwithstanding clause, section 33 of the Charter, which allows a government to pass legislation that violates certain Charter rights, is a testament to who the law targets and why.

"Do you think there's public support for Bill 21, or is this just something that politicians are doing on their own?" I asked my friend Jonathan Montpetit, a journalist who's been writing about Quebec politics for years. We had met at a conference hosted by the McGill Institute for the Study of Canada back in 2017, on "Canadian Exceptionalism: Are We Good or Are We Lucky?" Now, years later, we were sitting on a terrace drinking coffee on a beautiful summer day in 2021 and laughing about how the idea that Canada was either good or lucky—and nothing else—was just so very Canadian.

"There's clearly some degree of political support for it," he replied. "At the end of the day, Bill 21 was passed democratically. It was voted on by members of the National Assembly. Two parties supported it. Can you imagine the national constitutional crisis if the federal government used its rarely invoked legal power to squash the law? They just can't. And look," he continued, "Bill 21 is actually quite popular in the rest of the country, too. It's not just Quebec."[25]

"Sure, sure," I said, "and laws that are popular with a white majority are never, ever racist." Jonathan laughed. "So, you really believe there's some truth to the idea of Quebec-bashing?"

"No question." Jonathan shook his head. "The first part of my career was trying to correct other Canadians' misperceptions about Quebec. You know, Quebecers are annoying, they're the spoiled children of Confederation. There's a famous poem by Michèle Lalonde called 'Speak White'—that was a slur directed at French Canadians."

I was about to ask about that fascinating little historical tidbit, but Jonathan cut me off. "By the way," he warned, "don't use the term *French Canadian* in your book."

"What?" There were so many rules and cultural codes that I just didn't know, even though I grew up in Canada.

"Yeah," he said. "*French Canadian* is too broad—it could refer to Franco-Ontarians or any other French speakers in the country. But more importantly, it's antiquated. Part of the Quiet Revolution was about reclaiming Québécois identity . . ."

". . . without a reference to Canada," I finished. It reminded me of similar debates in the Black community in the late 1960s, when the term *Negro* was replaced with *African American* to lay claim to being part of the nation. Others, especially those in the Black Power movement, preferred *Black* instead, because why would we want to be part of something that doesn't want us back?

He nodded. "So you should use *Quebecer* or *Québécois*."

I thought for a moment. "Is there a difference between *Quebecer* and *Québécois*?" I asked.

Jonathan laughed again. "That's a very good question, Professor," he said diplomatically. "In French it's just Québécois. But in English, some draw a distinction between Quebecers, which would include anglophones and new immigrants to the province, and Québécois, which is more of an ethnic group."

"So, are you a Quebecer or a Québécois?" I asked. I mean, Jonathan Montpetit. It could go either way.

"Oh, I'd fight you if you say I'm not Québécois," he said earnestly. "We can trace our family back to the eighteenth century, and there's a statue of my great-grandfather in Quebec City." Jonathan's great-grandfather Joe Malone played hockey for the Quebec City Bulldogs and later the Montreal Canadiens. This is apparently a Very Big Deal.

"So wait a minute," I said. "Is being Québécois about language? Or is it more about lineage and longevity? Will my kids be Québécois?"

Jonathan said that it depends. It depends on what language they live and socialize in, the history they come to view as their own, who they associate with, what values they hold, whether Québécois cultural reference points in films, music, and books become part of the unspoken undercurrent of their worldviews. It depends on whether they come to see themselves as part of the Québécois nation, complete with long-standing anxieties about its resonance, resilience, and future.

It depends on who you ask.

There are more than a few Black folks in Quebec who don't feel like they are seen or accepted as part of this community. The brand of conservative nationalism that Legault promotes and others believe wholeheartedly is more akin to an ethnic nationalism than a civic one, meaning that access to belonging as a Québécois—a full-fledged member of the nation and recognized as such—is limited to white francophone Québécois. In this sense, lineage, and not language or longevity, defines the boundaries of the nation.

But the Black Montrealers I know say it's more complicated than that. Québécois is supposed to be a singular, primary, supra identity. It's not clear whether it's possible or acceptable to have multiple identities and still be considered Québécois, and so my friends' insistence that their Haitian heritage still matters is seen as troubling to those who want to claim them only as Québécois. Inclusion as Québécois comes with conditions attached—the low, low cost, but high, high price of abandoning all that your ancestors held dear.

And if being Québécois is defined by having anxieties about the perseverance of the French language and the survival of Quebec culture, as Jonathan claimed, then, my Black friends intoned, Black peoples' general indifference about these concerns is often seen as an unforgivable betrayal.[26]

"Look, we've got our own anxieties to worry about," one of them said seriously. "Affordable housing. Accessible health care. Not getting killed by the cops. And all of these are far more pressing than whether or not the number of people speaking French in their homes is on the decline."

Moreover, for decades Black activists in Montreal have worked across linguistic divides to build and solidify a sense of overarching Black identity in response to pervasive state and white citizen violence. In Black Montreal, language is not the singular, most important divisor that some make it out to be.[27] That being said, in the anglophone Black community, which has a long history in the Little Burgundy neighborhood of Montreal, the relationship to Quebec nationalism is even more complicated. Introduced in 1977, the Charter of the French Language, or Bill 101, famously made French the official language of political, economic, commercial, and social life in Quebec. It put restrictions on which children could attend English-language schools and in doing so forever changed the linguistic makeup of the province. The so-called "children of Bill 101"—especially the children of immigrants who were steered to the French school system—are often celebrated as a success story.

"That's not what happened to Black anglophones in Montreal," another one of my friends told me. "Bill 101 ended up pushing Black kids out of schools and after the 1995 referendum Black Anglos left Montreal in droves. They moved to Toronto. If you fast-forward to today, it's no wonder Quebec has this public discourse that claims there's no racism here. We don't have that many public voices able to counter that narrative. But we could have, had we not been systemically excluded from the places where these debates are happening, locked out of universities that would help us articulate our ideas, or just plain run out of town."

———

There is a general sense in the rest of Canada that Quebec, especially outside of Montreal, is particularly racist, xenophobic, and intolerant. Quebecers respond defensively (and sometimes dismissively) to this accusation, taking it as further evidence of rampant "Quebec-bashing." The more important work of these claims, however, is the way that imagining a problematically monolithic Quebec as exceptionally racist also allows the rest of Canada to leave their own institutionalized forms of racism intact, unexamined, and unquestioned. Quebec is a convenient scapegoat.

When I came back to Canada in this moment of racial reckoning, even as I was totally appalled by the blatant discrimination of Bill 21, I thought of Quebec as a success story, not a scapegoat. Decades of Quebec provincial governments set out to protect the French language and Québécois culture, and at the federal level the Bloc Québécois held enough sway to protect Quebec's interests on the national agenda. These policies, along with the Official Languages Act, were able to eliminate socioeconomic disparities between anglophones and francophones in a generation; they are the most effective set of affirmative action policies in North American history. Power over, or the separate administration of, certain policy areas that would normally be under the federal government's jurisdiction, such as immigration, statistics, some international relations, and taxation, have been granted to Quebec. Institutional safeguards to maintain Quebec's power vis-à-vis the rest of Canada have been fiercely protected; it has proven difficult to reduce the number of seats Quebec has in the House of Commons, even though it might be warranted according to redistricting formulas, there are a guaranteed number of senators, and a third of Supreme Court justices must be from Quebec. Quebecers as a national minority are indeed outnumbered in a mostly anglophone country, but Quebec as a political entity is, arguably, the most powerful province in the federation.

After a decade spent in the United States learning the details of many, varied, and violent attempts to destroy African American culture and communities, I found it all quite impressive. What could have happened, I wondered, if the United States had gone down this path after the Civil War? What life could Black people have made for themselves if they had the political, economic, and legal control that comes with having a state of our own? How many thousands of lives would not have ended swinging from trees while lynch mobs jeered from below? How much richer would our lives, our culture, our democracy be now, if Black freedom dreams had been institutionalized and protected the way Quebec's nationalist aspirations were?

I certainly wouldn't have called Quebec nationalism and autonomy impressive before I moved to the United States. Time and distance can do wondrous things. I may have repatriated to Canada, the land of my birth, but I came to Montreal as a twofold interloper—a settler/arrivant on Indigenous land and an anglophone living in a predominantly francophone province. My French-language skills are, for the record, horrendous. They were perhaps passable before 2010, but I lost nearly everything I knew during those years in America, when I was learning the language of Black love and resistance. My partner's French acquisition has been nothing short of astounding, but then again, he doesn't have any Anglo-Canadian feelings of shame and guilt for not being bilingual in the first place.

This is the first time in my life that language has intersected with race and gender to propel me to the outskirts of belonging. At least language is something I can learn and change. But still, I wonder: When I eventually improve my French, after years of dedicating those precious few hours in the evening after my children's bedtime to doing so; when I turn down the expected extra, unpaid labor of my actual job to make time to practice and learn, because there are only so many hours in the day; when I decide that I am willing to be a complete idiot as I make countless errors, relying on the kindness of strangers to help me struggle through everyday interactions—after all that, will I be accepted as a member of this nation?

Honestly, I doubt it. And it doesn't matter. I will learn, anyway, because I should and because it's the right thing to do. There are also dynamic worlds of non-white francophone

Returning to Canada, for the first time. Montreal's Pierre Trudeau International Airport, July 31, 2020.

culture in Montreal, which include novelists, poets, musicians, political activists, and more. The Black-owned publishing house Mémoire d'encrier has become a crucially important site of translation, Indigenous writing, and debates about race and diversity taking place in French. I want to access these insights, to be inspired by the brilliance of others, to learn from and take part in these conversations. More Black genius, more Black life and ways of living.

And maybe, one day, my children will have a chance to belong. I doubt they will ever be considered Québécois. But maybe, just maybe, they'll think of Montreal as home.

Neverwhere and Everyhere

I started writing this book while we were still in the middle of a moment of sheer potential. Many thought that the uprisings sparked by the murder of George Floyd would bring about a racial reckoning. Indeed, the protests around the world were a seismic disruption that seemed to catalyze a widespread acknowledgment that white supremacy was born and bred in the global sphere; an understanding that racism can manifest in the realm of ideas and can move across borders as easily as the wind; an appreciation that historical context and local circumstances still matter, but that they are nevertheless inflected with lessons and lesions from elsewhere; a resurrection of the disruptive and fracturing, conjugative and compounding potential diasporic consciousness.

Reckoning might not be the right word for all that has happened between then and now. The idea of a reckoning is about honored promises, debts repaid, and a balance restored. "To reckon" can also be used to express dreams and expectations, just as readily as a reckoning also faces the past, again and again, not unlike the way that a return involves circling back to the beginning of the journey.

That moment has now passed. The moment we are in now is much less clearly defined, much more indeterminate; it is a moment when "old horizons have collapsed or evaporated and new ones have not yet taken shape."[1] We are in a time of speculation and flux, vulnerability and risk, incoherence and possibility. And so, take heed: we might not like what emerges from the other side of this moment. Racial progress has always been shadowed by backlash.

The era of backlash has already begun. It came into the American public sphere most obviously and violently as the insurrection on the Capitol on January 6, 2021, when more than two thousand Trump supporters, outraged at the "stolen election," swarmed the national legislature. Months later, the backlash took the politer, more mainstream conservative shape of an orchestrated attack on critical race theory, led by Republican state lawmakers and echoed by "concerned" white parents.[2] It's highly doubtful that any of these adamant opponents have read the vast body of scholarship that comprises critical race theory. Instead, the war on critical race theory is a contrived conservative effort to galvanize Republican support. Critical race theory has become a bogeyman of white conservative politics, resuscitated in school board, PTA, and homeowners association meetings, shape-shifting into statewide book bans, the pearl-clutching claims of parental choice and childhood innocence, and mandated curricular revisions. If it all seems familiar, it's because we've been here before. Backlash doesn't have to be original, it just has to *work*, and using a contrived moral panic to stoke white racial resentment among the conservative base is a time-honored and effective Republican strategy, made even more auspicious as President Joe Biden's popularity plummets and the 2022 midterm elections loom.

In Quebec, the backlash has taken several different forms, including Premier Legault's denial that systemic racism exists in Quebec and his use of *woke* as a disparaging slur. But the backlash reprises itself, most frequently and most deceitfully, as the controversy surrounding the use of the n-word by white educators in classroom settings. After a University of Ottawa instructor and a Henri-Bourassa high school teacher were suspended for using the word in their classrooms, the Quebec National Assembly responded by passing a motion—supported by members of all four political parties—asserting the importance of freedom of expression in academic settings. The issue, several prominent white francophone journalists claim, orbits key beliefs about free speech and unnecessary censorship, academic freedom, freedom of expression, and the exaggeration of the harm that a simple word can do. The CAQ government then struck a committee on academic freedom, which issued a report in December 2021 proclaiming that Quebec university classrooms are not "safe spaces," and introduced legislation in April 2022 that confirmed "any word" that is used in an academic context can be spoken in a university classroom.[3]

I was pretty surprised to return to Canada in 2020 and find that the debate over whether white educators—or any non-Black people, for that matter—can say the n-word had not yet been resolved. The issue is very resolved in my mind. The answer is no. No, they cannot. Period. Of course, the real question isn't *whether* white people can say the n-word; it's why they want, *so badly*, to be able to say it.

Ta-Nehisi Coates, speaking about this very issue back in 2017, gave a potential answer: "When you're white in this country, you're taught that everything belongs to you. You think you have a right to everything. . . . You're conditioned this way." He continues, "So here comes this word that you feel you invented. And now somebody will tell you how to use the word you invented." Coates concludes by suggesting that since being Black in America is defined by walking through the world and watching others do the things we cannot possibly do, not being able to say the n-word actually gives white people a peek into what it means to be Black.[4]

Now, this same logic doesn't hold for white francophone Quebecers, who have certainly not been taught that the world belongs to them, without caveats or conditions. But two things most certainly do belong to white francophone Quebecers: one, a history of appropriating Black freedom struggles as their own and using the n-word in this cherished and sanctified effort; and two, the responsibility for protecting the French language in an anglophone-dominated continent. Combined, these undercurrents make the idea that there is a word—in French[5]—that white francophone Quebecers cannot say, *in French*, unfathomable.

And let's not pretend that there isn't some anti-Black racism happening here, too. It is easier to dismiss Black people's insistence that the word is violent when you don't care about Black people, when what we think or say or feel simply isn't enough to make you change your behavior. After all, there were other words once used as slurs against lesbian and gay people—including, of course, white lesbian and gay people—that have been jettisoned from the French language. Words we no longer say, because they are hurtful and unnecessary.

In the rest of Canada, the backlash was more of a shrug, coming in the form of a deep, obstinate ambivalence to specific policy demands. Nearly every large city in the country has increased its police budget since 2020. In Montreal, the city's proposed budget for 2022 includes a $45 million increase to the SPVM.[6] The Liberal federal government has made progress on some of the recommendations made by the Parliamentary Black Caucus in the summer of 2020,[7] but there's still a long, long way to go.

But nothing, *nothing*, would have happened without Black people taking to the streets. It is hard to come up with words to properly describe how different now feels from then. "Radical passion has been gutted, deflected, suppressed—and frozen into rhetoric, peddled as commodity," author and literary critic Tobi Haslett writes. "In the face of establishment cynicism and the promise of 'representation,' it can be hard to voice real outrage, and the ache of collective grief."[8] Now that we stand at the beginning—not the middle and certainly not the end—of this iteration of racial backlash, the very least we can do is remember and try to make sense of all that was. All that might still be.

I waited until I had both shots of the COVID-19 vaccine before going to visit my parents. It was a full year after I had moved back to Canada and more than two since I had last seen them in person. I was shocked to see how old they looked. How my father's hands now shake. How hard it was for my mother to climb the stairs. How neither of them seemed able to find the words they wanted to use. We sat in their tiny, cluttered living room chatting and drinking coffee, the art of my grandmother and my eldest sister adorning opposite walls, in silent conversation.

I told Dad that I was writing this book and that he ended up being something like the book's conscience, if a book can have a conscience. He gave me a puzzled, unimpressed kind of look and said, "Oh really?"

"Sure, Dad," I said. "You've always been full of advice."

"I don't know about that," he shrugged. "But then again, the older I get, the more I don't know."

"Me too, Dad," I said. "Me too."

I have tried to tread carefully in writing this history of the present, sandwiched in the space between what has come before and all that has not yet come to pass. It's not easy work, especially if you are, like me, hard on yourself about all the mistakes you've made, all you could have done better, if only you had the time, the know-how, the patience, the courage. Even now, in these final paragraphs, I know there is an abundance that I didn't get the chance to say, so many others who could have said all this better, too much that was left on the cutting-room floor.

Truth be known, using my experiences as an entry point into a broader inquiry about race, Blackness, and belonging makes me deeply uncomfortable. But in Black Studies, storytelling is tradition, repetition is sacred, and writing is the process of turning bewilderment to awe. The centuries-long curse of enforced exile and homelessness experienced by those of African descent has long served as a useful and critical standpoint from which to reconsider how the world came to be the way it is. Black Studies as vocation isn't just interdisciplinary but anti-disciplinary and un-disciplinary in that we seek the knowledge through which we can achieve racial justice in this world or we will remake it so those who follow will.

And so, Black people are not perpetual foreigners in search of our true home, because there are, in fact, many true homes. One of them, the one around which I have now orbited for two-hundred-odd pages, is the concept of diaspora, that which connects points A and B, balanced precariously on the line on the map, in the air among the clouds, in the ship on the sea, in a car with one hand on the wheel and the other on the ceiling. Diaspora, the inexplicable, liminal space of un/belonging, anchored by the Door of No Return and moored by those buried in the Deep.

What if being neither here nor there is, itself, a purposeful, emancipatory place? This, I think, is the liberatory power of belonging in and to the African diaspora.

It is animated by the shifting, amorphous, but nevertheless common political project of demanding and defending Black humanity in the face of commodification and relentless, ruinous violence. It is also, as Black Studies scholar Rinaldo Walcott has recently argued, the task of imagining a conceptualization of Black liberation that isn't intimately tied to Black enslavement.[9]

This potential exists in defiance of the "the," the idea that the Black diaspora is a singular, coherent formation. Instead, diasporic ways of being and becoming are multiple, overlapping, and dissonant. And so, to share a diasporic identity does not mean that all experiences within the Black diaspora are interchangeable; disagreement and disavowal, altercation and ambivalence are part of the conceptual, global history of Blackness. It turns out that no one and everyone is "authentically Black," and that racial authenticity is a false, impossible, grossly misused, and surveillance-ridden idea, anyway.

Instead, it's more useful to carefully take heed of the ways that time and space shape identities—to understand that Blackness is, as my former colleague and literary theorist Michelle Wright argues, a "where and a when," rather than a what; to extract the shared quest for freedom in the far-flung edges of the African diaspora, not as fictitious nor forced kinship connections, but as dissonant, always complicated, sometimes even contradictory freedom-seeking intimacy among strangers; to think through the ways that closeness and connections also exist alongside the fractures, fissures, frictions, and irritants that shape different parts of the whole; to find nuance in the translations, transcriptions, transferences of identities and political aspirations from one place to the next, from one time to another, including those times that we can only imagine; to embrace all that is unavoidably lost in translation and revel in all that which is simply untranslatable.[10]

With access to all this beauty, all this connectedness and complication, spirit and soul, across hundreds of years and the thousands of places where we have made homes simply by existing exactly where and as we are, shallow belonging in the nation-state pales by comparison.

"Beyond doubtful," Richard Iton wrote, "we might assert that for nonwhites—and for all others, *nous sommes tous des sans-papiers*—nationality is not only doubtful and improbable but indeed impossible and, furthermore, that these impossibilities themselves might be seen as desirable and appealing."[11]

We live together, here, in the impossible. We can struggle toward other impossible things, with other impossible peoples: no one is illegal; no one is illegal on stolen land; land back. Wherever we are is whenever we are. We rise, we fall, we bleed, we fight, we pray, we grieve, we disagree, we celebrate, we remember, together.

The truest thing about travel and movement, as anyone who has ever gone anywhere intrinsically knows, is how people change as they move. Our identities are not fixed; they are never once and for all. So, too, the very idea of a "return" is the stuff of fairy tales. Going back to a place where we once were, but no longer are, and yet desire to be—is a futility of the highest order. You can't go home again, not just because *home* changes, but because *you* do.

Acknowledgments

If citations are love letters, as my friend Ethel Tungohan contends, then acknowledgments are a testament to the potent and intricate threads of care, sanctuary, advocacy, and inspiration etched in every letter, word, sentence, paragraph, page. It's only through the graciousness and generosity of others that I've been able to turn an incoherent mess of ideas into whatever this has turned out to be, whatever it means to those who read it. If there are errors, the fault lies with me alone. But if you have found insight or resonance in these chapters, trust that there is an entire legion that made this possible.

To those who, without knowing very much about me at all, gave their time and wisdom, I remain in awe of the kindness of strangers: David Austin, Marjorie Bolgos, Desmond Cole, Natasha Henry, Tony Ince, Nantali Indongo, Katherine McKittrick, Samantha Meredith, Sean Mills, Charmaine Nelson, Antoni Nerestant, Angel Panag, Will Prosper, Rinaldo Walcott, and Barrington Walker.

To those who thought these ideas had potential from the earliest days, I couldn't have done this without you: my wonderful agent, Martha Webb, and my supportive, talented editors at Simon & Schuster Canada, Janie Yoon and Justin Stoller. A special shout-out to my old friend Mark Medley, who first suggested that these thoughts should be a book and then opened doors to make it happen.

To those who, knowing entirely too much about me, still read jumbled bits and pieces, or terrible draft upon draft, and loved me nevertheless, I am eternally grateful: Tari Ajadi, Cheryl Auger, Keith Banting, Susan Burgess, Marcus Carney, Michael Hanchard, Joe Lowndes, Sara Lewkowicz, Ted Rutland, Luc Turgeon, and Jenn Wallner. My best friend forever, Jonathan Montpetit, carefully read and enthusiastically discussed every single chapter draft, thrice; it was him, and not me, who realized this is a book about love. Kelly Gordon is the kindest person I know, and she'll hate that I wrote that. Jonathan Thompson is my favorite brother and therefore is the only one who can ruthlessly ask, "What's the point of this point?" Jack Byrne read, researched, commented, debated, fact-checked, distracted small humans, loved me endlessly, and never, ever complained; he believes in me more than anyone, and always has.

I had the unearned privilege of doing much of this work on the unceded territory of the Kanien'kehá:ka Nation, the custodians of the lands and waters of Tiohtià:ke/Montreal. We all play a role in upholding settler colonial violence, and so I will continue my imperfect attempts to be subversive within this structure of domination, to support Indigenous peoples' quests for sovereignty, and to struggle alongside them in word and deed. This work would not have been possible without funding from the Canada Research Chair program and the Social Science and Humanities Council of Canada, the exceptional research assistance of Dani Benavente, Danielle Gottlieb, Anushay Sheikh, Juliane Vandal, and the unstoppable Leïla Ahouman, and the freedom, support, and security I have because of my position at McGill University. Last, but never least, mad props to my students, who teach me far more than I teach them.

I am a work in progress.

Notes

Beginnings: We Came Back Too Soon

1 You're reading the endnotes; good for you! In this book, the notes aren't just about adhering to academic citational practices. Citations are, in the words of my forever-friend and migration scholar Dr. Ethel Tungohan, "love letters to fellow thinkers who came before me and who write alongside me." As Black Studies scholar Katherine McKittrick writes in her recent book, *Dear Science and Other Stories*, "perhaps the function of communication, referencing, citation, is not to master knowing and centralize our knowingness, but to share *how we know*, and share how we came to know imperfect and sometimes unintelligible but always hopeful and practical ways to live this world as black." Showing how we know, McKittrick continues, should be a painful undoing of who we think we are and how we come to share what we now know differently. It took me a long time to get here, I am not the same person I was when I started, and I have not traveled this road alone. What will become clear, if you choose to keep reading, is that while this book is many things, it most certainly is not a story of individual triumph. So let me start calling out the names of those who have come before me, all the giants on whose shoulders we stand, including: W. E. B. Du Bois, *The Souls of Black Folk* (A. C. McClurg, 1903).

2 Many thanks to Robyn Maynard, Rinaldo Walcott, and David

Austin, who have each spoken with me at length about this. See also Katherine McKittrick, "'Their Blood Is There, and They Can't Throw It Out': Honouring Black Canadian Geographies," *Topia: Canadian Journal of Cultural Studies* 7 (2002): 27–37; Katherine McKittrick, *Demonic Grounds: Black Women and the Cartographies of Struggle* (Minneapolis: University of Minnesota Press, 2006); David Chariandy, "'The Fiction of Belonging': On Second-Generation Black Writing in Canada," *Callaloo* 30, no. 3 (2007): 818–29; David Austin, "Narratives of Power: Historical Mythologies in Contemporary Quebec and Canada," *Race & Class* 52, no. 1 (2010): 19–32; George Elliot Clarke, "An Anatomy of the Originality of African-Canadian Thought," *CLR James Journal* 20, no. 1–2 (2014): 65–82; Peter James Hudson and Aaron Kamugisha, "On Black Canadian Thought," *CLR James Journal* 20, no. 1–2 (2014): 3–20; Rinaldo Walcott, "Shame: A Polemic," *CLR James Journal* 20, no. 1–2 (2014): 275–79.

3   It was later revealed during his murder trial that former Minneapolis police officer Derek Chauvin applied excess force to George Floyd's body for nine minutes and twenty-nine seconds.

4   Larry Buchanan, Quoctrung Bui, and Jugal K. Patel, "Black Lives Matter May Be the Largest Movement in U.S. History," *New York Times*, July 3, 2020, https://www.nytimes.com/interactive/2020/07/03/us/george-floyd-protests-crowd-size.html.

5   See Saidiya Hartman, *Lose Your Mother: A Journey Along the Atlantic Slave Route* (New York: Farrar, Straus & Giroux, 2007) and Christina Sharpe, *In the Wake: On Blackness and Being* (Durham, NC, and London: Duke University Press, 2016).

6   Neil Roberts, *Freedom as Marronage* (Chicago: University of Chicago Press, 2015).

7   The very ability to move across the border is an incredible privilege. My teenage self is in awe of how much time I now spend on airplanes. I didn't set foot on an international flight until my mid-twenties. I never fathomed I would have a life that required a passport. But it's not a passport that gives you the ability to leave

and return; it's your membership in the political community. Your citizenship. "Remember," my brother, who for years worked as an immigration agent for the Canadian Border Security Agency at Toronto's Pearson Airport would say before I went anywhere, "as a Canadian citizen you can't be denied entry to Canada. They have to let you come home."

8 See Taiaike Alfred, *Peace, Power, Righteousness: An Indigenous Manifesto* (New York: Oxford University Press, 1999); John Borrows, *Recovering Canada: The Resurgence of Indigenous Law* (Toronto: University of Toronto Press, 2002); Taiaike Alfred, *Wasáse: Indigenous Pathways of Action and Freedom* (Toronto: University of Toronto Press, 2005); Glen Coulthard, *Red Skin, White Masks: Rejecting the Colonial Politics of Recognition* (Minneapolis: University of Minnesota Press, 2014); Audra Simpson, *Mohawk Interruptus: Political Life Across the Borders of Settler States* (Durham, NC: Duke University Press, 2014); John Borrows, *Freedom and Indigenous Constitutionalism* (Toronto: University of Toronto Press, 2016); Leanne Betasamosake Simpson, *As We Have Always Done: Indigenous Freedom Through Radical Resistance* (Minneapolis: University of Minnesota Press, 2017).

9 Sharpe, *In the Wake*; Paul Gilroy, *The Black Atlantic: Modernity and Double Consciousness* (London and New York: Verso, 1993); Dionne Brand, *A Map to the Door of No Return: Notes to Belonging* (Toronto: Vintage Canada, 2001); Harsha Walia, *Border and Rule: Global Migration, Capitalism, and the Rise of Racist Nationalism* (Chicago: Haymarket Books, 2021).

Chapter 1: The Great White North

1 Afua Cooper, *The Hanging of Angélique: The Untold Story of Canadian Slavery and the Burning of Old Montreal* (Toronto: HarperCollins, 2006), p. 71. The historical record is unclear on Le Jeune's age, though most historians agree he was somewhere between six and nine years old.

2   This includes McGill University and Dalhousie University. See the international consortium, Universities Studying Slavery: https://slavery.virginia.edu/universities-studying-slavery/.

3   Nikole Hannah-Jones, "The Idea of America," 1619 Project, *New York Times Magazine*, August 18, 2019, pp. 14–26; Matthew Desmond, "Capitalism," *1619 Project, New York Times Magazine*, August 18, 2019, pp. 30–40. Quotation in Desmond, p. 33.

4   Eric Foner, *The Second Founding: How the Civil War and Reconstruction Remade the American Constitution* (New York: Norton, 2019).

5   Cooper, *The Hanging of Angélique*, pp. 100–106. See also the work of the Institute for the Study of Canadian Slavery at NSCAD University, led by Dr. Charmaine Nelson.

6   On the Black Loyalists, see James W. St. G. Walker, *The Black Loyalists: The Search for a Promised Land in Nova Scotia and Sierra Leone, 1783–1870* (Toronto: University of Toronto Press, 1992); Robin W. Winks, *The Blacks in Canada: A History*, 2nd ed. (Montreal and Kingston, ON: McGill-Queen's University Press, 1997), Chapters 2 and 3.

7   Winks, *The Blacks in Canada*, pp. 70–95.

8   This wave includes a substantial number of free Black people who lived in the free northern states, but feared being kidnapped and sold into slavery after the passage of the Fugitive Slave Act of 1850 and fled to Canada.

9   Daniel G. Hill, *The Freedom Seekers: Blacks in Early Canada* (Agincourt, ON: Book Society of Canada, 1981).

10 On the specific historic Black community of Buxton, see Sharon A. Roger Hepburn, "Crossing the Border from Slavery to Freedom: The Building of a Community at Buxton, Upper Canada," *American Nineteenth Century History* 3, no. 2 (2002): 25–68. Samantha Meredith, the executive director–curator of the Chatham-Kent Black Historical Society and Black Mecca Museum, and Angel Panag, the director of the 2021 documentary *The North Star: Finding Black Mecca*, were kind enough to speak with

me in October 2020 about the history of the Black communities in the area.

11 There is a growing interest in the "Black archive"—that is, the use of archival records as a mechanism through which Black people in Canada are made present or absented (or deployed as an absented-presence) in national histories. Archives are not just custodial repositories for objective information. They are not neutral, benign, accessible, or transparent. The lived experiences that become archival material are located, curated, retained, named, narrated, ordered, cataloged, classified, counted, shelved, marginalized, lost, destroyed, rediscovered, and reinterpreted. Archives privilege written documentation over oral histories, folklore, tall tales, and ghost stories and are intent on presenting history in incomplete but nevertheless recognizable forms. There is, as Saidiya Hartman and M. NourbeSe Philip both suggest, a violence of the archive, in that Black life is most often captured in records of Black incarceration, commodification, or death. The lesson here, I think, is to be relentlessly skeptical of anything that masquerades as truth. Thanks to historians Barrington Walker and Natasha Henry for taking the time to speak with me about the Black archive and other challenges of writing about Black Canadian history. See also Saidiya Hartman, "Venus in Two Acts," *small axe* 12, no. 2 (2008): 1–14; M. NourbeSe Philip, *Zong!* (Middletown, CT: Wesleyan University Press, 2008); Cheryl Thompson, "Black Canada and Why the Archival Logic of Memory Needs Reform," *Les ateliers de l'éthique/The Ethics Forum* 14, no. 2 (2019): 76–106.

12 See Tera W. Hunter's wonderful exploration of the meaning of marriage for free and enslaved African Americans, *Bound in Wedlock: Slave and Free Black Marriage in the Nineteenth Century* (Cambridge, MA: Harvard University Press, 2019).

13 Anne Milan and Kelly Tran, "Blacks in Canada: A Long History," *Canadian Social Trends* (Spring 2004), https://www150.statcan.gc.ca/n1/en/pub/11-008-x/2003004/article/6802-eng.pdf?st =vaVr9UGH.

14 See Sarah-Jane Mathieu, *North of the Color Line: Migration and Black Resistance in Canada, 1870–1955* (Chapel Hill: University of North Carolina Press, 2010); Robyn Maynard, *Policing Black Lives: State Violence in Canada from Slavery to the Present* (Halifax and Winnipeg: Fernwood, 2017); Cecil Foster, *They Call Me George: The Untold Story of Black Train Porters and the Birth of Modern Canada* (Windsor, ON: Biblioasis, 2019); Karina Vernon, ed., *The Black Prairie Archives: An Anthology* (Waterloo, ON: Wilfrid Laurier University Press, 2020).

15 Note that this includes people who identified as "Black or African American" alone or in combination with another racial group. Those who identify as "Black or African American" alone are 12.4 percent of the population, or 41.1 million people. Nicholas Jones, Rachel Marks, Roberto Ramirez, and Merarys Ríos-Vargas, "2020 Census Illuminates Racial and Ethnic Composition of the Country," United States Census Bureau, August 21, 2021, https://www .census.gov/library/stories/2021/08/improved-race-ethnicity-measures -reveal-united-states-population-much-more-multiracial.html.

16 Statistics Canada, *Diversity of the Black Population in Canada: An Overview* (Ottawa: Statistics Canada, 2019), https://www150.stat can.gc.ca/n1/pub/89-657-x/89-657-x2019002-eng.htm.

17 McKittrick, *Demonic Grounds*, p. 93.

Chapter 2: The Only One

1 Eduardo Bonilla-Silva, *Racism Without Racists: Color-Blind Racism and the Persistence of Racial Inequality in the United States* (Lanham, MD: Rowman & Littlefield, 2003). See also David Theo Goldberg, *The Threat of Race: Reflections on Racial Neoliberalism* (Oxford: Wiley-Blackwell, 2008); Ian Haney López, *Dog Whistle Politics: How Coded Racial Appeals Have Reinvented Racism and Wrecked the Middle Class* (Oxford: Oxford University Press, 2014).

2 There are a number of excellent critiques of multiculturalism from

this perspective. My favorites are Sunera Thobani, *Exalted Subjects: Studies in the Making of Race and Nation in Canada* (Toronto: University of Toronto Press, 2007); Jodi Melamed, *Represent and Destroy: Rationalizing Violence in the New Racial Capitalism* (Minneapolis: University of Minnesota Press, 2011); Eve Haque, *Multiculturalism Within a Bicultural Framework: Language, Race, and Belonging in Canada* (Toronto: University of Toronto Press, 2012); and Rinaldo Walcott, "The End of Diversity," *Public Culture* 31, no. 2 (2019): 393–408.

3 According to the city of Oshawa, the name means "the point at the crossing of the stream where the canoe was exchanged for the trail," but an Ojibwe dictionary I found defines it as "s/he goes across by boat; s/he crosses; go across by boat," and *aazhawa* just means "to cross" or "a crossing." The Ojibwe People's Dictionary, https://ojibwe.lib.umn.edu/main-entry/aazhawa-o-vai.

4 Michael Dawson, *Behind the Mule: Race and Class in African-American Politics* (Princeton, NJ: Princeton University Press, 1994). For ideas about a global sense of linked fate, see Michael Hanchard, *Party/Politics: Horizons in Black Political Thought* (Oxford: Oxford University Press, 2006), and Juliet Hooker, *Theorizing Race in the Americas: Douglass, Sarmiento, Du Bois, and Vasconcelos* (Oxford and New York: Oxford University Press, 2017). I also wrote a paper a few years ago about global linked fate and Marvel's 2018 *Black Panther* movie, which is a pretty fun read, if you're into that kind of thing: Debra Thompson, "Wakanda Forever: Black Panther in Black Political Thought," in *Representations of Political Resistance and Emancipation in Science Fiction*, ed. Judith Grant and Sean Parson (Lanham, MD: Lexington Books, 2021), pp. 93–112.

5 See Grace-Edward Galabuzi, *Canada's Economic Apartheid: The Social Exclusion of Racialized Groups in the New Century* (Toronto: Canadian Scholars' Press, 2006); Paul Attewell, Philip Kasinitz, and Kathleen Dunn, "Black Canadians and Black Americans: Racial Income Inequality in Comparative Perspective," *Ethnic and*

Racial Studies 33, no. 3 (2010): 473–95; Black Experience Project, *The Black Experience Project in the GTA: Overview Report* (Toronto: Environics, 2017), https://www.theblackexperienceproject .ca/wp-content/uploads/2017/07/Black-Experience-Project-GTA -OVERVIEW-REPORT-4.pdf; Eddy Ng and Suzanne Gagnon, *Skills Next: Employment Gaps and Underemployment for Racialized Groups and Immigrants in Canada: Current Findings and Future Directions* (Toronto: Public Policy Forum, 2020); Statistics Canada, *Canada's Black Population: Education, Labour and Resilience* (Ottawa: Statistics Canada, 2020); Martin Turcotte, *Results from the 2016 Census: Education and Labour Market Integration of Black Youth in Canada* (Ottawa: Statistics Canada, 2020); Ontario Human Rights Commission, *A Disparate Impact: Second Interim Report of the Inquiry into Racial Profiling and Racial Discrimination of Black Persons by the Toronto Police Service* (Toronto: Government of Ontario, 2020), http://www.ohrc.on.ca/en/disparate -impact-second-interim-report-inquiry-racial-profiling-and-racial -discrimination-black; Office de consultation publique de Montréal, *Summary Report: Public Consultation on Systemic Racism and Discrimination within the Jurisdiction of the City of Montreal* (Montreal: Office de consultation publique de Montréal, 2020), https://ocpm.qc.ca/sites/ocpm.qc.ca/files/pdf/P99/resume-reds _english.pdf.

6   In 2020 the *Globe and Mail* published a multiyear investigation into racial bias in federal inmates' risk assessments. The results are shocking. See Tom Cardoso, "Bias Behind Bars: A Globe Investigation Finds a Prison System Stacked against Black and Indigenous Inmates," *Globe and Mail*, October 24, 2020, https:// www.theglobeandmail.com/canada/article-investigation-racial -bias-in-canadian-prison-risk-assessments/.

7   The situation is even more dire for Indigenous peoples, who are just over 4 percent of the population, but 16 percent of fatal police encounters. See CBC's Deadly Force database: https://newsinter actives.cbc.ca/fatalpoliceencounters/.

8   Michelle Alexander, *The New Jim Crow: Mass Incarceration in the Age of Colorblindness* (New York and London: The New Press, 2010).

Chapter 3: The Freedom Trail

1   See Aziz Rana, *The Two Faces of American Freedom* (Cambridge, MA: Harvard University Press, 2010), Chapter 1.

2   Edmund Morgan, *American Slavery, American Freedom: The Ordeal of Colonial Virginia* (New York: Norton, 1975).

3   Joel Olson, *The Abolition of White Democracy* (Minneapolis: University of Minnesota Press, 2004). Some other great books on the emergence and reproduction of "white" as a racial category are Ian Haney López, *White by Law: The Legal Construction of Race*, 10th anniversary ed. (New York: New York University Press, 2006); Ariela Gross, *What Blood Won't Tell: A History of Race on Trial in America* (Cambridge, MA: Harvard University Press, 2010); Nell Irvin Painter, *The History of White People* (New York and London: Norton, 2010).

4   And these forces—racism and heart disease—are related. In the United States, where racial health data is more readily accessible, there are persistent health disparities between white and Black Americans, especially in terms of access to care. Greater public awareness of Black maternal health followed a cover story on Serena Williams in *Vogue* in January 2018, in which she describes knowing something was wrong following the birth of her daughter and having those concerns dismissed by hospital employees. A series on "Lost Mothers," copublished by ProPublica and NPR, demonstrates that the rates of maternal mortality in the United States are shockingly high for Black women, who die at rates three to four times higher than white mothers. In 2017 there were more than 700 studies on the link between racial discrimination and physical and mental well-being; even before the COVID-19 pandemic, an estimated 100,000 Black people died prematurely every year. See Douglas Jacobs, "We're Sick of Racism, Literally,"

New York Times, November 11, 2017, https://www.nytimes.com /2017/11/11/opinion/sunday/sick-of-racism-literally.html; Nina Martin and Renee Montagne, "Nothing Protects Black Women from Dying in Pregnancy and Childbirth," ProPublica, December 7, 2017, https://www.propublica.org/article/nothing-protects -black-women-from-dying-in-pregnancy-and-childbirth; Rob Haskill, "Serena Williams on Motherhood, Marriage, and Making Her Comeback," *Vogue*, January 10, 2018, https://www.vogue .com/article/serena-williams-vogue-cover-interview-february-2018; Roni Caryn Rabin, "Racial Inequalities Persist in Health Care Despite Expanded Insurance," *New York Times*, August 17, 2021, https://www.nytimes.com/2021/08/17/health/racial-disparities -health-care.html

5   To be fair, it's a little more complicated than this. The ruling party typically loses seats in the first midterms after coming to power. And the twenty state legislatures that became Republican-controlled were largely a result of "Operation REDMAP," short for "Redistricting Majority Project," an effort of the Republican State Leadership Committee to use partisan gerrymandering and strategically drawn electoral districts to increase control of congressional seats and state legislatures.

6   Jake Silverstein, "Editor's Note: 1619," *New York Times Magazine*, August 18, 2019, https://pulitzercenter.org/sites/default/files/full _issue_of_the_1619_project.pdf.

7   Nikole Hannah-Jones, *The 1619 Project: A New Origin Story* (New York: Random House, 2021). For a recap on the Project's popularity, see Sarah Ellison, "How the 1619 Project Took Over 2020," *Washington Post*, October 13, 2020, https://www.washingtonpost .com/lifestyle/style/1619-project-took-over-2020-inside-story /2020/10/13/af537092-00df-11eb-897d-3a6201d6643f_story.html.

8   MSNBC, "The 1619 Project: How Slavery Has Defined America Today," August 18, 2019, https://www.youtube.com/watch?v =NseZ3SRCJWY.

9   This is the idea of "contingent consent." See Phillipe C. Schmitter

and Terry Lynn Karl, "What Democracy Is . . . and Is Not," *Journal of Democracy* 2, no. 3 (1991): 75–88.

10 Danielle S. Allen, *Talking to Strangers: Anxieties of Citizenship since* Brown v. Board of Education (Chicago and London: University of Chicago Press, 2004).

11 This article, and Hooker's entire body of work, has been hugely influential on my thinking. Juliet Hooker, "Black Lives Matter and the Paradoxes of U.S. Black Politics: From Democratic Sacrifice to Democratic Repair," *Political Theory* 44, no. 4 (2016): 448–69.

12 Carol Anderson, *White Rage: The Unspoken Truth of Our Racial Divide* (New York: Bloomsbury, 2016).

13 Glen Sean Coulthard, *Red Skin, White Masks: Rejecting the Colonial Politics of Recognition* (Minneapolis: University of Minnesota Press, 2014), p. 13, italics in original.

14 "The arc of the moral universe is long, but it bends toward justice" is a famous quote of Dr. Martin Luther King Jr., often repeated by President Barack Obama. But there's an interesting historical context to the quotation, discussed in Mychal Denzel Smith, "The Truth About 'The Arc of the Moral Universe,'" *HuffPost*, January 18, 2018, https://www.huffpost.com/entry/opinion -smith-obama-king_n_5a5903e0e4b04f3c55a252a4.

Chapter 4: Appalachian Elegies

1 Janell Ross, "Obama Revives His 'Cling to Guns or Religion' Analysis—for Donald Trump Supporters," *Washington Post*, December 21, 2015, https://www.washingtonpost.com/news/the-fix /wp/2015/12/21/obama-dusts-off-his-cling-to-guns-or-religion -idea-for-donald-trump/; Domenico Montanaro, "Hillary Clinton's 'Basket of Deplorables,' in Full Context of This Ugly Campaign," NPR, September 10, 2016, https://www.npr.org/2016 /09/10/493427601/hillary-clintons-basket-of-deplorables-in-full -context-of-this-ugly-campaign.

2   J. D. Vance, *Hillbilly Elegy: A Memoir of a Family and Culture in Crisis* (New York: HarperCollins, 2016). For worthy critiques and amendments, see Elizabeth Catte, *What You're Getting Wrong About Appalachia* (Cleveland: Belt, 2018); Sarah Smarsh, *Heartland: A Memoir of Working Hard and Being Broke in the Richest Country on Earth* (New York: Scribner, 2018); Cassie Chambers, *Hill Women: Finding Family and a Way Forward in the Appalachian Mountains* (New York: Ballantine Books, 2020).

3   Hanna Love and Tracy Hadden Loh, "The 'Rural-Urban Divide' Furthers Myths about Race and Poverty—Concealing Effective Policy Solutions," Brookings Institution, December 8, 2020, https://www.brookings.edu/blog/the-avenue/2020/12/08/the-rural-urban-divide-furthers-myths-about-race-and-poverty-concealing-effective-policy-solutions/.

4   See Noel Ignatiev, *How the Irish Became White* (New York: Routledge, 1995); David R. Roediger, *The Wages of Whiteness: Race and the Making of the American Working Class*, rev. ed. (London and New York: Verso Books, 2007).

5   See Melissa Phruksachart, "The Literature of White Liberalism," *Boston Review*, August 21, 2020, http://bostonreview.net/race/melissa-phruksachart-literature-white-liberalism. And, if you must: Robin DiAngelo, *White Fragility: Why It's So Hard for White People to Talk About Racism* (Boston: Beacon Press, 2018); Reni Eddo-Lodge, *Why I'm No Longer Talking to White People About Race* (London and New York: Bloomsbury, 2017); Crystal M. Fleming, *How to Be Less Stupid About Race: On Racism, White Supremacy, and the Racial Divide* (Boston: Beacon Press, 2018); Ibram X. Kendi, *How to Be an Antiracist* (New York: Random House, 2019); Ijeoma Oluo, *So You Want to Talk About Race* (New York: Seal Press, 2018).

6   Dr. Martin Luther King Jr., "Letter from Birmingham Jail," April 16, 1963, https://kinginstitute.stanford.edu/sites/mlk/files/letterfrombirmingham_wwcw_0.pdf.

7 Toni Morrison, "A Humanist View," speech at Portland State University, May 30, 1975.

8 See Sara Ahmed, *On Being Included: Racism and Diversity in Institutional Life* (Durham, NC, and London: Duke University Press, 2012); Kecia M. Thomas, Juanita Johnson-Bailey, Rosemary E. Phelps, Ny Mia Tran, and Lindsay N. Johnson, "Women of Color at Midcareer: Going from Pet to Threat," in *Psychological Health of Women of Color: Intersections, Challenges, and Opportunities*, ed. Lillian Comas-Díaz and Beverly Greene (Santa Barbara, CA: Praeger, 2013), pp. 275–86; and Natasha Warikoo, *The Diversity Bargain: And Other Paradoxes of Race, Admissions, and Meritocracy at Elite Universities* (Chicago: University of Chicago Press, 2016). There's been some excellent recent work done in Canada on racism in higher education: Frances Henry, Enakshi Dua, Carl E. James, Audrey Kobayashi, Peter Li, Howard Ramos, and Malinda S. Smith, *The Equity Myth: Racialization and Indigeneity at Canadian Universities* (Vancouver: University of British Columbia Press, 2017); Rita Dhamoon, "Racism as a Workload and Bargaining Issue," *Socialist Studies* 14, no. 1 (2020); rosalind hampton, *Black Racialization and Resistance at an Elite University* (Toronto: University of Toronto Press, 2020). Nisha Nath, a brilliant assistant professor of equity studies at Athabasca University, has recently been researching what she calls "the letters"—that is, all the open letters, private letters, emails written both by universities and those whom the institution bears down upon, tracing the act of letter writing within institutions as a psychologically heavy social practice that attempts, but often fails, to challenge racism in higher education.

9 I first encountered this turn of phrase in philosopher Charles Mills's wonderful treatise *The Racial Contract* (Ithaca, NY: Cornell University Press, 1997). Charles was incredibly kind to me and a strong advocate of my work, even as we often disagreed on the merits and potential of liberalism. "Why are you always trying

to save liberalism, Charles?" I'd ask him. "It's the only game in town, Deb," he'd reply. He passed away in September 2021 at just seventy years old. Another icon, gone too soon. Rest in power, friend.

Chapter 5: The Black Metropolis

1   There are many excellent books on the various contours of Black political thought. If you're looking for a place to start, I'd recommend the collection of essays in Melvin L. Rogers and Jack Turner, eds., *African American Political Thought: A Collected History* (Chicago: University of Chicago Press, 2021).

2   Ta-Nehisi Coates, *We Were Eight Years in Power: An American Tragedy* (New York: One World, 2018), p. 110.

3   Ta-Nehisi Coates, *Between the World and Me* (New York: Spiegel & Grau, 2015), p. 11.

4   Matt Taibbi, "Why Baltimore Blew Up," *Rolling Stone*, May 26, 2015, https://www.rollingstone.com/culture/culture-news/why-baltimore-blew-up-75167/; United States Department of Justice, Civil Rights Division, *Investigation of the Baltimore City Police Department*, August 10, 2016, https://www.justice.gov/crt/file/883296/download; Lynh Bui and Peter Hermann, "Federal Officials Indict Seven Baltimore Police Officers on Racketeering," *Washington Post*, March 1, 2017, https://www.washingtonpost.com/local/public-safety/federal-officials-to-announce-indictments-against-seven-baltimore-police-officers/2017/03/01/0380ab96-fe8f-11e6-8f41-ea6ed597e4ca_story.html?utm_term=.c3bbc4f96106.

5   The title for this chapter is a reference to St. Clair Drake and Horace R. Cayton's 1945 landmark study of race and urban life. St. Clair Drake and Horace R. Cayton, *Black Metropolis: A Study of Negro Life in a Northern City* (Chicago: University of Chicago Press, 1945).

6   Richard Iton, *In Search of the Black Fantastic: Politics and Popular Culture in the Post–Civil Rights Era* (Oxford and New York:

Oxford University Press, 2008), p. 16. See also Richard Iton, *Solidarity Blues: Race, Culture, and the American Left* (Chapel Hill: University of North Carolina Press, 2000); Richard Iton, "Still Life," *small axe* 17, no. 1 (2013): 22–39.

7   To my mind, this requirement was not nearly as problematic as the one that asked my marital status. "I don't answer that question," I'd say, whenever asked. "I don't see how my marital status is relevant to my health in any way." "That's a good point," the admin person would sometimes admit. But then they would just fill it in for me. The next time I'd go to the doctor, they'd ask if I was still "single" while confirming my other personal information and we'd start the whole ordeal over again.

8   Mary Pattillo, *Black Picket Fences: Privilege and Peril among the Black Middle Class* (Chicago: University of Chicago Press, 1999), p. 3. But see also her subsequent book, which detailed the divergent class interests among middle- and working-class African Americans that shaped the North Kenwood–Oakland neighborhood of Chicago; Mary Pattillo, *Black on the Block: The Politics of Race and Class in the City* (Chicago, University of Chicago Press, 2007).

9   Richard Rothstein, *The Color of Law: A Forgotten History of How Our Government Segregated America* (New York: Norton, 2017). See also the excellent books by political scientists Chloe Thurston, *At the Boundaries of Homeownership: Credit, Discrimination, and the American State* (New York: Cambridge University Press, 2018), and Jessica Trounstine, *Segregation by Design: Local Politics and Inequality in American Cities* (New York: Cambridge University Press, 2018).

10 Thomas M. Shapiro, *The Hidden Cost of Being African American: How Wealth Perpetuates Inequality* (New York: Oxford University Press, 2005); Melvin L. Oliver and Thomas M. Shapiro, *Black Wealth/White Wealth: A New Perspective on Racial Inequality* (New York: Routledge, 2006); Anne Helen Petersen, "The Mirage of the Black Middle Class," *Vox*, January 26, 2021, https://www.vox.com/the-goods/22245223/black-middle-class-racism-reparations;

William Darity Jr., Fenaba R. Addo, and Imari Z. Smith, "A Subaltern Middle Class: The Case of the Missing 'Black Bourgeoise' in America," *Contemporary Economic Policy* 39, no. 3 (2020): 494–502.

11 Spencer Ackerman, "Homan Square Revealed: How Chicago Police 'Disappeared' 7,000 People," *Guardian*, October 19, 2015, https://www.theguardian.com/us-news/2015/oct/19/homan-square-chicago-police-disappeared-thousands.

12 In November 2015 the Independent Police Review Authority recommended that Servin be terminated. Servin, who had been on desk duty since May 2012, resigned from the Chicago Police Department in May 2016, days before a departmental hearing that could have resulted in his termination from the force. Ray Sanchez, "Chicago Officer Who Shot Rekia Boyd Resigns," CNN, May 18, 2016, https://edition.cnn.com/2016/05/18/us/rekia-boyd-shooting-officer-resigns/.

13 I'm not an activist or an organizer. I'm not claiming to be. It's not my skill set. There are many excellent books written by people more closely connected to grassroots movements than me. I also don't pretend to be an expert on Black Lives Matter by any stretch of the imagination. Those doing the on-the-ground work can certainly speak for themselves. But I am a researcher, a writer, and, importantly, a teacher. My only talent is that I see invisible things, and so I can teach others to see them, too. On Black Lives Matter, see Keeanga-Yamahtta Taylor, *From #BlackLivesMatter to Black Liberation* (Chicago: Haymarket Books, 2016); Patrisse Khan-Cullors and asha bandele, *When They Call You a Terrorist: A Black Lives Matter Memoir* (New York: St. Martin's Griffin, 2017); Charlene Carruthers, *Unapologetic: A Black, Queer, and Feminist Mandate for Radical Movements* (Boston: Beacon Press, 2018); Barbara Ransby, *Making All Black Lives Matter: Reimagining Freedom in the Twenty-First Century* (Oakland: University of California Press, 2018); Rodney Diverlus, Sandy Hudson, and Syrus Marcus Ware, eds., *Until We Are Free: Reflections on*

Black Lives Matter in Canada (Regina, SK: University of Regina Press, 2020); Deva R. Woodly, *Reckoning: Black Lives Matter and the Democratic Necessity of Social Movements* (New York: Oxford University Press, 2022).

14 Bruce Drake, "Divide Between Blacks and Whites on Police Runs Deep," Pew Research Center, April 28, 2015, https://www.pew research.org/fact-tank/2015/04/28/blacks-whites-police/.

15 Evelyn Brooks Higginbotham, *Righteous Discontent: The Women's Movement in the Black Baptist Church, 1880–1920* (Cambridge, MA: Harvard University Press, 1993). There is an incredibly interesting history of the fight for African American civil rights in the international sphere and the influence of Cold War dynamics on the concessions made by the American government. See, for example, Mary L. Dudziak, *Cold War Civil Rights: Race and the Image of American Democracy* (Princeton, NJ: Princeton University Press, 2000), and Al Tillery, *Between Homeland and Motherland: Africa, U.S. Foreign Policy, and Black Leadership in America* (Ithaca, NY: Cornell University Press, 2011).

16 Naomi Murakawa, *The First Civil Right: How Liberals Built Prison America* (Princeton, NJ: Princeton University Press, 2014); see also Khalil Gibran Muhammad, *The Condemnation of Blackness: Race, Crime, and the Making of Modern Urban America* (Cambridge, MA: Harvard University Press, 2010).

17 Angela Y. Davis, *Are Prisons Obsolete?* (New York: Seven Stories Press, 2003); Robyn Maynard, "Police Abolition/Black Revolt," *TOPIA: Canadian Journal of Cultural Studies* 41 (2020): 70–78; William C. Anderson, *The Nation on No Map: Black Anarchism and Abolition* (Chico, CA: AK Press, 2021); Mariame Kaba, *We Do This 'Til We Free Us: Abolitionist Organizing and Transforming Justice* (Chicago: Haymarket Books, 2021); Colin Kaepernick, ed., *Abolition for the People: The Movement for a Future Without Policing and Prisons* (Kaepernick Publishing, 2021); Geo Maher, *A World Without Police: How Strong Communities Make Cops Obsolete* (Brooklyn: Verso, 2021); Dereka Purnell, *Becoming*

Abolitionists: Police, Protests, and the Pursuits of Freedom (New York: Astra House, 2021); Angela Y. Davis, Gina Dent, Erica R. Meiners, and Beth E. Richie, *Abolition. Feminism. Now.* (Chicago: Haymarket Books, 2022); Shiri Pasternak, Kevin Walby, and Abby Stadnyk, eds., *Disarm, Defund, Dismantle: Police Abolition in Canada* (Toronto: Between the Lines Press, 2022); Ruth Wilson Gilmore, *Change Everything: Racial Capitalism and the Case for Abolition* (Chicago: Haymarket Books, 2022); Robyn Maynard and Leanne Betasamosake Simpson, *Rehearsals for Living* (Chicago: Haymarket Books, 2022).

Chapter 6: The Western Frontier

1   This is a fascinating account of white nationalist and antifascist mobilizations in Portland: Luke Mogelson, "In the Streets with Antifa," *The New Yorker*, October 25, 2020, https://www.newyorker.com/magazine/2020/11/02/trump-antifa-movement-portland.

2   I first heard of the idea of rhizomatic formulations from my friend and colleague Kelly Gordon, a political scientist at McGill University. She uses the concept of the rhizome to describe the flexibility and adaptive nature of conservatism in Canada, and she doesn't mind that I stole her idea. I checked.

3   Jefferson Cowie, "Is Freedom White?" *Boston Review*, September 23, 2020, https://bostonreview.net/articles/jefferson-cowie-is-freedom-white/.

4   Some Joe Lowndes work: *From the New Deal to the New Right: Race and the Southern Origins of Modern Conservatism* (New Haven, NY: Yale University Press, 2008); Daniel Martinez HoSang and Joseph Lowndes, *Producers, Parasites, Patriots: Race and the New Right-Wing Politics of Precarity* (Minneapolis: University of Minnesota Press, 2019); "Far-right Extremism Dominates the GOP. It Didn't Start—and Won't End—with Trump," *Washington Post*, November 8, 2021, https://www.washingtonpost.com/outlook/2021/11/08/far-right-extremism-dominates-gop-it-didnt

-start-wont-end-with-trump/. Also check out his blog: www.joe lowndes.org.

5   There is some fantastic recent work on the intersection of Black and Indigenous histories: see Aileen Moreton-Robinson, *The White Possessive: Property, Power, and Indigenous Sovereignty* (Minneapolis: University of Minnesota Press, 2015); Kyle T. Mays, *An Afro-Indigenous History of the United States* (Boston: Beacon Press, 2021); Alaina E. Roberts, *I've Been Here All the While: Black Freedom on Native Land* (Philadelphia: University of Pennsylvania Press, 2021); Samantha Seeley, *Race, Removal, and the Right to Remain: Migration and the Making of the United States* (Chapel Hill: University of North Carolina Press, 2021).

6   The term *arrivants* appears in Jodi A. Byrd, *The Transit of Empire: Indigenous Critiques of Colonialism* (Minneapolis: University of Minnesota Press, 2011). On the possibilities of Black/Indigenous solidarity, see also Eve Tuck, Allison Guess, and Hannah Sultan, "Not Nowhere: Collaborating on Selfsame Land," *Decolonization: Indigeneity, Education & Society*, June 26, 2014, https:// decolonization.files.wordpress.com/2014/06/notnowhere-pdf.pdf; Justin Leroy, "Black History in Occupied Territory: On the Entanglements of Slavery and Settler Colonialism," *Theory & Event* 19, no. 4 (2016); Tiffany Lethabo King, *The Black Shoals: Offshore Formations of Black and Native Studies* (Durham, NC: Duke University Press, 2019); Tiya Miles, "Beyond a Boundary: Black Lives and the Settler-Native Divide," *William and Mary Quarterly* 76, no. 3 (2019): 417–26.

7   Steven Levitsky and Daniel Ziblatt, *How Democracies Die* (New York: Crown, 2018); see also Suzanne Mettler and Robert C. Lieberman, *Four Threats: The Recurring Crises of American Democracy* (New York: St. Martin's Press, 2020).

8   Haley Sweetland Edwards, "How Christine Blasey Ford's Testimony Changed America," *Time*, October 4, 2018. https://time .com/5415027/christine-blasey-ford-testimony/; Emma Brown, "California Professor, Writer of Confidential Brett Kavanaugh

Letter, Speaks Out about Her Allegation of Sexual Assault," *Washington Post*, September 16, 2018. https://www.washingtonpost .com/investigations/california-professor-writer-of-confidential -brett-kavanaugh-letter-speaks-out-about-her-allegation-of-sexual -assault/2018/09/16/46982194-b846-11e8-94eb-3bd52dfe917b _story.html.

9   It did happen. Following Justice Ruth Bader Ginsburg's death in September 2020, President Trump appointed Amy Coney Barrett to the United States Supreme Court. Justice Stephen Breyer's re- tirement at the end of the Supreme Court's session in 2022 was clearly timed to allow President Joe Biden the chance to appoint a liberal justice. On February 25, 2022, the president nominated Judge Ketanji Brown Jackson to become the 116th associate jus- tice of the United States Supreme Court.

Chapter 7: Borderlands

1   Michael H. Schill, "The Misguided Student Crusade Against 'Fascism,'" *New York Times*, October 23, 2017, https://www.ny times.com/2017/10/23/opinion/fascism-protest-university-oregon .html. To be fair, President Schill came to Pancake Sunday in the spring of 2018, answered students' questions, and took their pointed criticisms for over two hours.

2   Warsan Shire, "Home," https://www.facinghistory.org/standing -up-hatred-intolerance/warsan-shire-home.

3   White House Task Force on New Americans, *Strengthening Com- munities by Welcoming All Residents: A Federal Strategic Action Plan on Immigrant and Refugee Integration*, April 2015, https:// obamawhitehouse.archives.gov/sites/default/files/docs/final_tf _newamericans_report_4-14-15_clean.pdf.

4   Ayelet Shachar, *The Birthright Lottery: Citizenship and Global In- equality* (Cambridge, MA: Harvard University Press, 2009). See also Joseph H. Carens, *The Ethics of Immigration* (New York: Ox- ford University Press, 2013).

5   See Astra Taylor, *Democracy May Not Exist, But We'll Miss It When It's Gone* (New York: Metropolitan Books, 2019), Chapter 3. If the most basic definition of democracy includes the citizenry's ability to participate in determining elected representatives without exclusion (for example, without restrictions based on race, gender, religion, etc.) and without the use of force (for example, without coercion or the threat of violence that could prevent one from voting) then when did Canada and the United States really become democracies? Perhaps in 1965 in the United States, when the Voting Rights Act was passed? Or in 1969, when Quebec was the last province to allow Indigenous people the right to vote without losing their Indian status, or in 1993, when the government of Canada removed the voter disqualification on the basis of mental disability? Or in 2002, when the Supreme Court of Canada ruling in *Sauvé v. Canada (Chief Electoral Officer)* granted all prisoners the right to vote? Should our ideas of "the people" also include corporations (already considered "persons" under the American Constitution), animals, robots, or nature?

6   Hannah Arendt, *The Origins of Totalitarianism* (New York: Meridian Books, 1958).

7   I want to point out the link between time and power here. Doing complicated paperwork takes *time*. In public policy, the concept of "administrative burden" speaks to the difficulties that citizens have in navigating complicated and layered bureaucracies and regulations. As Annie Lowrey writes, administrative burdens embedded in many social policies are a "'time tax'—a levy of paperwork, aggravation, and mental effort imposed on citizens in exchange for benefits that putatively exist to help them." And, it needs to be emphasized, often those who are the most vulnerable have the least amount of time to spare. Annie Lowrey, "The Time Tax," *The Atlantic*, July 27, 2021, https://www.theatlantic.com /politics/archive/2021/07/how-government-learned-waste-your -time-tax/619568/.

8   I have so many thoughts about this. I could probably write an entire

book on the relationship between race and sports. Taylor Branch's article, "The Shame of College Sports," *The Atlantic*, October 15, 2011, is no longer accurate, but still provides a detailed account of how the NCAA came to be and the ways that it relies on the unpaid labor of mostly Black student-athletes in college basketball and football. NPR's *Code Switch* podcast did a great breakdown of the core issues surrounding the exploitation of student-athletes back in 2018; see *Code Switch*, "The Madness of March," March 21, 2018, https://www.npr.org/2018/03/21/594911280/the-madness-of-march. In June 2021 the NCAA agreed to allow college athletes to "strike endorsement deals, profit off their social media accounts, sell autographs and otherwise make money from their names, images, and likenesses. . . ." Alan Blinder, "College Athletes May Earn Money from Their Fame, NCAA Rules," *New York Times*, June 30, 2021, https://www.nytimes.com/2021/06/30/sports/ncaabasketball/ncaa-nil-rules.html. In addition, the National Labor Relations Board, which in 2015 prevented football players from Northwestern University from unionizing (yes, the same university where I taught; those players were in my classes and they were amazing), issued a memo in September 2021 conceding that the term *student-athlete* was created to disguise what is clearly an employment relationship between universities and college athletes, and therefore subject to all statutory protections, including the right to unionize.

9   Luin Goldring, Carolina Berinstein, and Judith K. Bernhard, "Institutionalizing Precarious Migratory Status in Canada," *Citizenship Studies* 13, no. 3 (2009): 239–65.

10   Karla Cornejo Villavicencio, *The Undocumented Americans* (New York: One World, 2020).

11   Based on data from 2017. Jeffrey S. Passel and D'Vera Cohn, "Mexicans Decline to Less than Half the U.S. Unauthorized Immigrant Population for the First Time," Pew Research Center, June 12, 2019, https://www.pewresearch.org/fact-tank/2019/06/12/us-unauthorized-immigrant-population-2017/.

12   Harsha Walia, *Border and Rule: Global Migration, Capitalism, and the Rise of Racist Nationalism* (Chicago: Haymarket Books, 2021), p. 70, and Red Nation, *The Red Deal: Indigenous Action to Save Our Earth* (Brooklyn: Common Notions, 2021).

13   A lot of my thinking on the use of time in immigration policy has been shaped by Elizabeth Cohen, *The Political Value of Time: Citizenship, Duration, and Democratic Justice* (Cambridge: Cambridge University Press, 2018).

14   Fay Faraday, *Canada's Choice: Decent Work or Entrenched Exploitation for Canada's Migrant Workers?* Metcalf Foundation, 2016, https://metcalffoundation.com/publication/canadas-choice/. Political scientists Yasmeen Abu-Laban, Ethel Tungohan, and Christina Gabriel also address the inequities of Canadian immigration policy in their forthcoming book, *Containing Diversity: Canada and the Politics of Immigration in the 21st Century* (Toronto: University of Toronto Press).

15   Adam Serwer, *The Cruelty Is the Point: The Past, Present, and Future of Trump's America* (New York: One World, 2021), and especially his essay, "The Nationalist's Delusion," *The Atlantic*, November 20, 2017, https://www.theatlantic.com/politics/archive/2017/11/the-nationalists-delusion/546356/. For a more academic take, see Cristina Beltrán's persuasive book, *Cruelty as Citizenship: How Migrant Suffering Sustains White Democracy* (Minneapolis: University of Minnesota Press, 2020).

16   *Jennings v. Rodriguez*, 583 U.S. ___ (2018), https://www.supremecourt.gov/opinions/17pdf/15-1204_f29g.pdf.

17   Marlene Daut, "When France Extorted Haiti—the Greatest Heist in History," *The Conversation*, June 30, 2020, https://theconversation.com/when-france-extorted-haiti-the-greatest-heist-in-history-137949. The Haitian Revolution was nevertheless an epochal moment in world history—the only successful revolution against colonial slavery, the founding of the first Black republic, and the beginning of a radical experiment of universal citizenship. See, first and foremost, C. L. R. James, *The Black Jacobins:*

Toussaint L'Ouverture and the San Domingo Revolution, 2nd ed., rev. (New York: Random House, 1963), and then, Laurent Dubois, *Haiti: The Aftershocks of History* (New York: Picador, 2013) and Adom Getachew, "Universalism After the Post-colonial Turn: Interpreting the Haitian Revolution," *Political Theory* 44, no. 6 (2016): 821–45.

18 Months later, the Société de l'assurance automobile du Québec did, in fact, confiscate my Oregon driver's license.

19 Michael German, "The FBI Targets a New Generation of Black Activists," Brennan Center for Justice, June 26, 2020, https://www .brennancenter.org/our-work/analysis-opinion/fbi-targets-new -generation-black-activists.

20 I'm drawing here from some rich literature that brings together the idea of a "fugitive democracy" and practices of Black fugitivity. In particular, see Stephen Best and Saidiya Hartman, "Fugitive Justice," *Representations* 92, no. 1 (2005): 1–15; Barnor Hesse, "Escaping Liberty: Western Hegemony, Black Fugitivity," *Political Theory* 42, no. 3 (2014): 288–313; Neil Roberts, *Freedom as Marronage* (Chicago: University of Chicago Press, 2015); and Lia Haro and Romand Coles, "Reimagining Fugitive Democracy and Transformative Sanctuary with Black Frontline Communities in the Underground Railroad," *Political Theory* 47, no. 5 (2019): 646–73.

Chapter 8: Je reviendrai parmi vous

1 Hi again. You might notice that this chapter has more citations and notes than the others. I've tried to be both fair and thorough in my take on race politics in Montreal and Quebec, especially since I haven't been here for all that long and in many ways I'm still an interloper. There are also embedded peculiarities of being in Quebec, which is and isn't Canada, in Montreal, which is and isn't Quebec, and at the predominantly anglophone McGill University, which is and isn't Montreal.

2 Jonathan Montpetit and John MacFarlane, "At Huge Anti-Racism

Demonstrations in Quebec, Premier Called Out for Downplaying Problem," CBC News, June 7, 2020, https://www.cbc.ca/news /canada/montreal/police-racism-george-floyd-montreal-june-7 -1.5601984.

3　Robyn Maynard, "Black Life and Death Across the U.S.–Canada Border: Border Violence, Black Fugitive Belonging, and a Turtle Island View of Black Liberation," *Journal of the Critical Ethnic Studies Association* 5, nos. 1–2 (2019): 124–51. Robyn Maynard is also currently writing a fantastic dissertation on the intersection of Black politics and Black migration. It's going to be a landmark piece of scholarship.

4　See Gerald Alfred, *Heeding the Voices of Our Ancestors: Kahnawake Mohawk Politics and the Rise of Native Nationalism* (New York: Oxford University Press, 1995). On Kanehsatà:ke and Kahnawake land defense today, see Katsi'tsakwas Ellen Gabriel, "Violence Against Indigenous Land Defenders Must Stop," *Ricochet*, December 2, 2021, https://ricochet.media/en/3822/violence-against-indigenous-land-defenders-must-stop.

5　Alicia Elliott, "This Entire Country Is Haunted," *Maclean's*, July 12, 2021, https://www.macleans.ca/opinion/this-entire-country-is-haunted/.

6　Tari Ajadi and Debra Thompson, "The Two Pandemics," *Globe and Mail*, May 22, 2021, https://www.theglobeandmail.com/opinion /article-the-two-pandemics-of-anti-black-racism-and-covid-19-are -tied-together/.

7　The short answer: nope, not really. See Vanmala Subramaniam, Clare O'Hara, James Bradshaw, and Jaren Kerr, "Companies Show Little Progress on Diversity a Year after Committing to BlackNorth Initiative," *Globe and Mail*, July 20, 2021, https:// www.theglobeandmail.com/business/article-companies-show -little-progress-on-diversity-a-year-after-committing-to/.

8　Keith Banting (a professor emeritus at Queen's University) and I spent six years writing an article that makes precisely this argument. It would make a great book, but Keith says he's "retired."

Keith Banting and Debra Thompson, "The Puzzling Persistence of Racial Inequality in Canada," *Canadian Journal of Political Science* 54, no. 4 (2021): 870–91.

9   In their own words: Desmond Cole, *The Skin We're In: A Year of Black Resistance and Power* (Toronto: Doubleday Canada, 2020), and Rodney Diverlus, Sandy Hudson, and Syrus Marcus Ware, eds., *Until We Are Free: Reflections on Black Lives Matter in Canada* (Regina, SK: University of Regina Press, 2020).

10   This statistic is from the 2019 General Social Survey on Canadians' Safety. According to a crowdsourcing initiative of 36,000 respondents conducted in August 2020 (after the May/June 2020 protests), 23 percent reported having low levels of trust in the police. But there were significant differences among population groups. Among Indigenous respondents, 40 percent expressed distrust in the police; Black respondents had even higher levels of distrust, at 52 percent. This is compared to 19 percent of white respondents that expressed distrust in the police. See Dyna Ibrahim, "Public Perceptions of the Police in Canada's Provinces, 2019," Statistics Canada, November 25, 2020, https://www150.statcan .gc.ca/n1/pub/85-002-x/2020001/article/00014-eng.htm.

11   https://www.defundthespvm.com/main-page. See also the work of #MTLsansprofilage.

12   Ted Rutland, Karl Beaulieu, and Jade Bourdages, "Moral Panic over Gun Violence Encourages Racism and Repression," *Ricochet*, February 22, 2021, https://ricochet.media/en/3498/moral-panic -over-gun-violence-encourages-racism-and-repression. Ted Rutland, an associate professor in the Department of Geography, Planning, and Environment at Concordia University, has done a lot of excellent work keeping tabs on the SPVM and racial profiling.

13   "Under city regulations, the city is compelled to hold public hearings on the subjects of any petition signed by at least 15,000 citizens." CBC News, "Public Consultations on Systemic Racism to Be Held in Montreal for the First Time," August 17, 2018,

https://www.cbc.ca/news/canada/montreal/ocpm-public-consul ations-systemic-racism-and-discrimination-racism-against-visible -minorities-1.4788925.

14 Hugo Pilon-Larose, "PK Subban Played by 'Blackface' Actor in Montreal Show," *Toronto Star*, January 15, 2015, https://www .thestar.com/news/canada/2015/01/15/pk-subban-played-by-black face-actor-in-montreal-show.html.

15 A Quebec Superior Court judge declared that the shooter, twenty-seven-year-old Alexandre Bissonnette, was "truly motivated by race, and a visceral hatred toward Muslim immigrants." Julia Page, "Quebec City Mosque Shooter Sentenced to at Least 40 Years in Prison," CBC News, February 8, 2019, https://www.cbc .ca/news/canada/montreal/alexandre-bissonnette-sentence-quebec -city-mosque-shooting-1.4973655.

16 Black activists in the city, however, have been trying to push for the province to recognize the realities of racism since the 1960s; thanks to Will Prosper for taking the time to give me an overview of the brave and substantial efforts of community actors.

17 A quick word on French-language media in Quebec. It is a near-hegemonic, tightly knit, often fractious, and highly influ-ential ecosystem where debates, anxieties, and warnings about the state of Quebec nationalism often take center stage. French-language newspapers, especially *Le Journal de Montréal*, along-side other influential media platforms in radio (including two popular talk shows hosted by journalists Paul Arcand and Pat-rick Lagacé, respectively), television (especially *Tout le monde en parle*, hosted by Guy Lepage), films, and books, form a power-ful, self-sustaining entertainment and media industry, capable of shaping both the public opinion of its captive, attentive audience and political agendas of politicians seeking to keep a finger on the pulse of the Québécois public sphere. This Quebec mediascape is popular and powerful in the province, and public sentiment about issues such as the existence of systemic racism, the permissibility of white educators using the n-word, the ban on religious symbols in

Bill 21, and the prevalence of police brutality is shaped by a small cadre of almost entirely white media opinion-makers. In particular, *Journal de Montréal* journalists Mathieu Bock-Côté, Denise Bombardier, and Richard Martineau have written about systemic racism as a façade, Bill 21 as necessary to protect Quebec values, and "woke-ism" as a scourge, while *La Presse* journalist Isabelle Hachey has written a number of articles vehemently defending the right of white educators to use the n-word in their classrooms. There are a few well-known Black francophone journalists working to counter these narratives, such as Émilie Nicolas (*Le Devoir*) and Fabrice Vil (a lawyer, who has also written in *La Presse* and *Le Devoir*), but they are vastly outnumbered. Thanks to my research assistant, Juliane Vandal, for compiling a giant spreadsheet of media coverage of racism in Quebec.

18 I write more in the epilogue about whether non-Black people can say the n-word, in any language. Spoiler: No. Absolutely not.

19 Pierre Vallières was a francophone Québécois journalist and a member of the Front de liberation du Québec (FLQ), a militant separatist organization that, by the mid-1960s, was using bombing campaigns to send a message about the group's commitment to Quebec independence. Vallières and his compatriot, Charles Gagnon, fled to the United States and were arrested in September 1966 in front of the United Nations in New York, where they had initiated a hunger strike to demand the status of imprisoned members of the FLQ. He spent four months in prison in New York, awaiting extradition to Canada. According to Bruno Cornellier, an associate professor of English at the University of Winnipeg, "Vallières allegedly wrote the book without interruption during his and his fellow revolutionary Charles Gagnon's imprisonment at the Manhattan House of Detention for Men, amid a mostly black prison population. As an inmate himself, Vallières's physical propinquity with imprisoned black bodies would predictably become a legitimizing tool for his argument, most notably in his insistence of shared, affective experiences of suffering." See Bruno

Cornellier, "The Struggle of Others: Pierre Vallières, Quebecois Settler Nationalism, and the N-Word Today," *Discourse* 39, no. 1 (2017): 31–66.

20 Corrie Scott, "How French Canadians Became White Folks, or Doing Things with Race in Quebec," *Ethnic and Racial Studies* 39, no. 7 (2016): 1291.

21 Everyone in Canada should read Eve Tuck and K. Wayne Yang, "Decolonization Is Not a Metaphor," *Decolonization: Indigeneity, Education & Society* 1, no. 1 (2012): 1–40.

22 In addition, historians David Austin and Sean Mills have each documented the skeptical responses of anticolonial intellectuals of the time to the idea that white francophone Quebecers could lay claim to these struggles and comparisons. See David Austin, *Fear of a Black Nation: Race, Sex, and Security in Sixties Montreal* (Toronto: Between the Lines, 2013), and Sean Mills, *The Empire Within: Postcolonial Thought and Political Activism in Sixties Montreal* (Montreal and Kingston, ON: McGill-Queen's University Press, 2010). For a history of Black Montreal, see Dorothy Williams, *The Road to Now: A History of Blacks in Montreal* (Montreal: Vehicule Press, 1997).

23 Luc Turgeon and Antoine Bilodeau, "Minority Nations and Attitudes Towards Immigration: The Case of Quebec," *Nations and Nationalism* 20, no. 2 (2014): 317–36; Yannick Dufresne et al., "Religiosity or Racism? The Basis of Opposition to Religious Accommodation in Quebec," *Nations and Nationalism* 25, no. 2 (2019): 673–96.

24 Supriya Dwivedi, "Our National Silence on Bill 21," *The Walrus*, October 18, 2019, https://thewalrus.ca/our-national-silence-on-bill-21/.

25 According to a January 2022 poll, 33 percent of Canadians outside Quebec were in favor of banning religious symbols worn by public school teachers, 55 percent against, and 12 percent undecided. In contrast, 55 percent of Quebecers supported the ban. This number represents a drop in previous survey results published in September

2021 that found 64 percent of Quebecers in favor. The decline is likely because of a widely publicized case of a Grade 3 teacher, Fatemah Anvari, who was reassigned from teaching duties at her school in Chelsea, Quebec, because she wore a hijab. Morgan Lowrie, "Poll Suggests Support for Bill 21 Provision May Have Dropped in Quebec," CBC News, January 16, 2022, https://www.cbc.ca/news/canada/montreal/bill-21-support-poll-1.6316859.

26 The folks I talked to asked not to be identified by name in this book for these same reasons. They have careers that could be harmed because they spoke frankly to me about these matters. Once again, indiscernibility is a crucial strategy of Black survival.

27 See Délice Mugabo, "Black in the City: On the Ruse of Ethnicity and Language in an Antiblack Landscape," *Identities: Global Studies in Culture and Power* 26, no. 6 (2019): 631–48.

Epilogue: Neverwhere and Everyhere

1 David Scott, *Conscripts of Modernity: The Tragedy of Colonial Enlightenment* (Durham, NC: Duke University Press, 2004), p. 168.

2 See David Theo Goldberg, "The War on Critical Race Theory," *Boston Review*, May 7, 2021, https://bostonreview.net/articles/the-war-on-critical-race-theory/; Ibram X. Kendi, "There Is No Debate Over Critical Race Theory," *The Atlantic*, July 9, 2021, https://www.theatlantic.com/ideas/archive/2021/07/opponents-critical-race-theory-are-arguing-themselves/619391/; and Elizabeth Harris and Alexandra Alter, "Book Ban Efforts Spread Across the U.S.," *New York Times*, January 30, 2022, https://www.nytimes.com/2022/01/30/books/book-ban-us-schools.html.

3 See, for example, Isabelle Hachey, "L'étudiant a toujours raison," *La Presse*, October 15, 2020, https://www.lapresse.ca/actualites/2020-10-15/l-etudiant-a-toujours-raison.php; some useful counterpoints are provided by Émilie Nicolas, "Comment te faire confiance avec cette arme sans me fatiguer," *Le Devoir*, October 21, 2020, https://www.ledevoir.com/opinion/chroniques/588151/comment

-te-faire-confiance-avec-cette-arme-sans-me-fatiguer, and Jonathan Montpetit, "In Vow to Protect Campus Free Speech, Quebec
Premier Joins 'War on Woke,'" CBC News, February 18, 2021,
https://www.cbc.ca/news/canada/montreal/quebec-campus-free
-speech-academic-freedom-legault-1.5917113.

4 German Lopez, "Ta-Nehisi Coates Has an Incredibly Clear Explanation for Why White People Shouldn't Use the N-word,"
Vox, November 9, 2017, https://www.vox.com/identities/2017/11
/9/16627900/ta-nehisi-coates-n-word.

5 Bruno Cornellier points out that there are also slippery translation
issues at play: "French users of the term [*nègre*] have too often
found solace in the convenient ambiguity provided by the French
language between, on the one hand, the inflammatory and un-
equivocal N-word and, on the other, something assumed by white
Francophone speakers to be less so by attaching the world nè***
to something that would be more akin to the antiquated English
term 'Negro'—or, by any measure, to mean nè*** as a term that
could be used to mean the English N-word but not necessarily. . . .
I consider such strategic recourse to the ambiguity of the French
word nè*** a way for white Francophone Quebecers to use or
imply with ease—when convenient—the N-word and get away
with it." Cornellier, "The Struggle of Others," p. 35.

6 A few caveats are in order. According to the data my research
assistant, Danielle Gottlieb, has collected, Edmonton is the
only large city that has voted to reduce its police budget in the
coming year. It's also worth noting that the Halifax Board of
Police Commissioners appointed a community advisory committee to develop a definition of defunding the police; the report *Defunding the Police: Defining the Way Forward for HRM*,
was made public in January 2022: https://www.halifax.ca/sites
/default/files/documents/city-hall/boards-committees-commis
sions/220117bopc1021.pdf. On police funding in Montreal, see
Ted Rutland, "Defund the Police? In Montreal, We're Super-
funding the Cops," *Ricochet*, January 21, 2022, https://ricochet

.media/en/3831/defund-the-police-in-montreal-were-super funding-the-cops.

7   David Thurton, "One Year after Trudeau Took a Knee, Is His Government Living Up to Its Anti-racism Promises?" CBC News, August 5, 2021, https://www.cbc.ca/news/politics/trudeau-black -racism-1.6122821.

8   Tobi Haslett has written the most beautiful and devastating essay I've ever read on the George Floyd uprisings—or anything else for that matter. Tobi Haslett, "Magic Actions: Looking Back on the George Floyd Rebellion," *n+1 magazine*, no. 40, May 7, 2021, https://www.nplusonemag.com/issue-40/politics/magic-actions-2/.

9   Rinaldo Walcott, *The Long Emancipation: Moving Toward Black Freedom* (Durham, NC: Duke University Press, 2021).

10 My thinking on this has been shaped by Kim D. Butler, "Defining Diaspora, Refining a Discourse," *Diaspora: A Journal of Transnational Studies* 10, no. 2 (2001): 189–219; Brent Hayes Edwards, *The Practice of Diaspora: Literature, Translation, and the Rise of Black Internationalism* (Cambridge, MA: Harvard University Press, 2003); Jacqueline Nassy Brown, *Dropping Anchor, Setting Sail: Geographies of Race in Black Liverpool* (Princeton, NJ: Princeton University Press, 2005); Michael Hanchard, *Party /Politics*; Michelle M. Wright, *Physics of Blackness: Beyond the Middle Passage Epistemology* (Minneapolis: University of Minnesota Press, 2015); and Keguro Macharia, *Frottage: Frictions of Intimacy Across the Black Diaspora* (New York: New York University Press, 2019), among many, many others.

11 Last(ing) words belong to Richard Iton, *In Search of the Black Fantastic*, p. 195.

Further Reading

Alexander, Michelle. *The New Jim Crow: Mass Incarceration in the Age of Colorblindness*. New York: Basic Books, 2010.

Austin, David. *Fear of a Black Nation: Race, Sex, and Security in Sixties Montreal*. Toronto: Between the Lines, 2013.

Beltrán, Cristina. *Cruelty as Citizenship: How Migrant Suffering Sustains White Democracy*. Minneapolis: University of Minnesota Press, 2020.

Benjamin, Ruha. *Race After Technology: Abolitionist Tools for the New Jim Code*. New York: Polity, 2019.

Brand, Dionne. *A Map to the Door of No Return: Notes to Belonging*. Toronto: Vintage Canada, 2001.

Chariandy, David. *I've Been Meaning to Tell You: A Letter to My Daughter*. Toronto: McClelland & Stewart, 2018.

Coates, Ta-Nehisi. *We Were Eight Years in Power: An American Tragedy*. New York: One World, 2018.

Cole, Desmond. *The Skin We're In: A Year of Black Resistance and Power*. Toronto: Doubleday Canada, 2020.

Cooper, Afua. *The Hanging of Angélique: The Untold Story of Canadian Slavery and the Burning of Old Montréal*. Toronto: HarperCollins, 2006.

Coulthard, Glen Sean. *Red Skin, White Masks: Rejecting the Colonial Politics of Recognition*. Minneapolis: University of Minnesota Press, 2014.

Davis, Angela Y., Gina Dent, Erica R. Meiners, and Beth E. Richie. *Abolition. Feminism. Now*. Chicago: Haymarket Books, 2022.

Du Bois, W. E. B. *The Souls of Black Folk*. A. C. McClurg, 1903.

Foster, Cecil. *They Call Me George: The Untold Story of Black Train Porters and the Birth of Modern Canada*. Windsor: Biblioasis, 2019.

Gilmore, Ruth Wilson. *Change Everything: Racial Capitalism and the Case for Abolition*. Chicago: Haymarket Books, 2022.

Gilroy, Paul. *The Black Atlantic: Modernity and Double Consciousness*. London and New York: Verso, 1993.

hampton, rosalind. *Black Racialization and Resistance at an Elite University*. Toronto: University of Toronto Press, 2020.

Hanchard, Michael. *Party/Politics: Horizons in Black Political Thought*. Oxford: Oxford University Press, 2006.

Hartman, Saidiya. *Lose Your Mother: A Journey Along the Atlantic Slave Route*. New York: Farrar, Straus & Giroux, 2007.

Hill, Lawrence. *The Book of Negroes*. Toronto: HarperCollins, 2011.

Hinton, Elizabeth. *America on Fire: The Untold Story of Police Violence and Black Rebellions Since the 1960s*. New York: Liveright, 2021.

Hooker, Juliet. *Theorizing Race in the Americas: Douglass, Sarmiento, Du Bois, and Vasconcelos*. New York: Oxford University Press, 2017.

HoSang, Daniel Martinez, and Joseph Lowndes. *Producers, Parasites, Patriots: Race and the New Right-Wing Politics of Precarity*. Minneapolis: University of Minnesota Press, 2019.

Iton, Richard. *In Search of the Black Fantastic: Politics and Popular Culture in the Post–Civil Rights Era*. Oxford and New York: Oxford University Press, 2008.

James, C. L. R. *The Black Jacobins: Toussaint L'Ouverture and the San Domingo Revolution*. 2nd ed., rev. New York: Random House, 1963.

Kaba, Mariame. *We Do This 'Til We Free Us: Abolitionist Organizing and Transforming Justice*. Chicago: Haymarket Books, 2021.

Kaepernick, Colin, ed. *Abolition for the People: The Movement for a Future Without Policing and Prisons*. Kaepernick Publishing, 2021.

Kelley, Robin D. G. *Freedom Dreams: The Black Radical Imagination*. Boston: Beacon Press, 2002.

Laymon, Kiese. *Heavy: An American Memoir*. New York: Scribner, 2018.

Maher, Geo. *A World Without Police: How Strong Communities Make Cops Obsolete*. Brooklyn: Verso, 2021.

Mathieu, Sarah-Jane. *North of the Color Line: Migration and Black Resistance in Canada, 1870–1955*. Chapel Hill: University of North Carolina Press, 2010.

Maynard, Robyn. *Policing Black Lives: State Violence in Canada from Slavery to the Present*. Halifax and Winnipeg: Fernwood, 2017.

Maynard, Robyn, and Leanne Betasamosake Simpson. *Rehearsals for Living*. Toronto: Penguin Random House Canada, 2022.

Mays, Kyle T. *An Afro-Indigenous History of the United States*. Boston: Beacon Press, 2021.

McKittrick, Katherine. *Dear Science and Other Stories*. Durham, NC: Duke University Press, 2021.

Mills, Charles. *The Racial Contract*. Ithaca, NY: Cornell University Press, 1997.

Mills, Sean. *The Empire Within: Postcolonial Thought and Political Activism in Sixties Montreal*. Montreal and Kingston, ON: McGill-Queen's University Press, 2010.

Morrison, Toni. *The Source of Self-Regard: Selected Essays, Speeches, and Meditations*. New York: Knopf, 2019.

Murakawa, Naomi. *The First Civil Right: How Liberals Built Prison America*. Princeton, NJ: Princeton University Press, 2014.

Olson, Joel. *The Abolition of White Democracy*. Minneapolis: University of Minnesota Press, 2004.

Philip, M. NourbeSe. *Zong!* Middletown, CT: Wesleyan University Press, 2008.

Prescod-Weinstein, Chanda. *The Disordered Cosmos: A Journey into Dark Matter, Spacetime, & Dreams Deferred*. New York: Bold Type Books, 2021.

Purnell, Dereka. *Becoming Abolitionists: Police, Protests, and the Pursuits of Freedom*. New York: Astra House, 2021.

Roberts, Neil. *Freedom as Marronage*. Chicago: University of Chicago Press, 2015.

Rogers, Melvin L., and Jack Turner, eds. *African American Political Thought: A Collected History*. Chicago: University of Chicago Press, 2021.

Rothstein, Richard. *The Color of Law: A Forgotten History of How Our Government Segregated America*. New York: Norton, 2017.

Serwer, Adam. *The Cruelty Is the Point: The Past, Present, and Future of Trump's America*. New York: One World, 2021.

Sharpe, Christina. *In the Wake: On Blackness and Being*. Durham, NC, and London: Duke University Press, 2016.

Simpson, Leanne Betasamosake. *As We Have Always Done: Indigenous Freedom Through Radical Resistance*. Minneapolis: University of Minnesota Press, 2017.

Taylor, Candacy. *Overground Railroad: The Green Book and the Roots of Black Travel in America*. New York: Abrams Press, 2020.

Taylor, Keeanga-Yamahtta. *From #BlackLivesMatter to Black Liberation*. 2nd edition. Chicago: Haymarket Books, 2021.

Thobani, Sunera. *Exalted Subjects: Studies in the Making of Race and Nation in Canada*. Toronto: University of Toronto Press, 2007.

Trouillot, Michel-Rolph. *Silencing the Past: Power and the Production of History*. Twentieth anniversary ed. New York: Penguin Random House, 2015.

Vernon, Karina, ed. *The Black Prairie Archives: An Anthology*. Waterloo, ON: Wilfrid Laurier University Press, 2020.

Villavicencio, Karla Cornejo. *The Undocumented Americans*. New York: One World, 2020.

Walcott, Rinaldo. *The Long Emancipation: Moving Toward Black Freedom*. Durham, NC: Duke University Press, 2021.

Waldron, Ingrid R. G. *There's Something in the Water: Environmental Racism in Indigenous & Black Communities*. Halifax: Fernwood, 2018.

Walia, Harsha. *Border and Rule: Global Migration, Capitalism, and the Rise of Racist Nationalism*. Chicago: Haymarket Books, 2021.

Walker, James W. St. G. *The Black Loyalists: The Search for a Promised Land in Nova Scotia and Sierra Leone, 1783–1870*. Toronto: University of Toronto Press, 1992.

Winks, Robin W. *Blacks in Canada: A History*. Fiftieth anniversary ed. Montreal and Kingston, ON: McGill-Queen's University Press, 2021.

Woodly, Deva R. *Reckoning: Black Lives Matter and the Democratic Necessity of Social Movements*. New York: Oxford University Press, 2022.

Permissions

Every reasonable effort has been made to trace ownership of copyright materials. The publisher will gladly rectify any inadvertent errors or omissions in credits in future editions.

Page 22: The students of S.S. Harwich No. 13, 1929. Courtesy of author, from deep in my parents' basement.

Page 30: Cornelius Thompson, year unknown. This picture was passed along to my cousin Erica Murphy by Karolyn Smardz Frost, a historian of the Underground Railroad.

Page 49: The author and her sisters. Image courtesy of Jessica Thompson.

Page 67: The Robert Gould Shaw 54th Regiment Memorial in Boston Common. Courtesy of National Park Service.

Page 84: *The Soiling of Old Glory*, by Stanley Forman, 1977. Image credit: © Stanley Forman.

Page 88: Image of United States president Lyndon B. Johnson outside of Memorial Auditorium of Ohio University, May 7, 1964. Courtesy of Ohio University Archives.

Page 118: #BlackLivesMatter protest, Chicago. Image credit: © Lorie Shaull.

Page 121: Laquan McDonald protest, Chicago. Courtesy of Wikicommons. Image Credit: © C. Presutti/VOA.

Page 136: The Ku Klux Klan in Portland, Oregon, circa 1922. Courtesy of Oregon Historical Society.

Page 143: Kalapuya Ilihi Residence Hall at the University of Oregon. Courtesy of the University of Oregon.

Page 178: Citizenship letter. Courtesy of the author.

Page 207: Montreal's Pierre Trudeau International Airport, July 31, 2020. Courtesy of the author.

Index

NOTE: Page references in *italics* refer to information in captions.

THE
LONG ROAD
HOME

Debra Thompson

READING GROUP GUIDE

This reading group guide for *The Long Road Home* includes an introduction and discussion questions. The suggested questions are intended to help your reading group find new and interesting angles and topics for your discussion. We hope that these ideas will enrich your conversation and increase your enjoyment of the book.

INTRODUCTION

In this profound and personal narrative, Debra Thompson, an internationally recognized expert on race and ethnic politics, follows the *roots* of Black identities in North America and the *routes* taken by those who have crisscrossed the world's longest undefended border in search of freedom and belonging, starting with her own family, who travelled the Underground Railroad to Shrewsbury, Ontario, and then traces her journey across the United States in search of Blackness and belonging.

TOPICS AND QUESTIONS
FOR DISCUSSION

1. In the opening to the book, Debra Thompson quotes her father saying to her in early 2020: "You know, Debra, your daughter was the first Thompson born in America since Cornelius Thompson escaped slavery. It's been over a hundred and fifty years, and some days I think we came back too soon." What do you think Debra's father means? What is the significance of him saying, "*we* came back too soon"?

2. Debra discusses the differences between racism in Canada and the United States. What are some of the ways in which racism manifests differently in each country? How does one country influence the other?

3. Debra talks about the idea of home for Black North Americans. What are some possible meanings of "home" within the context of Black history and for the African diaspora? Why is the idea of a "return" so complex?

4. Why is the question "Where are you really from?" so problematic? What does it assume of the person being asked the question? What does it say about Blackness and belonging?

5. Debra points out that "many Canadians still don't know or acknowledge that slavery existed here, for more than two hundred years." How much did you know about the history of slavery in Canada? What aspects did you learn here?

6. How does Debra define the Canadian national project versus the American national project, especially in terms of how systemic racism manifests in each country?

7. What does Debra mean when she talks about the "absented-presence" of Black Canada in the narratives of Canadian identity? How does it compare to the way Black America is included, or not included, in the narratives of American identity?

8. Debra talks about the harmful effects of being the Only One—the only Black person in so many white spaces. What are some of these harmful effects? What does this imply about the idea of whiteness?

9. Boston, Massachusetts, is known as one of the birthplaces of American freedom. What are the distinctive ways that white and Black Americans might conceive of freedom? How does that dual reality relate to what W. E. B. Du Bois called the "double consciousness" experienced by Black people?

10. In Athens, Ohio, Debra experiences two kinds of racism. How does the racism commonly associated with the white working class differ from the racism of white liberals?

11. Debra finally feels at home in Chicago, the famous Black metropolis. What makes her feel at home here? What is it about Chicago that makes her feel at one with her Blackness for the very first time? And what are the very serious issues she sees affecting the Black population here?

12. Oregon was founded as a white ethno-state on Indigenous land. How does Debra reconcile being a Black person on Indigenous land? Does she?

13. What are the complexities of citizenship? How does citizenship relate to ideas of home? And how does citizenship relate to ideas of personal identity?

14. What are the forces that gave rise to the 2020 Black Lives Matter protests? Why do you think the Black Lives Matter protests spread across the globe?

15. What are the tensions that rise between Quebec nationalism and identity and immigrant populations? How do Black Canadians fit into the Quebec narrative?

16. Debra says that every movement, every period of racial progress, has been followed by a backlash. Can you give examples of both progress and pushback now?